CONTINUING ISSUES IN U.S. NATIONAL SECURITY POLICY

Edited by

DEMETRIOS CARALEY
MARYLENA MANTAS

Special Introduction by

ROBERT JERVIS

THE ACADEMY OF POLITICAL SCIENCE
NEW YORK

Copyright © 2016 by The Academy of Political Science

All rights reserved. No part of this publication may be reproduced, stored in a retrieval system, or transmitted in any form or by any means, electronic, mechanical, photocopying, recording, or otherwise, without the prior written permission of the publisher.

Published by
The Academy of Political Science
475 Riverside Drive, Suite 1274
New York, NY 10115

Cover design: Loren Morales Kando

Cover credits: U.S. Marine Corps, U.S. Department of Defense, and U.S. Department of State photos.

Library of Congress Cataloging-in-Publication Data

Names: Caraley, Demetrios, editor. | Mantas, Marylena, editor.
Title: Continuing issues in U.S. national security policy / edited by
   Demetrios James Caraley, Marylena Mantas ; special introduction by Robert
   Jervis.
Other titles: Continuing issues in United States national security policy
Description: New York : The Academy of Political Science, [2016]
Identifiers: LCCN 2016032050 | ISBN 9781884853111 (pbk.)
Subjects: LCSH: Presidents—United States—Election. | United States—Foreign
   relations. | United States—Politics and government. | National
   security—United States.
Classification: LCC E183 .C784 2016 | DDC 324.973—dc23 LC record available at
   https://lccn.loc.gov/2016032050

Printed in the United States of America
P 5 4 3 2 1

CONTENTS

Publisher's Preface
DEMETRIOS JAMES CARALEY v

Introduction: Presidents and Foreign Policy
ROBERT JERVIS 1

Will More Countries Become Democratic?
SAMUEL P. HUNTINGTON 7

Limits of American Power
JOSEPH S. NYE, JR. 37

Understanding the Bush Doctrine: Preventive Wars and
Regime Change
ROBERT JERVIS 55

Globalization as a Security Strategy: Power and
Vulnerability in the "China Model"
ANDREW J. NATHAN and ANDREW SCOBELL 83

Creating a Disaster: NATO's Open Door Policy
ROBERT J. ART 111

The Role of Villain: Iran and U.S. Foreign Policy
PAUL R. PILLAR 135

Pakistani Opposition to American Drone Strikes
C. CHRISTINE FAIR, KARL KALTENTHALER, and
WILLIAM J. MILLER 157

The Rationality of Radical Islam
QUINTAN WIKTOROWICZ and KARL KALTENTHALER 191

The Soft Underbelly of American Primacy: Tactical
Advantages of Terror
RICHARD K. BETTS 219

Publisher's Preface

DEMETRIOS JAMES CARALEY

THIS BOOK IS ONE OF A SERIES of publications released by the Academy of Political Science on timely subjects of special importance in the fields of public and international affairs. *Continuing Issues in U.S. National Security Policy* brings together essays that explore topics of central and ongoing importance to American foreign policy.

The Academy of Political Science is a nonpartisan, nonprofit organization founded in 1880 with a threefold mission: to contribute to the scholarly examination of political institutions, processes, and public policies; to enrich political discourse and channel the best social science research in an understandable way to political leaders for use in public policy making and the process of governing; and to educate members of the general public so that they become informed participants in the democratic process. The major vehicles for accomplishing these goals are its journal, *Political Science Quarterly*, Academy conferences, and special books.

Published continuously since 1886, *PSQ* is the most widely read and accessible scholarly journal on government, politics, and policy, both international and domestic. Dedicated to objective analysis based on evidence, *PSQ* has no ideological or methodological slant and is edited for both specialists and general readers who have a serious interest in public and foreign affairs.

I thank the authors of the essays in this collection. As is normal, the views expressed are those of the authors and not of the institutions with which they are affiliated. I am especially grateful to Robert Jervis, a long-term member of *PSQ*'s editorial board, for writing an overview discussing the intersection between the presidency and foreign policy issues, and how the selected essays can inform our understanding of critical foreign policy mistakes and opportunities. My warm thanks to Loren Morales Kando, who as Vice President for Operations and Executive Director of the Academy oversaw final details of the book's publication and distribution. Ms. Kando also designed the cover. Such thanks also go to Marylena Mantas, *PSQ*'s Managing Editor, who did the lion's share of the work in converting a set of articles into a well-integrated book.

DEMETRIOS JAMES CARALEY is President of the Academy of Political Science and Editor of the *Political Science Quarterly*. He is also Janet H. Robb Professor of the Social Sciences Emeritus at Barnard College and Professor of International and Public Affairs Emeritus at Columbia University.

Introduction: Presidents and Foreign Policy

ROBERT JERVIS

AS THE WORLD'S ONLY SUPERPOWER, THE UNITED STATES both influences and is influenced by events across the globe. Although American prosperity is less dependent on trade than is true for most countries, with almost 14 percent of the American economy consisting of exports, prosperity at home is in part the product of what is happening abroad.

Even in an era dominated by domestic concerns, foreign policy issues matter for the national welfare, and many of them are discussed in the articles that follow. Written earlier, they show that while foreign policy problems often can be managed, they are rarely solved and instead bedevil us for prolonged periods.

Democracy, in the form of representative government, is more than the bedrock of American politics; it is built into foreign policy not only through elections but also through American ideology. From the first years of the Republic, American leaders and public opinion have generally favored the spread of representative governments abroad and believed that they are more likely to share our interests than unrepresentative and repressive regimes. Woodrow Wilson wanted to teach our southern neighbors to elect good men, and the two world wars drove home the lesson that dictatorships are dangerous.[1] After World War II, the United States devoted

---

[1] This view has been confirmed—or at least supported—by a generation of political science research arguing that democracies rarely, if ever, fight each other and are more prone to keep their commitments. It is interesting both that these findings, unlike many others in the field, have found widespread acceptance in the wider public and that this school of thought has few proponents outside of the United States.

ROBERT JERVIS is Adlai E. Stevenson Professor of International Politics at Columbia University and author most recently of *Why Intelligence Fails: Lessons from the Iranian Revolution and the Iraq War*.

significant resources to seeing that Germany and Japan became democracies, and the American perception of the danger that these countries would return to revisionism declined as democracy took root. This is not to say, of course, that the United States did not maintain good relations with dictatorships, especially because of the felt need to combat communism. The classic statement is Kennedy's in the wake of the assassination of Rafael Trujillo, the brutal dictator of the Dominican Republic, in 1961: "There are three possibilities in descending order of preference: a decent democratic regime, a continuation of the Trujillo regime, or a Castro regime. We ought to aim at the first, but we really cannot renounce the second until we are sure that we can avoid the third."[2] The dilemma is a bit weaker today, but Barack Obama could have paraphrased this when considering whether to try to overthrow the Bashar al-Assad regime in Syria, and his successor is sure to face similar conundrums.

Democracies were favored for reasons both instrumental and intrinsic. One thing almost everyone across the political spectrum could agree on was that for most countries, democracy was the best form of government, at least when certain prerequisites in terms of education and economic development had been reached. There was also a widespread belief that the interests of the general populations in most, if not all foreign countries, were compatible with those of the United States. During the Cold War, it was believed that if the Soviet leadership loosened its hold on the people, the conflict would end, as a representative and responsive government would stop seeking to spread communism abroad and would see great common interests with the United States. It was Mikhail Gorbachev's domestic policies at least as much as his foreign policies that led many in the United States to believe that a fundamental change was taking place. When Reagan was asked on his trip to Moscow in 1988 how he could square the friendship that he was now expressing with his earlier statement that the Soviet Union was an evil empire, he replied, "I was talking about another time, another era."

After the Cold War, the American prodemocracy impulses were strengthened because the danger of domestic turmoil leading to a communist regime receded. So the article by Samuel Huntington, written in 1984, retains its relevance. What is particularly important is his argument that there are important economic, political, and social preconditions that strongly influence the likelihood that a country can become democratic and that, while American support does play a role, "the ability of the United

---

[2] Quoted in Arthur Schlesinger, Jr., *A Thousand Days: John F. Kennedy in the White House* (Boston: Houghton Mifflin, 1965), 769.

States to affect the development of democracy elsewhere is limited." Most, although certainly not all, political scientists and many political leaders agreed at the time. The end of the Cold War, the establishment of democracy in the states of Central and Eastern Europe (and for 10 years or so in the Soviet Union), coupled with the amazing peaceful transition to democracy in South Africa, produced a wave of optimism. Preconditions may have been helpful but did not appear to have been necessary. If the end of communism and the Cold War reinforced the perceived links between regime type and foreign policy, the successful transitions led people to believe there were no inherent barriers to democracy. Once dictators were overthrown, representative government could emerge.

The academic debate over whether this optimistic view is correct continues to rage, but this is not merely an academic concern, as presidents will have to base their policies in part on estimates of how easy or difficult it will be to establish democracies where they have not flourished before and the likely consequences of intervening in order to do so. It was optimistic beliefs that interacted with the great fear generated by the terrorist attacks on September 11, 2001, to produce the American invasion of Iraq and the Bush Doctrine that it represented. As I discuss in my article, one major assumption underlying George W. Bush's policy was that countries that oppress their own people are very likely to attack their neighbors and ally with terrorists. This very American view that foreign policy comes more from the nature of the regime than from the external environment led to the conclusion that Saddam Hussein's Iraq was a grave menace. By itself, this might not have been sufficient to generate a policy of overthrow, even in the environment of heightened fear in the wake of September 11. Another pillar of the Bush doctrine was that once Saddam was removed from power, democracy would emerge without a prolonged American military occupation. Obviously, the results did not conform to these hopes or confirm the underlying theory. The three fundamental questions of the extent to which foreign policy is a product of the nature of the domestic regime, how difficult it is to establish a democratic regimes, and how much the United States can do to help in this regard remain fundamental to the political campaign and the choices the future presidents will make.

Presidents will also have to decide how to deal with "rogue" regimes and whether it is wiser to try to change the behavior of recalcitrant governments like that of North Korea, a policy that is likely to require rewards as well as punishments, or to revert to a policy of regime change.

Central to American foreign policy are questions of how to maintain American power. Joseph S. Nye, Jr., analyzes it in his contribution. Going beyond the distinction he initially drew between hard and soft power, he stresses that "how others react to American power is equally important to the question of stability and governance in this global information age." Power is never in the possession of one state but rather grows out of the continuing relationships among states.[3] This is true for Chinese as well as American power. Andrew Nathan and Andrew Scobell show that under Mao Zedong, ideology combined with external hostility led China to seek autarky, but this was ultimately unsustainable politically or economically. China is now deeply entangled in the world political and economic system, and it faces Western fears that it will throw its weight around or shirk its global responsibilities. Deep involvement not only increases China's power, however, it also gives others new leverage over it. While China's importance to the rest of the world means that it is hard to imagine it ever being isolated again, or even being the target of strong sanctions, its "global engagement also made China more vulnerable to pressure from other countries' soft power." Its economy, furthermore, while strongly influencing other countries is now vulnerable to economic downturns elsewhere. China has gained much influence, but it has also lost autonomy.

For those who seek or hold the American presidency, China presents puzzles, challenges, and opportunities. In previous elections, the opposition candidate invariably attacked the incumbent for being "soft" on China on issues ranging from economic practices to human rights to policies toward its neighbors, and vowed to be much tougher. Once in office, however, and sometimes after a few false starts, the new president pretty much picked up where the old one left off. Future presidents will have to face difficult choices about how to deal with China, especially in the East and South China seas. Judging Chinese intentions and motives, charting a course that keeps American alliances together, and discerning the nature and extent of American vital interests in the region are extremely troublesome questions that are sure to preoccupy new administrations.

Parallel questions arise about Russia. Putin's annexation of Crimea and occupation of parts of eastern Ukraine, coupled with his bellicose rhetoric and domestic authoritarianism, have resurrected an unpleasant history that many analysts and leaders had thought was buried. To simplify, many analysts see Putin's policy as stemming largely from his own personality, preferences, and domestic political calculations. To the extent that the United States triggered what he did, it was by being insufficiently strong and failing to adopt a credible policy of deterrence. Others argue that the United States is responsible at least in part for the undesired Russian

---

[3]For a magisterial treatment of power, see David A. Baldwin, *Power and International Relations: A Conceptual Approach* (Princeton, NJ: Princeton University Press, 2016).

behavior, more specifically, by supporting the "color revolutions" in former Soviet republics, sponsoring the independence of Kosovo and, especially, expanding NATO to the East, including pledges that Ukraine and Georgia would eventually be admitted—all actions that have deeply threatened Russian security interests. Robert Art argues against the twin possibilities of further encircling Russia or admitting it to NATO. The deterioration of relations since he wrote in 1998 rules out the latter course of action, but the former, although also unwise, continues to receive attention. Presidents have to try to understand the causes of undesired Russian behavior as part of charting the way forward.

Iran has been even more controversial, with Democrats supporting the 2015 nuclear agreement with some reservations and Republicans vying to be the most vehement in their rejection. I have explained my own support for the agreement elsewhere,[4] and here Paul Pillar explores the extraordinary attention this issue has received. His perspective is that of both a scholar and a former national intelligence officer for Iran and its region, and so he combines a knowledge of the relevant scholarship with having witnessed many of the government debates. He argues that leaders and public opinion tend to exaggerate the threats to American security: "one has to ask—and future historians are sure to ask—how the sole superpower of the early twenty-first century could come to see this state along the Persian Gulf as posing such a supposedly immense threat." Part of the reason, he suggests, is the dysfunctional history of Iranian-American relations. Other factors are at work as well: foolish Iranian policies, the influence of Israel, and the domestic advantages of demonizing the other side.

He also argues that a compounding reason is the perception of Iranian leaders as irrational religious fanatics. In their contribution, Quintan Wiktorowicz and Karl Kaltenthaler join Pillar in disputing this image. Examining one radical Islamist group, they show how spiritual incentives are deployed to inspire costly and risky activism. Although these group members were not terrorists, their demonstrations did lead to public shunning, arrests, and loss of employment. Considered from the outside, this seems irrational because little came of these activities, but spiritual desires and support from fellow believers are powerful: "if we accept that religion does matter, seemingly irrational behavior becomes understandable as a rational choice."

Rational or not from the standpoint of the perpetrator, terrorism can have a great impact on the major powers. Presidential administrations will

---

[4]Robert Jervis, "Turn Down for What: The Iran Deal and What Will Follow," *Foreign Affairs*, 15 July 2015, accessed at https://www.foreignaffairs.com/articles/iran/2015-07-15/turn-down-what, 19 January 2015.

have to decide the scope and pace of drone attacks. Started by Bush, under Obama, they became a central instrument of American policy for several years until growing opposition, and perhaps a decline in the number of appropriate targets, led to a marked reduction. Used in several countries, Pakistan was the one that was hit most often and in which the attacks have generated most domestic opposition. The complexities of the situation in that country and in its relations with the United States are well known and epitomized by the dual facts that the United States could not have conducted its operations in Afghanistan without Pakistan's assistance and that Pakistan has supported branches of the Taliban. Public opinion in Pakistan is very unfavorable toward the United States, and as a cause and an effect of this, opposition to drone strikes is widespread among those who express an opinion. But, as C. Christine Fair, Karl Kaltenthaler, and William J. Miller show, "only about one third of the public is aware that drones are being used to kill militants on Pakistan's soil."

Furthermore, there does not appear to be a relationship between Pakistani attitudes toward al Qaeda or support for Islamism, on the one hand, and opposition to drone strikes, on the other. Instead, what matters most is level of education, with those who are less educated being most opposed. The reason appears to be that those with less education get their information from the Urdu media, which is uniformly hostile to drones, and those with more education read or hear English-language outlets, which present a more balanced picture. Drone strikes are likely to remain controversial. Abroad, they represent the enormous disparity between American technology and the resources available to poor countries. For Americans, they embody new ways of warfare that seem simultaneously humane in minimizing (although not eliminating) civilian casualties and inhumane by literally removing the soldier from the battlefield. Drones enable the United States to undertake military missions that were previously unthinkable, but they also raise new questions and call up new sources of opposition.

As Richard Betts explains in a fitting final chapter in this volume, many of the factors that make the United States so powerful are to little avail against terrorism and indeed, by making it an obvious target, increase its vulnerability. Of course, being a rich and powerful state allows the United States to deploy massive resources against terrorism both for offense and defense. Unfortunately, however, the latter can never be perfect, and the former may provoke and create terrorists as much as it destroys and deters them.

Will More Countries Become Democratic?

SAMUEL P. HUNTINGTON

WHAT ARE THE PROSPECTS FOR THE EMERGENCE of more democratic regimes in the world? This question has intellectual and policy relevance for the 1980s. During the 1950s and early 1960s, scholars concerned with this issue were generally optimistic that decolonization and economic development would lead to the multiplication of democratic regimes. The history of the next decade dealt roughly with these expectations, and people became more pessimistically preoccupied with the reasons for the breakdown of democratic systems. By the late 1970s and early 1980s, however, the prospects for democracy seemed to have brightened once again, and social scientists have responded accordingly. "Transitions to democracy" became the new focus of attention. The optimists of the 1950s were rather naively optimistic; those of the 1980s have been more cautiously optimistic, but the optimism and the hope are still there. Coincidentally, the Reagan administration moved far beyond the Carter administration's more limited concern with human rights and first launched "Project Democracy" and "The Democracy Program" to promote democratic institutions in other societies, and then persuaded Congress to create a "National Endowment for Democracy" to pursue this goal on a permanent basis. In the early 1980s, in short, concern with the development of new democratic regimes has been increasing among academics and policymakers. The purpose of this article is to use social science theory

---

SAMUEL P. HUNTINGTON was Eaton Professor of the Science of Government and director of the Center for International Affairs at Harvard University. He was the author of many books and articles on American government, comparative politics, and military affairs and strategy.

and comparative political analysis to see to what extent this new, more cautious optimism may be justified.

This issue is important for at least four reasons. First, the future of democracy is closely associated with the future of freedom in the world. Democracies can and have abused individual rights and liberties, and a well-regulated authoritarian state may provide a high degree of security and order for its citizens. Overall, however, the correlation between the existence of democracy and the existence of individual liberty is extremely high. Indeed, some measure of the latter is an essential component of the former. Conversely, the long-term effect of the operation of democratic politics is probably to broaden and deepen individual liberty. Liberty is, in a sense, the peculiar virtue of democracy; hence, if one is concerned with liberty as an ultimate social value, one should also be concerned with the fate of democracy.

Second, the future of democracy elsewhere in the world is of importance to the United States. The United States is the world's premier democratic country, and the greater the extent to which democracy prevails elsewhere in the world, the more congenial the world environment will be to American interests generally and the future of democracy in the United States in particular. Michael Doyle has argued quite persuasively that no two liberal societies have ever fought each other.[1] His concept of liberalism differs from the concept of democracy employed in this paper, but the point may well be true of democratic regimes as well as liberal ones. Other things being equal, non-democratic regimes are likely to pose more serious challenges to American interests than democratic regimes.

Third, "a house divided against itself," Abraham Lincoln said, "cannot stand.... This government cannot endure permanently half-slave and half-free." At present the world is not a single house, but it is becoming more and more closely integrated. Interdependence is the trend of the times. How long can an increasingly interdependent world survive part-democratic and part-authoritarian and totalitarian? At what point does interdependence become incompatible with coexistence? For the Soviet bloc and the Western World, that point may still be some distance in the future, but tensions arising out of the growing interaction between totally different political systems are almost inevitably bound to increase. At some point, coexistence may require a slowing down or halting of the trends toward interdependence.

---

[1] Michael W. Doyle, "Kant, Liberal Legacies, and Foreign Affairs, Part I," *Philosophy and Public Affairs* 12 (1983): 213ff.

Fourth, the extension or decline of democracy has implications for other social values, such as economic growth, socioeconomic equity, political stability, social justice, and national independence. In societies at one level of development, progress toward one or more of these goals may be compatible with a high level of democracy. At another level of socioeconomic development, conflicts may exist. The question of the appropriateness of democracy for poor countries is, in this context, a central issue. But even highly developed societies may achieve their democracy at some sacrifice of other important values, such as national security.

In addition, if it is desirable to extend the scope of democracy in the world, obviously it is necessary to know what conditions favor that in the late twentieth century. Empirical analysis is necessary to answer the question: What policies should governments, private institutions, and individuals espouse to encourage the spread of democracy? To what extent do efforts such as those of the Reagan administration have an impact, positive or negative, on the state of democracy in the world, and at what cost in terms of other social values and national goals?

The first step in evaluating the prospects for democracy is to define the dependent variable with which we are concerned. Definitions of democracy are legion. The term has been applied to areas and institutions far removed from politics. It has also been defined as an ideal impossible of human achievement. For Peter Bachrach, for instance, a democratic system of government has for its paramount objective "maximization of the self-development of every individual." Robert Dahl says a democratic political system is one which is "completely or almost completely responsible to all its citizens."[2] Such definitions may be relevant to normative political theory, but they are not very useful for comparative empirical analysis. First, they are often so vague and general that it is virtually impossible to apply them in practice. How does one judge whether a political system is attempting to maximize the self-development of individuals or is completely responsive to all its citizens? Second, democracy may also be defined in such broad terms as to make it identical with almost all civic virtues, including social justice, equality, liberty, fulfillment, progress, and a variety of other good things. Hence it becomes difficult if not impossible to analyze the relationship between democracy and other social goals.

---

[2]Peter Bachrach, *The Theory of Democratic Elitism: A Critique* (Washington, D.C.: University Press of America, 1980), 24, 98ff.; Robert A. Dahl, *Polyarchy: Participation and Opposition* (New Haven: Yale University Press, 1971), 2. For a useful analysis of "rationalist" and "descriptive" concepts of democracy, see Jeane J. Kirkpatrick, "Democratic Elections, Democratic Government, and Democratic Theory," in David Butler, Howard R. Penniman, and Austin Ranney, eds., *Democracy at the Polls* (Washington, D.C.: American Enterprise Institute for Public Policy Research, 1981), 325–48.

For comparative analysis a more empirical and institutional definition is desirable, and this paper follows in the tradition of Joseph A. Schumpeter. A political system is defined as democratic to the extent that its most powerful collective decision-makers are selected through periodic elections in which candidates freely compete for votes and in which virtually all the adult population is eligible to vote. So defined, a democracy thus involves the two dimensions—contestation and participation—that Dahl sees as critical to his realistic democracy or polyarchy.[3]

THE RECORD OF DEMOCRATIC DEVELOPMENT

The historical emergence of modern democratic regimes falls into four phases. What could reasonably be called a democratic political system at the national level of government first appeared in the United States in the early nineteenth century. During the following century democratic regimes gradually emerged in northern and Western Europe, in the British dominions, and in a few countries in Latin America. This trend, which Alexis de Tocqueville had foreseen in 1835 and which James Bryce documented in 1920, appeared to be irreversable if not necessarily universal. Virtually all significant regime changes were from less democracy to more democracy. Writing at the end of this period, Bryce could well speculate as to whether this "trend toward democracy now widely visible, is a natural trend, due to a general law of social progress."[4]

The trend was reversing, however, even as he wrote. The year 1920 was in many aspects the peak of democratic development among the independent nations of the world.[5] During the following two decades, democracy or democratic trends were snuffed out in Germany, Italy, Austria, Poland, the Baltic states, Spain, Portugal, Greece, Argentina, Brazil, and Japan. The war fought to make the world safe for democracy seemed instead to have brought its progress to an abrupt halt and to have unleashed social movements from the Right and the Left intent on destroying it.

The aftermath of World War II, on the other hand, marked another dramatic, if brief, spurt in the multiplication of democratic regimes. With the support of its allies, the United States imposed democracy on West

---

[3] Dahl, *Polyarchy*, 4–9. See also Joseph A. Schumpeter, *Capitalism, Socialism, and Democracy*, 2nd ed. (New York: Harper and Bros., 1947), 269: "the democratic method is that institutional arrangement for arriving at political decisions in which individuals acquire the power to decide by means of a competitive struggle for the people's vote."

[4] James Bryce, *Modern Democracies*, 2 vols. (New York: Macmillan, 1921), 1:24.

[5] The proportion of independent states that were democratic was roughly 19 percent in 1902, 34 percent in 1920, 32 percent in 1929–30, and 24 percent in 1960. See G. Bingham Powell, Jr., *Contemporary Democracies* (Cambridge: Harvard University Press, 1982), 238.

Germany, Austria, Italy, and Japan (where it took root), and attempted to do so in South Korea (where it did not). Coincidentally, the process of decolonizaton got underway with newly independent countries usually adopting at first the political forms of the imperial powers. In at least some cases, such as India, Israel, Ceylon, and the Philippines, the forms of democracy were accompanied by the substance also. Other countries, such as Turkey and some Latin American states, moved to emulate the political systems of the victorious Western powers. By the early 1950s, the proportion of democracies among the world's independent states had reached another high.

The fourth period in the evolution of democratic regimes, from the early 1950s to the 1980s, differs from the other three. In each of them, there was an overwhelmingly dominant trend, either toward the extension of democracy (1820–1920 and 1942–1953), or toward its reduction (1920–1942). In each period there were very few, if any, significant regime shifts against the dominant trend. The thirty years from the early 1950s to the early 1980s, however, were not characterized by a strong move in either direction. The trends were mixed. As we have seen, the number of democratic regimes seemed to expand in the 1950s and early 1960s, to shrink in the middle-late 1960s and early 1970s, and then to expand again in the late 1970s and early 1980s. Overall, however, the net record of change in the state of democracy in the world was not very great. It would be difficult to argue that the world was more or less democratic in 1984 than it had been in 1954. Indicative of this relative stability, albeit for a much shorter period of time, are Freedom House's estimates of the proportion of the world's population living in "free" states. In the first such estimate, in January 1973, 32.0 percent of the world's population was found to live in "free" states. In the next year, the percentage increased to 36.0 percent. During the following ten years, except for the two years India was under emergency rule (when it was 19.8 percent and 19.6 percent), the proportion of the world's population living in free states never went above 37.0 percent and never dropped below 35.0 percent. In January 1984 it was 36.0 percent, exactly where it had been ten years earlier.[6]

---

[6]See "The Comparative Survey of Freedom" compiled annually for Freedom House by Raymond D. Gastil, particularly *Freedom at Issue*, no. 17 (1973): 2–3; no. 70 (1983): 4; no. 76 (1984): 5. Freedom House classifies a state as "free" if it rates in first or second place on a seven-place scale for both political rights and civil liberties. The countries so classified all have the minimum features of a democratic political system, at least at the time of classification. While recognizing the importance of institutionalization, the Freedom House survey does not attempt to measure the extent to which democracy has become institutionalized. Thus, its 1984 survey, published at the very beginning of 1984, rated both New Zealand and Nigeria as "free," although the latter had presumably left the category as a result of the coup on New Year's Day.

The overall stability in the extent of democracy does, however, conceal some important developments in both directions. With a few notable exceptions, almost all colonies that achieved independence after World War II shifted from democratic to nondemocratic systems. In contrast, a few countries moved in the opposite direction. These include Spain, Portugal, Colombia, Venezuela, Greece, and the Dominican Republic. Several South American countries, including two with long-standing democratic systems (Chile, Uruguay) and two with less stable populist systems (Brazil, Argentina), became bureaucratic-authoritarian states, with military governments intent upon fairly sustained rule. By the end of 1983, however, Brazil had made substantial progress back towards a democratic system, and Argentina had a democratically elected government. Many other countries (including Peru, Ecuador, Ghana, Nigeria, and Turkey) seemed to oscillate back and forth between democratic and undemocratic systems, in a pattern traditionally characteristic of praetorian societies. In East Asia: Korea, Singapore, Indonesia, and the Philippines became less democratic, Taiwan remained undemocratic; the Indochinese states succumbed to a ruthless Vietnamese totalitarianism; and Thailand and Malaysia remained partially democratic. Finally, efforts to move Hungary, Czechoslovakia, and Poland toward more democratic politics were halted directly or indirectly by Soviet action.

Any estimate of the future of democracy in the world must be rooted in an explanation of why these mixed trends prevailed between the 1950s and the 1980s, and hence whether the overall stability in the prevalence of democratic regimes in the world will continue. Ancient and modern political analysts have many theories to explain the rise and fall of democratic regimes. To what extent do these various and conflicting theories explain what happened and did not happen after World War II and what could happen in the 1980s?

Thinking about the reasons for the emergence of democratic regimes has typically had two foci. One approach has focused on the preconditions in society that favor democratic development. A second approach has focused on the nature of the political processes by which that development has occurred. Each will be considered in turn.

PRECONDITIONS OF DEMOCRATIZATION

In 1970, Dankwart Rustow published a penetrating article on "transitions to democracy," in which he criticized studies that focused on "preconditions" for democratization because they often tended to jump from the correlation between democracy and other factors to the conclusion that those other factors were responsible for democracy. They also tended, he argued, to look for the causes of democracy primarily in economic, social, cultural, and psychological, but not political, factors.[7] Rustow's criticisms were well taken and helped to provide a more balanced view of the complexities of democratization. It would, however, be a mistake to swing entirely to the other extreme and ignore the environmental factors that may affect democratic development. In fact, plausible arguments can be and have been made for a wide variety of factors or preconditions that appear to be associated with the emergence of democratic regimes. To a large extent these factors can be grouped into four broad categories—economic, social, external, and cultural.

Economic Wealth and Equality
In his critique, Rustow gave special attention to an influential article published by Seymour Martin Lipset a decade earlier. In that piece, Lipset highlighted the seeming correlation between high levels of economic development and the prevalence of democratic political systems among European, English-speaking, and Latin American nations. The "more well-to-do a nation," he postulated, "the greater the chances that it will sustain democracy."[8] His study stimulated a flood of further analyses that criticized, qualified, and refined his argument. Whatever the academic hairsplittings, however, his basic point seemed to make sense. "There is," as another scholar put it in 1960, "a positive correlation between economic development and political competitiveness."[9] A quarter century later, that correlation still seemed to exist. In 1981, for instance, a comparison of the World Bank's ratings of countries in terms of economic development with Freedom House's ratings of them in terms of liberty showed these results—two of thirty-six low-income countries were classified "free" or democratic, fourteen out of sixty middle-income countries were so classified, and eighteen out of twenty-four countries with industrial economies were so classified.[10] As one moves up the economic ladder, the greater are the chances that a country will be democratic.

---

[7]Dankwart A. Rustow, "Transitions to Democracy: Toward a Dynamic Model," *Comparative Politics* 2 (1970): 337ff.
[8]Seymour Martin Lipset, "Some Social Requisites of Democracy: Economic Development and Political Legitimacy," *American Political Science Review* 53 (1959): 75.
[9]James S. Coleman, "Conclusion," in Gabriel A. Almond and James S. Coleman, eds., *The Politics of the Developing Areas* (Princeton, N.J.: Princeton University Press, 1960), 538.
[10]World Bank, *World Development Report 1981* (New York: Oxford University Press, 1981), 134–35; and *Freedom at Issue*, no. 64 (1982): 8–9. See also Seymour Martin Lipset's update of his earlier analysis, *Political Man: The Social Bases of Politics*, 2nd ed. (Baltimore: Johns Hopkins University Press, 1981), 469–76.

The correlation between wealth and democracy is thus fairly strong. How can it be explained? There are three possibilities. First, both democracy and wealth could be caused by a third factor. Protestantism has, for instance, been assigned by some a major role in the origins of capitalism, economic development, and democracy. Second, democracy could give rise to economic wealth. In fact, however, high levels of economic wealth require high rates of economic growth and high rates of economic growth do not correlate with the prevalence of democratic political systems.[11] Hence, it seems unlikely that wealth depends on democracy, and, if a connection exists, democracy must depend on wealth.

The probability of any causal connection running from wealth to democracy is enhanced by the arguments as to why this would be a plausible relationship. A wealthy economy, it is said, makes possible higher levels of literacy, education, and mass media exposure, all of which are conducive to democracy. A wealthy economy also moderates the tensions of political conflict; alternative opportunities are likely to exist for unsuccessful political leaders and greater economic resources generally facilitate accommodation and compromise. In addition, a highly developed, industrialized economy and the complex society it implies cannot be governed efficiently by authoritarian means. Decision-making is necessarily dispersed, and hence power is shared and rule must be based on consent. Finally, in a more highly developed economy, income and possibly wealth also tend to be more equally distributed than in a poorer economy. Since democracy means, in some measure, majority rule, democracy is only possible if the majority is a relatively satisfied middle class, and not an impoverished majority confronting an inordinately wealthy oligarchy. A substantial middle class, in turn, may be the product of the relatively equal distribution of land in agrarian societies that may otherwise be relatively poor, such as the early nineteenth century United States or twentieth century Costa Rica. It may also be the result of a relatively high level of development, which produces greater income equality in industrial as compared to industrializing societies.

If these arguments are correct, economic development in the Communist world and the Third World should facilitate the emergence of

---

[11]This is not to argue that authoritarian regimes necessarily have higher economic growth rates than democratic ones, although they may. See Robert M. Marsh, "Does Democracy Hinder Economic Development in the Latecomer Developing Nations," *Comparative Social Research* 2 (1979): 215–48; G. William Dick, "Authoritarian Versus Nonauthoritarian Approaches to Economic Development," *Journal of Political Economy* 82 (1974): 817–27; and Erich Weede, "Political Democracy, State Strength and Economic Growth in LDCs: A Cross-National Analysis" (Paper presented at the Annual Meeting of the American Political Science Association, Chicago, Ill., September 1983).

democratic regimes. Yet one must be skeptical as to whether such an easy conclusion is warranted. In the first place, there is the question as to what level of economic development is required to make possible the transition to democracy. As Jonathan Sunshine has conclusively shown, the countries of Western Europe generally became democratic when their per capita gross domestic products were in the range of $300-$500 (in 1960 dollars). By 1981, perhaps two-thirds of the middle-income developing countries had reached or exceeded that level of development. Most of them, however, had not become democratic. If the economic theory holds, the level of economic development necessary to facilitate the transition to democracy must be higher in the late twentieth century than it was in the century prior to 1950.[12] In addition, different countries may still transit to democracy at widely varying levels of development. Spain, after all, did grow extremely rapidly during the 1950s and 1960s and did become democratic after the death of Francisco Franco in the mid-1970s. Could this have happened without the industrialization, urbanization, and development of the middle class that were central to Spmish economic growth? Quite probably not. Lopez Rodo was at least partially right when he had earlier predicted that Spain would become democratic when its per capita income reached $2,000 per head.[13] But then what about Portugal? It made a simultaneous transition to democracy, without having experienced the massive economic development of Spain and while still at a much lower level of economic well-being.

In addition, what about the experience of the southern cone states of Latin America? They too went through major processes of economic development and yet turned away from democracy, a phenomenon that led Guillermo O'Donnell to develop his theory of bureaucratic authoritarianism that posited just the opposite of the Lipset wealth-democracy theory. Instead, O'Donnell argued that economic development and particularly the strains produced by a heavy emphasis on import substitution led to the emergence of new, stronger, and more lasting forms of authoritarian rule.[14]

---

[12]Jonathan Sunshine, "Economic Causes and Consequences of Democracy: A Study in Historical Statistics" (Ph.D. diss., Columbia University, 1972), 115ff.
[13]John F. Coverdale, *The Political Transformation of Spain after Franco* (New York: Praeger Publishers, 1979), 1.
[14]Guillermo A. O'Donnell, *Modernization and Bureaucratic-Authoritarianism* (Berkeley: University of California, Institute for International Studies, 1973), 3-15, 113-14. For analysis of this theory, see David Collier, ed., *The New Authoritarianism in Latin America* (Princeton, N.J.: Princeton University Press, 1979).

There is also the experience of the East Asian newly industrializing countries. In the 1960s and 1970s, these countries not only had the highest economic growth rates in the world, but they also achieved those rates while in most cases maintaining very equitable systems of income distribution. Yet none became more democratic and two of the most notable economic achievers, Korea and Singapore, became less so.

At the same time, the economic theory may still serve a purpose in terms of focusing attention on those countries where transitions to democratic or other types of modern political systems are most likely to occur. As countries develop economically, they can be conceived of moving into a zone of transition or choice, in which traditional forms of rule become increasingly difficult to maintain and new types of political institutions are required to aggregate the demands of an increasingly complex society and to implement public policies in such a society. In the 1981 World Bank ordering of countries by level of economic development, the zone of choice might be conceived as comprising the top one-third of the middle-income countries, that is, those running from Number 77 (the Republic of Korea) up to Number 96 (Spain). To these should be added Taiwan, which in terms of per capita income fits in the middle of this group. Of these twenty-one countries:

> 7 were democracies, including 4 (Spain, Venezuela, Portugal, Greece) that transited to democracy after World War II, 2 that became democratic on independence (Israel, 1tinidad and Tobago), and 1 that had sustained democracy for many years (Costa Rica);
>
> 4 were the bureaucratic-authoritarian (B-A) states of the southern cone (Brazil, Chile, Argentina, Uruguay);
>
> 4 were the newly industrializing countries (NICs) of East Asia (the Republic of Korea, Taiwan, Singapore, Hong Kong);
>
> 2 were Communist (Rumania and Yugoslavia);
>
> and the remaining 4 (Algeria, Mexico, Iran, and South Africa) were resource rich, ideologically diverse, and politically undemocratic.

Two years later, this group of countries, now labeled by the World Bank as "upper middle income countries" had been reduced by the graduation of Spain into the category of "industrial market economies," but had been enlarged by the movement upward of Malaysia, Lebanon, and Panama, and by the Bank's transfer into it of Iraq from the category of "high income oil exporters."[15]

---

[15]World Bank, *Development Report 1981*, 134–35, and *World Development Report 1983* (New York: Oxford University Press, 1983), 148–49.

If the wealth theory of democracy were valid, one would predict further movement toward democracy among the twenty-odd states in this group, perhaps particularly on the part of the East Asian NICs and the B-A states of South America. Experience suggests, however, that what is predictable for these countries in the transition zone is not the advent of democracy but rather the demise of previously existing political forms. Economic development compels the modification or abandonment of traditional political institutions; it does not determine what political system will replace them. That will be shaped by other factors, such as the underlying culture of the society, the values of the elites, and external influences.

In the late 1950s, for instance, both Cuba and Venezuela were reaching the level of economic development where the traditional sort of military despotism to which each had been subjected for years (Fulgencio y Batista Zaldivar, Marcos Perez Jimenez) was no longer adequate for the needs of the society. These military despotisms came to their ends in 1958 and 1959. Batista collapsed in the face of an armed revolutionary movement that rapidly seized and consolidated power, nationalized private property, and installed a pervasive Marxist-Leninist dictatorship. The Perez Jimenez regime collapsed as a result of the withdrawal of support by virtually all the major groups of Venezuelan society. That collapse was accompanied, however, by the negotiation of a series of pacts among Venezuelan leaders representing the major political and social groups that set the framework for a democratic political system.[16] By the late 1950s, the days of traditional personalistic despotism in Cuba and Venezuela were numbered; what was not fixed was what would replace them. Fidel Castro chose to lead Cuba in one direction; Rómulo Betancourt chose to lead Venezuela in a very different one. Fifteen years later in somewhat comparable circumstances King Juan Carlos and Adolfo Suarez in Spain and Antonio Ramalho Eanes in Portugal made similar choices on behalf of democracy. In another case, by the mid-1970s the rapid economic development of Iran had clearly undermined the basis for the shah's regime. The shah did not attempt to develop a broader, more participatory set of democratic institutions. His inaction, combined with the decision or lack of decision by the military leaders and the political skill of the mullahs, opened Iran to a religious revolution. Different and earlier decisions by Iranian leaders in the 1960s and 1970s might have moved Iran in a more democratic direction.

---

[16]See Terry Karl, "Petroleum and Political Pacts: The Transition to Democracy in Venezuela" (Latin American Program Working Paper 107, The Wilson Center, 1981).

If the concept of a transition zone is valid, economic development produces a phase in a nation's history where political elites and the prevailing political values can shape choices that decisively determine the nation's future evolution. The range of choice may be limited. In 1981, for instance, all countries with per capita gross national products of $4,220 or more (aside from the small oilexporting states and Singapore) were either democratic or Communist. Conceivably, transition zone countries could make other choices. Iran is obviously in the fanatic pursuit of a different course; possibly the East Asian NICs and the Latin American B-A regimes may find other alternatives. To date, however, those countries that have come through the transition zone have almost always emerged as either democracies or as Communist dictatorships.

Social Structure

A second set of often-discussed preconditions for democracy involves the extent to which there is a widely differentiated and articulated social structure with relatively autonomous social classes, regional groups, occupational groups, and ethnic and religious groups. Such groups, it is argued, provide the basis for the limitation of state power, hence for the control of the state by society, and hence for democratic political institutions as the most effective means of exercising that control. Societies that lack autonomous intermediate groups are, on the other hand, much more likely to be dominated by a centralized power apparatus—an absolute monarchy, an oriental despotism, or an authoritarian or totalitarian dictatorship.[17] This argument can be made on behalf of groups and pluralism in general or on behalf of particular groups or types of pluralistic structure which are singled out as playing a decisive role in making democracy possible.

According to one line of argument, pluralism (even highly stratified pluralism) in traditional society enhances the probability of developing stable democracy in modern society. The caste system may be one reason why India has been able to develop and to maintain stable democratic institutions.[18] More generally, the argument is made that societies with a highly developed feudalism, including an aristocracy capable of limiting

---

[17] Those who hold a more Rousseauistic conception of democracy will, of course, tend to see intermediate groups as obstacles to the realization of true democracy. For a balanced analysis of these issues, see Robert A. Dahl, *Dilemmas of Pluralist Democracy: Autonomy vs. Control* (New Haven: Yale University Press, 1982). For a general argument for intermediate groups as a bulwark against totalitarianism, see William Kornhauser, *The Politics of Mass Society* (Glencoe, Ill.: Free Press, 1959).

[18] See Lloyd I. and Susanne Roeber Rudolph, *The Modernity of Tradition: Political Development in India* (Chicago: University of Chicago Press, 1967), 15-154.

the development of state power, are more likely to evolve into democracies than those that lack such social pluralism. The record of Western Europe versus Russia and of Japan versus China suggests that there may well be something to this theory. But the theory fails to account for differences between North America and South America. Tocqueville, Louis Hartz, and others attribute democracy in the former to the absence of feudalism. The failure of democracy in South America has, conversely, often been attributed precisely to its feudal heritage, although the feudalism that existed there was, to be sure, highly centralized.[19]

The theory that emphasizes traditional pluralism is, in a sense, the opposite of the one that emphasizes wealth as a precondition of democracy. The latter makes democracy dependent on how far the processes of economic development and modernization have gone. The traditional pluralism theory, in contrast, puts the emphasis on where the process started, on the nature of traditional society. Was it, in Gaetano Mosca's terms, primarily a "feudal" or a "bureaucratic" society? If pushed to the extreme, of course, this theory implies societal predestination: it is all determined in advance that some societies will become democratic and others will not.

The most significant manifestation of the social structure argument, however, concerns not the existence of a feudal aristocracy, but rather the existence of an autonomous bourgeoisie. Democracy, the Marxists argue, is bourgeois democracy, reflecting the interests of that particular social class. Barrington Moore has restated the proposition succinctly in a more limited formulation: "No bourgeois, no democracy."[20] This argument would seem to have much to commend it. The failure of democracy to develop in Third World countries despite their economic growth can, perhaps, be related to the nature of that growth. The leading roles have been played by the state and by multinational enterprises. As a result, economic development runs ahead of the development of a bourgeoisie. In those circumstances where a bourgeoisie has developed, however, the prospects for democracy have been greater. The move to democracy in Turkey in the 1940s coincided with the move away from the etatisme of Kemalism and the appearance of a group of independent businessmen. More significantly, the ability of a

---

[19]For elaboration of these themes, see, among others: Louis Hartz, *The Liberal Tradition in America* (New York: Harcourt Brace, 1955), and idem, ed., *The Founding of New Societies* (New York: Harcourt Brace, 1964), especially Richard M. Morse, "The Heritage of Latin America"; James M. Malloy, ed., *Authoritarianism and Corporatism in Latin America* (Pittsburgh: University of Pittsburgh Press, 1977); Howard J. Wiarda, "Toward a Framework for the Study of Political Change in the Iberio-Latin Tradition," *World Politics* 25 (1973): 206–35; Claudio Veliz, *The Centralist Tradition of Latin America* (Princeton, N.J.: Princeton University Press, 1979).

[20]Barrington Moore, Jr., *Social Origins of Dictatorship and Democracy* (Boston: Beacon Press, 1966), 418.

developing country to have an autonomous, indigenous bourgeoisie is likely to be related to its size. Countries with small internal markets are unlikely to be able to sustain such a class, but large ones can. This may be one factor explaining why India (with one short interlude) has sustained a democratic system, and why Brazil, which is also developing a vigorous indigenous bourgeoisie, steadily moved away from bureaucratic authoritarianism in the 1970s and early 1980s. In South Africa, businessmen have been among those most active in attempting to ameliorate apartheid and broaden democracy in that country.

The seemingly important role of an autonomous bourgeoisie for the development of democracy highlights the question of the relation between economic system and political system. Clearly political democracy is compatible with both a substantial role in the economy for state-owned enterprises and a substantial state welfare and social security system. Nonetheless, as Charles Lindblom has pointed out (in a volume that otherwise highlights the conflict between the business corporation and democracy), all political democracies have market-oriented economies, although quite clearly not all market-oriented economies are paired with democratic political systems.[21] Lindblom's message would seem to be like Moore's—a market-oriented economy, like a bourgeoisie, is a necessary but not sufficient condition for the existence of a democratic political system.

Why should this be the case? At least two reasons suggest themselves. Politically, a market economy requires a dispersion of economic power and in practice almost invariably some form of private property. The dispersion of economic power creates alternatives and counters to state power and enables those elites that control economic power to limit state power and to exploit democratic means to make it serve their interests. Economically, a market economy appears more likely to sustain economic growth than a command economy (although the latter may, as the Soviet and East European cases suggest, do so for a short period of time), and hence a market economy is more likely to give rise to the economic wealth and the resulting more equitable distribution of income that provide the infrastructure of democracy.

A third source of autonomous social pressure in a democratic direction may be provided by labor unions. Historically, unions played this role in Western Europe and the United States. In the contemporary world, unions have also had a role in the struggles against the racist

---

[21]Charles E. Lindblom, *Politics and Markets* (New York: Basic Books, 1977), 161–69.

oligarchy in South Africa, against military rule in the southern cone, and against the Communist dictatorship in Poland. At the same time, the experience of these cases also suggests the limits on the extent to which, in the absence of affiliated political parties, labor unions can affect political change.

Under some conditions, communal (that is, ethnic, racial, or religious) pluralism may be conducive to the development of at least limited forms of democracy. In most cases of communal pluralism, democracy can operate only on a consociational rather than a majoritarian basis.[22] And even when it is organized on a consociational basis, it will often break down as a result of social mobilization that undermines the power of elites or as a result of the intrusion of external political and military forces (as in Cyprus or Lebanon). Even in the best of circumstances, consociational democracy can often only remain stable by in effect becoming consociational oligarchy (as in Malaysia), that is, by sacrificing contestation in order to maintain representation.

External Environment
External influences may be of decisive importance in influencing whether a society moves in a democratic or non-democratic direction. To the extent that such influences are more important than indigenous factors, democratization is the result of diffusion rather than development. Conceivably, democracy in the world could stem from a single source. Clearly it does not. Yet it would be wrong to ignore the extent to which much of the democracy in the world does have a common origin. In 1984, Freedom House classified fifty-two countries (many of them extremely small) as "free."[23] In thirty-three of those fifty-two countries, the presence of democratic institutions could be ascribed in large part to British and American influence, either through settlement, colonial rule, defeat in war, or fairly direct imposition (such as in the Dominican Republic). Most of the other nineteen "free" countries where democracy had other sources were either in Western Europe or in South America. The extension of democracy into the non-Western world, insofar as that has occurred, has thus been largely the product of Anglo-American efforts.

Ever since the French Revolution, armies have carried political ideologies with them. As we have indicated, where American armies went in

---

[22]See primarily the works of Arend Lijphart, particularly *The Politics of Accommodation: Pluralism and Democracy in the Netherlands*, 2nd ed. (Berkeley: University of California Press, 1975) and *Democracy in Plural Societies: A Comparative Evaluation* (New Haven: Yale University Press, 1977).
[23]*Freedom at Issue*, no. 76 (1984): 8–9.

World War II, democracy followed (in four cases enduringly, in one case temporarily). Where Soviet armies went, communism followed. Military conquest is clearly one way of extending democracy and other political systems. Historically, however, Western colonialism has been the most important means of diffusing democratic ideas and institutions. The enduring results of such colonialism have, however, been rather limited. As of 1983, no former French, U.S., Dutch, Portuguese, or Belgian colony was rated "free" by Freedom House. Several former British colonies were. Myron Weiner has, indeed, emphasized that *"very single country in the third world that emerged from colonial rule since the second world war with a population of at least one million (and almost all the smaller countries as well) with a continuous democratic experience is a former British colony."*[24] British rule seemingly had a significantly different impact from that of other colonial powers. Only six countries meet Weiner's condition, however, and a much larger number of former British colonies have *not* sustained democracy. The question then becomes how to distinguish among former British colonies. One possibility is that the duration of democratic institutions after independence is a function of the duration of British rule before independence. The colonies where democratic institutions appear to have taken the firmest root are those such as India, Sri Lanka, and the West Indian Anglophone states, where British rule dates from the eighteenth century. The record of former British colonies in Africa, on the other hand, where British rule dates only from the late nineteenth century, is not all that different from that of the former African colonies of other European powers.

In large measure, the rise and decline of democracy on a global scale is a function of the rise and decline of the most powerful democratic states. The spread of democracy in the nineteenth century went hand in hand with the Pax Britannica. The extension of democracy after World War II reflected the global power of the United States. The decline of democracy in East Asia and Latin America in the 1970s was in part a reflection of the waning of American influence.[25] That influence is felt both directly, as a result of the efforts of the American government to affect political processes in other societies, and also indirectly by providing a powerful and successful model to be followed.

---

[24]Myron Weiner, "Empirical Democratic Theory," in Myron Weiner and Ergun Ozbudun, eds., *Comparative Elections in Developing Countries* (Washington, D.C.: American Enterprise Institute, manuscript, 26 [italics in original]).

[25]Samuel P. Huntington, *American Politics: The Promise of Disharmony* (Cambridge: Harvard Univerity Press, 1981), 246–59.

Regional external influences can also have a significant effect on political development within a society. The governments and political parties of the European Community (EC) helped to encourage the emergence of democratic institutions in Spain and Portugal, and the desire of those two countries plus Greece to join the community provided an additional incentive for them to become democratic. Even beyond the confines of the EC, Western Europe has generally become defined as a community of democratic nations, and any significant departure by one nation from the democratic norm would clearly create a major crisis in intra-European relations. In some measure, a similar development may be taking place among the countries of the Andean Pact. The departure from the Pact of Chile and the addition of Venezuela in the mid-1970s, plus the transitions to democracy in Ecuador and Peru, then laid the basis for identifying pact membership with the adherence to democratic government.

In some regions, but most notably in Latin America, regional trends may exist. By and large, Latin American governments moved in a democratic direction in the late 1950s and early 1960s, then in an authoritarian direction in the late 1960s and early 1970s, and then once again in a democratic direction in the late 1970s and early 1980s. The reasons for these regional shifts are not entirely clear. They could be a result of four factors: simultaneous parallel socioeconomic development in Latin American societies; the triggering of a trend by the impact of one "pace-setting" Latin American society on its neighbors; the impact on Latin America of a common external influence (such as the United States); or some combination of these factors.

Cultural Context

The political culture of a society has been defined by Sidney Verba as "the system of empirical beliefs, expressive symbols, and values which defines the situation in which political action takes place."[26] Political culture is, presumably, rooted in the broader culture of a society involving those beliefs and values, often religiously based, concerning the nature of humanity and society, the relations among human beings, and the relation of individuals to a transcendent being. Significant differences in their receptivity to democracy appear to exist among societies with different cultural traditions.

---

[26]Sidney Verba, "Comparative Political Culture," in Lucian W. Pye and Sidney Verba, eds., *Political Culture and Political Development* (Princeton, N.J.: Princeton University Press, 1965), 513.

Historically, as many scholars have pointed out, a high correlation existed between Protestantism and democracy. In the contemporary world, virtually all countries with a European population and a Protestant majority (except East Germany) have democratic governments.[27] The case of Catholicism, particularly in Latin countries, on the other hand, is more ambivalent. Historically, it was often argued that a natural opposition existed between Catholicism and democracy. By and large, democratic institutions developed later and less surely in European Catholic countries than in Protestant ones. By and large, however, these countries also developed later economically than the Protestant countries, and hence it is difficult to distinguish between the impact of economics and that of religion. Conceivably, the influence of the latter on politics could have been mediated through its impact on economic development and the rise of an entrepreneurial class. With economic development, however, the role of the church changed, and in most Catholic countries now the church is identified with support for democracy.

Islam, on the other hand, has not been hospitable to democracy. Of thirty-six countries with Moslem majorities, Freedom House in 1984 rated twenty-one as "not free," fifteen as "partially free," none as "free." The one Islamic country that sustained even intermittent democracy after World War II was Turkey, which had, under Mustapha Kemal, explicitly rejected its Islamic tradition and defined itself as a secular republic. The one Arab country that sustained democracy, albeit of the consociational variety, for any time was Lebanon, 40 to 50 percent of whose population was Christian and whose democratic institutions collapsed when the Moslem majority asserted itself in the 1970s. Somewhat similarly, both Confucianism and Buddhism have been conducive to authoritarian rule, even in those cases where, as in Korea, Taiwan, and Singapore, economic preconditions for democracy have come into being. In India and Japan, on the other hand, the traditional Hindu and Shinto cultures at the very least did not prevent the development of democratic institutions and may well have encouraged it.

How can these differences be explained? Both doctrinal and structural aspects of the religions could play a role. At the most obvious level, those cultures that are consummatory in character—that is, where intermediate and ultimate ends are closely connected—seem to be less favorable to democracy. In Islam, for instance, no distinction exists between religion

---

[27]For the statistical correlation between Protestantism and democracy, see Kenneth A. Bollen, "Political Democracy and the Timing of Development," *American Sociological Review* 44 (1979): 572–87.

and politics or between the spiritual and the secular, and political participation was historically an alien concept.[28] Somewhat similarly, Confucianism in China was generally hostile to social bodies independent of the state, and the culture was conceived as a total entity, no part of which could be changed without threatening the whole. Instrumental cultures, in contrast, are "characterized by a large sector of intermediate ends separate from and independent of ultimate ends" and hence "ultimate ends do not color every concrete act."[29] The Hindu tradition, for example, is relatively tolerant of diversity. S. N. Eisenstadt has written that "the basic religious and cultural orientations, the specific cultural identity of Indian civilization were not necessarily associated with any particular political or imperial framework. . . ."[30]

As a whole, consummatory culture is thus more resistant to change, and when change comes in one significant element of the culture, the entire culture is thrown into question or is displaced and destroyed. In the instrumental culture, on the other hand, change can come gradually and incrementally. Hence, less resistance exists to the adaptation of new political forms, such as democratic institutions, and the process of adaptation can be an extended one that in itself facilitates the development of stable democracy.

With respect to the more narrowly political culture of a society, it seems reasonable to expect that the prevalence of some values and beliefs will be more conducive to the emergence of democracy than others. A political culture that values highly hierarchical relationships and extreme deference to authority presumably is less fertile ground for democracy than one that does not. Similarly, a culture in which there is a high degree of mutual trust among members of the society is likely to be more favorable to democracy than one in which interpersonal relationships are more generally characterized by suspicion, hostility, and distrust. A willingness to tolerate diversity and conflict among groups and to recognize the legitimacy of compromise also should be helpful to democratic development. Societies in which great stress is put on the need to acquire power and little on the need to accommodate others are more likely to have authoritarian or totalitarian regimes. Social scientists have attempted to compare societies

---

[28]See Daniel Pipes, *In the Path of God: Islam and Political Power* (New York: Basic Books, 1983), 48–69, 144–47.
[29]David E. Apter, *The Politics of Modernization* (Chicago: University of Chicago Press, 1965), 85.
[30]S.N. Eisenstadt, "Transformation of Social, Political, and Cultural Orders in Modernization," *American Sociological Review* 30 (1965): 668. In contrast to the Hindu tradition, Eisenstadt writes, "the identity between political and religious communities represents a very important similarity between the Chinese and Islamic societies" (p. 663).

along these various dimensions, but the evidence remains fragmented and difficult to systematize.[31] In addition, of course, even if some beliefs and values are found to correlate with the presence of democratic institutions, the question still remains concerning the relationship among these in a developmental sense. To what extent does the development of a pro-democratic political culture have to precede the development of democratic institutions? Or do the two tend to develop more simultaneously with the successful operation of democratic institutions, possibly created for other reasons, generating adherence to democratic values and beliefs?[32]

PROCESSES OF DEMOCRATIZATION

The classic model of democratization that has infused much discussion of the subject is that of Britain, with its stately progression from civic rights to political rights to social rights, gradual development of parliamentary supremacy and cabinet government, and incremental expansion of the suffrage over the course of a century. It is basically a linear model. Dankwart A. Rustow's model, based on Swedish experience—national unity, prolonged and inconclusive political struggle, a conscious decision to adopt democratic rules, habituation to the working of those rules—also involves a relatively simple linear progression. These "ingredients," he has argued, "must be assembled one at a time."[33] These linear models primarily reflect European experience during the century ending in 1920 and the experience of some Latin American countries (such as Argentina until 1930 and Chile until 1973).

Two other models have generally been more relevant than the linear model to the experience of Third World countries. One is the cyclical model of alternating despotism and democracy. In this case, key elites normally accept, at least superficially, the legitimacy of democratic forms. Elections are held from time to time, but rarely is there any sustained succession of governments coming to power through the electoral process. Governments are as often the product of military interventions as they are of elections. Such interventions tend to occur either when a radical party wins or appears about to win an election, when the government in power threatens or appears to threaten the prerogatives of the armed forces, or when the

---

[31] See Pye and Verba, *Political Culture and Political Development*; Dahl, *Polyarchy*, 124–87; Gabriel A. Almond and Sidney Verba, *The Civic Culture* (Princeton, N.J.: Princeton University Press, 1963); David McClelland, *The Achieving Society* (Princeton, N.J.: D. Van Nostrand, 1961).

[32] For arguments on the priority of democratic values, see the case Dahl makes on Argentina, *Polyarchy*, 132–40, and Jonathan Tumin's amendment of Barrington Moore in "The Theory of Democratic Development: A Critical Revision," *Theory and Society* 11 (1982): 143–64.

[33] Rustow, "Transitions to Democracy," 361.

government appears incapable of effectively guiding the economy and maintaining public order. Once a military junta takes over, it will normally promise to return power to civilian rule. In due course, it does so, if only to minimize divisiveness within the armed forces and to escape from its own inability to govern effectively. In a praetorian situation like this, neither authoritarian nor democratic institutions are effectively institutionalized. Once countries enter into this cyclical pattern, it appears to be extremely difficult for them to escape from it. In many respects, countries that have had relatively stable authoritarian rule (such as Spain and Portugal) are more likely to evolve into relatively stable democracies than countries that have regularly oscillated between despotism and democracy (such as Peru, Ecuador, Bolivia, Argentina, Ghana, Nigeria). In the latter, neither democratic nor authoritarian norms have deep roots among the relevant political elites, while in the former a broad consensus accepting of authoritarian norms is displaced by a broad consensus on or acceptance of democratic ones. In the one case, the alternation of democracy and despotism *is* the political system; in the other, the shift from a stable despotism to a stable democracy *is a change* in political systems.

A third model is neither linear nor cyclical but rather dialectical. In this case, the development of a middle class leads to increased pressures on the existing authoritarian regimes for expanded participation and contestation. At some point, there is then a sharp break, perhaps in the form of what I have elsewhere called the "urban breakthrough," the overthrow of the existing authoritarian regime, and the installation of a democratic one.[34] This regime, however, finds it difficult or impossible to govern effectively. A sharp reaction occurs with the overthrow of the democratic system and installation of a (usually right-wing) authoritarian regime. In due course, however, this regime collapses and a transition is made to a more stable, more balanced, and longer-lasting democratic system. This model is roughly applicable to the history of a number of countries, including Germany, Italy, Austria, Greece, and Spain.

Most theories of political development in general and of democratization in particular see these processes as involving a number of different elements. The sequence in which those components appear may have important implications for the overall results of the process. Several theorists have suggested, for instance, that the preferable overall process of development for a country is first to define its national identity, next to

---

[34]Samuel P. Huntington, *Political Order in Changing Societies* (New Haven: Yale University Press, 1968), 72–78.

develop effective institutions of authority, and then to expand political participation. The "probabilities of a political system's development in a nonviolent, nonauthoritarian, and eventually democratically stable manner are maximized," Eric Nordlinger has argued, when this sequence occurs.[35] In somewhat parallel fashion, it has been argued that the development of broad-gauged political institutions for political participation, such as electoral and party systems, must coincide with or precede the expansion of political participation if instability and violence are to be avoided. Similarly, Robert A. Dahl emphasizes the greater probability of success in transitions to democracy (or polyarchy in his terms) if the expansion of contestation precedes the expansion of participation.[36]

All these theories thus emphasize the desirability for the eventual development of stable democracy of the expansion of political participation occurring relatively late in the sequence of change. However, given the widely accepted desirability of political participation (including in totalitarian regimes) and the major increases in social mobilization (such as urbanization, literacy, and media consumption) produced by economic development, the prevailing tendencies in the contemporary world are for participation to expand early in the process of development, and before or concurrently with contestation. This may be one reason why economic development in the Third World has not stimulated the emergence of more stable democratic regimes. At present, the one notable case where contestation has clearly developed in advance of participation is South Africa. Hence, according to the Dahl thesis, the prospects for democratic development should be greater in South Africa than elsewhere in Africa.

It is often assumed that since democracy, to a greater degree than other forms of government, involves rule by the people, the people therefore play a greater role in bringing it into existence than they do with other forms of government. In fact, however, democratic regimes that last have seldom, if ever, been instituted by mass popular action. Almost always, democracy has come as much from the top down as from the bottom up; it is as likely to be the product of oligarchy as of protest against oligarchy. The passionate dissidents from authoritarian rule and the crusaders for democratic principles, the Tom Paines of this world, do not create democratic

---

[35] Eric A. Nordlinger, "Political Development: Time Sequences and Rates of Change," *World Politics* 20 (1968): 494–530; Dankwart A. Rustow, *A World of Nations* (Washington, D.C.: Brookings Institution, 1967), 126ff.; Leonard Binder et al., *Crises and Sequences in Political Development* (Princeton, N.J.: Princeton University Press, 1971), 310–313.

[36] Dahl, *Polyarchy*, 33–40; Huntington, *Political Order*, esp. pp. 32–59, 78–92. See also Richard A. Pride, *Origins of Democracy: A Cross-National Study of Mobilization, Party Systems, and Democratic Stability*, Comparative Politics Series, Vol. 1, (Beverly Hills: Sage Publications, 1970).

institutions; that requires James Madisons. Those institutions come into existence through negotiations and compromises among political elites calculating their own interests and desires. They are produced when, as Rustow argued, political leaders decide "to accept the existence of diversity in unity and, to that end, to institutionalize some crucial aspect of democratic procedure." The political leaders may do this because they are convinced of the ethical and political superiority of democracy and hence view democracy as a desirable goal in itself. More likely, however, they will view democracy as a means to other goals, such as prolonging their own rule, achieving international legitimacy, minimizing domestic opposition, and reducing the likelihood of civil violence, from which they will probably suffer. Hence, whatever institutions are agreed on will, in Rustow's words, "seem second-best to all major parties involved."[37] One could paraphrase Reinhold Niebuhr: the ability of elites to compromise makes democracy possible; the inclination of elites to vengeance makes democracy desirable—for the elites.

In the decades after World War II, democratic regimes have usually been introduced in independent countries through one or some combination of two processes. *Replacement* occurs when an authoritarian regime collapses or is overthrown as a result of military defeat, economic disaster, or the withdrawal of support from it by substantial groups in the population. Its leaders are killed, imprisoned, flee the country, or withdraw from politics. The leaders of the now-dominant groups, which had not been actively involved with the authoritarian regime, agree among themselves to institute a democratic system. This agreement may be reached very quickly because of previous experience with democracy and because its inauguration is seen as the "obvious" solution by the relevant political elites, as in Venezuela in 1958 and Greece in 1974. Or it may come about as a result of political struggle among elites with differing views as to the future of their country, out of which the leaders committed to democracy emerge successfully (as in Portugal in 1975–76). This process may involve, as it did in the case of Venezuela, a series of carefully negotiated pacts among the relevant groups that can cover economic policy and the role of institutions (such as the church and the army), as well as the procedures for choosing a government. One critical issue on which the constitutive elites must agree is how to treat those actively involved in the previous authoritarian regime.[38]

---

[37]Rustow, "Transitions to Democracy," 355–57.
[38]John H. Herz, "On Reestablishing Democracy after the Downfall of Authoritarian or Dictatorial Regimes," *Comparative Politics* 10 (1978): 559–62.

The alternative process for inaugurating a democratic regime might be termed *transformation*. In this case, the elites within an authoritarian system conclude that, for some reason or another, that system which they have led and presumably benefited from no longer meets their needs or those of their society. They hence take the lead in modifying the existing political system and transforming it into a democratic one. In this case, while there may well be a variety of internal and external pressures favoring change, the initiative for such change comes from the rulers. Transformation involves, as Juan Linz put it, "change through *reforma* rather than *ruptura*."[39] Notable examples include, of course, Britain in the nineteenth century, and after World War II, Turkey in the 1940s, Spain in the 1970s, and Brazil in the 1970s and 1980s. The leaders of the transformation process typically confront all the problems of the political reformer, having to maneuver skillfully between the stand-patters opposed to any democratization, on the one hand, and the committed dissident and opposition groups demanding the immediate dissolution of the authoritarian system, on the other. Essential to their success is that they be seen as keeping control, acting from a position of strength and not under duress, and dictating the pace of change.

The replacement process requires compromise and agreement among elites who have not been part of the authoritarian regime. The transformation process requires skilled leadership from and agreement among the elites who are part of that regime. In neither case is agreement necessarily required between elites who are within the regime and those opposing the regime. This situation makes replacement and transformation possible, since reaching an agreement between out-groups and in-groups is far more difficult than reaching an agreement among out-groups or among in-groups. Except for Costa Rica in 1948, it is hard to think of a case where a democratic system of any duration was inaugurated by explicit agrement between the leaders of a regime and the leaders of the armed opposition to that regime.

"As long as powerful vested interests oppose changes that lead toward a less oppressive world," Barrington Moore has argued, "no commitment to a free society can dispense with some conception of revolutionary coercion."[40] His thesis is that liberty and democracy can be inaugurated by bloody revolution and that such a course may well impose fewer costs than the alternative of gradual reform. When in world history, however, has

---

[39] Juan Linz, "Crisis, Breakdown, and Reequilibration," in Juan Linz and Alfred Stepan, eds., *The Breakdown of Democratic Regimes* (Baltimore: Johns Hopkins University Press, 1978), 35.
[40] Moore, *Social Origins of Dictatorship*, 508.

violent revolution produced a stable democratic regime in an independent state? "Revolutionary coercion" may bring down an authoritarian regime, but, except again for Costa Rica in 1948, guerrilla insurgencies do not inaugurate democratic regimes. All revolutionary opponents of authoritarian regimes claim to be democrats; once they achieve power through violence, almost all turn out to be authoritarian themselves, often imposing an even more repressive regime than the one they overthrew. Most authoritarian regimes are thus replaced by new authoritarian regimes, and a democratic succession usually requires minimum violence. "In the future as in the past," as Dahl concluded his study of this issue, "stable polyarchies and near-polyarchies are more likely to result from rather slow evolutionary processes than from revolutionary overthrow of existing hegemonies."[41]

THE PROSPECTS FOR DEMOCRACY

This brief and informal survey of the preconditions and processes conducive to the emergence of democratic regimes argues for caution in any effort to predict whether more countries will become democratic. It may, however, be useful to attempt to sum up the modest conclusions which seem to emerge from this review.

With respect to preconditions, the emergence of democracy in a society is helped by a number of factors: higher levels of economic well-being; the absence of extreme inequalities in wealth and income; greater social pluralism, including particularly a strong and autonomous bourgeoisie; a more market-oriented economy; greater influence vis-à-vis the society of existing democratic states; and a culture that is less monistic and more tolerant of diversity and compromise. No one of these preconditions is sufficient to lead to democratic development. With the possible exception of a market economy, no single precondition is necessary to produce such development. Some combination of some of these preconditons is required for a democratic regime to emerge, but the nature of that combination can vary greatly from one case to another. It is also necessary, however, to look not only at what preconditons must be present but also at the negative strength of any preconditon that may be absent. The powerful absence of one favorable condition, or, conversely, the presence of a powerful negative condition, that overrides the presence of otherwise favorable conditions, may prevent democratic development. In terms of cultural tradition, economic development, and social structure, Czechoslovakia would

---

[41]Dahl, *Polyarchy*, 45.

certainly be a democracy today (and probably Hungary and Poland also) if it were not for the overriding veto of the Soviet presence. In similar fashion, extreme poverty, extreme economic inequalities, or deeply ingrained Islamic and Confucian cultural traditions could have comparable effect in Africa, Central America, or the Middle East and East Asia.

With respect to the processes necessary to bring about democratic development, a central requirement would appear to be that either the established elites within an authoritarian system or the successor elites after an authoritarian system collapses see their interests served by the introduction of democratic institutions. The probability of stable democracy emerging will be enhanced to the extent that the transition can be a gradual one, that the introduction of contestation precedes the expansion of political participation, and that the role of violence in the transition is minimized. The probability of democratization decreases sharply to the extent that political life in a society becomes highly polarized and involves violent conflict between social forces.

Possibility of Regime Changes

In terms of these generalizations, prospects for democratic development in the 1980s are probably greatest in the bureaucratic-authoritarian states of South America. Cultural traditions, levels of economic development, previous democratic experience, social pluralism (albeit with weak bourgeoisies outside Brazil), and elite desires to emulate European and North American models all favor movement toward democracy in these countries. On the other hand, the polarization and violence that has occurred (particularly in Argentina and Chile) could make such movement difficult. The prospects for a relatively stable democratic system should be greatest in Brazil. Beginning in the early 1970s, the leadership of the Brazilian regime began a process of *distensão*, gradually relaxing the authoritarian controls that had been imposed in the 1960s. By the early 1980s, Brazil had acquired many of the characteristics of a democratic system. The principal deficiency was the absence of popular elections for the chief executive, but those were generally viewed as certain to come sometime in the 1980s. The gradualness of the Brazilian process, the relative low level of violence that accompanied it, and the general recognition among elite groups of the importance of not disrupting it in any way, all seemed to enhance the prospects for democracy.

In Argentina, the economic and military failures of the authoritarian regime led to a much more dramatic and rapid transit to democracy in 1983. The probabilities of this replacement being sustained would seem to depend on three factors: the ability of the Alfonsin government to deal with the economic problems it confronted; the extent to which Peronista, as well as Radical, elites were willing to abide by democratic rules; and the extent to which military leadership was effectively excluded from power or came to identify its interests with the maintenance of a democratic regime. The two other southern cone countries with bureaucratic-authoritarian regimes, Chile and Uruguay, are the two South American countries that did have the strongest democratic traditions. As of 1984, however, in neither country had authoritarian rule lost its legitimacy and effectiveness to the point where it could no longer be maintained and a replacement process could occur (as in Argentina). Nor had the leaders of either regime embarked on a meaningful transformation process to democratize their system (as in Brazil). The Brazilian and Argentine changes, however, cannot fail to have impact on political development in the smaller countries.

The probability of movement in a democratic direction in the East Asian newly industrializing countries is considerably less than it is among the Latin American B-A states. The economic basis for democracy is clearly coming into existence, and if their economic development continues at anything like the rates it did in the 1960s and 1970s, these states will soon constitute an authoritarian anomaly among the wealthier countries of the world. The East Asian countries generally have also had and maintained a relatively equal distribution of income. In addition, the United States, Britain, and Japan are the principal external influences on these societies. All these factors favor democratic development. On the other side, cultural traditions, social structure, and a general weakness of democratic norms among key elites all impede movement in a democratic direction. In some measure, the East Asian states dramatically pose the issue of whether economics or culture has the greater influence on political development. One can also speculate on whether the spread of Christianity in Korea may create a cultural context more favorable to democracy.

Among other less economically developed East Asian societies, the prospects for democracy are undoubtedly highest but still not very high in the Philippines. The Marcos government is not likely to attempt to transform itself, and hence efforts to create a democratic system must await its demise. At that time, American influence, previous experience with democracy, social pluralism (including the influence of the Catholic Church), and the general agreement among opposition political leaders on the desirability of a return to democracy, should all provide support for movement in that direction. On the other hand, military leaders may not support democratic norms, and the existence of a radical insurgency committed to violence, plus a general proclivity to the use of violence in the society, might make such a transition difficult. Conceivably, Philippine development could follow the lines of the dialectical model referred to earlier, in which (as in Venezuela) an initial experience with democracy is broken by a personalistic authoritarian interlude that then collapses and a new, more stable democratic regime is brought into existence by agreement among political leaders. The Philippine Betancourt, however, may well have been gunned down at the Manila airport.

Among Islamic countries, particularly those in the Middle East, the prospects for democratic development seem low. The Islamic revival, and particularly the rise of Shi'ite fundamentalism, would seem to reduce even further the likelihood of democratic development, particularly since democracy is often identified with the very Western influences the revival strongly opposes. In addition, many of the Islamic states are very poor. Those that are rich, on the other hand, are so because of oil, which is controlled by the state and hence enhances the power of the state in general and of the bureaucracy in particular. Saudi Arabia and some of the smaller Arab oil-rich Gulf countries have from time to time made some modest gestures toward the introduction of democratic institutions, but these have not gone far and have often been reversed.

Most African countries are, by reason of their poverty or the violence of their politics, unlikely to move into a democratic direction. Those African and Latin American countries that have adhered to the cyclical pattern of alternating democratic and authoritarian systems in the past are not likely to change this basic pattern, as the example of Nigeria underlines, unless more fundamental changes occur in their economic and social infrastructure. In South Africa, on the other hand, the relatively high level of economic development by African standards, the intense contestation that occurs within the minority permitted to participate in politics, the modest expansion of that minority to include the Coloureds and Asians, and the influence of Western democratic norms, all provide a basis for moving in a more democratic direction. However, that basis is countered on the other side by the inequalities, fears, and hatreds that separate blacks and whites.

In some small countries, democratic institutions may emerge as a result of massive foreign effort. This did happen in the Dominican Republic; in 1984 it was, presumably, happening in Grenada; it could, conceivably, happen at extremely high cost in El Salvador.

The likelihood of democratic development in Eastern Europe is virtually nil. The Soviet presence is a decisive overriding obstacle, no matter how favorable other conditions may be in countries like Czechoslovakia, Hungary, and Poland. Democratization could occur in these societies only if either the Soviet Union were drastically weakened through war, domestic upheaval, or economic collapse (none of which seems likely), or if the Soviet Union came to view Eastern European democratization as not threatening to its interests (which seems equally unlikely).

The issue of Soviet intervention apart, a more general issue concerns the domestic pattern of evolution within Communist states. For almost four decades after World War II, no democratic country, with the dubious possible exception of Czechoslovakia in 1948, became Communist and no Communist country became democratic through internal causes. Authoritarian regimes, on the other hand, were frequently replaced by either democratic or Communist regimes, and democratic regimes were replaced by authoritarian ones. In their early phase, Communist states usually approximated the totalitarian model, with ideology and the party playing central roles and massive efforts being made to indoctrinate and mobilize the population and to extend party control throughout all institutions in the society. Over time, however, Communist regimes also tend to change and often to become less totalitarian and more authoritarian. The importance of ideology and mobilization declines, bureaucratic stagnation replaces ideological fervor, and the party becomes less a dedicated elite and more a mechanism for patronage. In some cases, military influence increases significantly. The question thus arises: Will Communist authoritarian regimes, absent Soviet control, be more susceptible to movement toward democracy than Communist totalitarian regimes?

The answer to that question may well depend on the extent to which Communist authoritarian regimes permit the development of a market-oriented economy. The basic thrust of communism suggests that such a development is unlikely. Communism is not, as Karl Marx argued, a product of capitalist democracy; nor is it simply a "disease of the transition" to capitalist democracy, to use Rostow's phrase.[42] It is instead an alternative to capitalist democracy and one whose guiding principle is the subjection of economic development to political control. Even if it becomes more authoritarian and less totalitarian, the Communist political system is likely to ensure that economic development neither achieves a level nor assumes a form that will be conducive to democracy.

The United States and Global Democracy
The ability of the United States to affect the development of democracy elsewhere is limited. There is little that the United States or any other

---

[42]Walt W. Rostow, *The Stages of Economic Growth* (Cambridge: Cambridge University Press, 1960), 162.

foreign country can do to alter the basic cultural tradition and social structure of another society or to promote compromise among groups of that society that have been killing each other. Within the restricted limits of the possible, however, the United States could contribute to democratic development in other countries in four ways.

First, it can assist the economic development of poor countries and promote a more equitable distribution of income and wealth in those countries. Second, it can encourage developing countries to foster market economies and the development of vigorous bourgeois classes. Third, it can refurbish its own economic, military, and political power so as to be able to exercise greater influence than it has in world affairs. Finally, it can develop a concerted program designed to encourage and to help the elites of countries entering the "transition zone" to move their countries in a more democratic direction.

Efforts such as these could have a modest influence on the development of democracy in other countries. Overall, however, this survey of the preconditions for and processes of democratization leads to the conclusion that, with a few exceptions, the prospects for the extension of democracy to other societies are not great. These prospects would improve significantly only if there were major discontinuities in current trends—such as if, for instance, the economic development of the Third World were to proceed at a much faster rate and to have a far more positive impact on democratic development than it has had so far, or if the United States reestablished a hegemonic position in the world comparable to that which it had in the 1940s and 1950s. In the absence of developments such as these, a significant increase in the number of democratic regimes in the world is unlikely. The substantial power of anti-democratic governments (particularly the Soviet Union), the unreceptivity to democracy of several major cultural traditions, the difficulties of eliminating poverty in large parts of the world, and the prevalence of high levels of polarization and violence in many societies all suggest that, with a few exceptions, the limits of democratic development in the world may well have been reached.*

---

*This article was originally published in *Political Science Quarterly* 99 (Summer 1984): 193–218.

Limits of American Power

JOSEPH S. NYE, JR.

NOT SINCE ROME HAS ONE NATION LOOMED so large above the others. In the words of *The Economist*, "the United States bestrides the globe like a colossus. It dominates business, commerce and communications; its economy is the world's most successful, its military might second to none."[1] French foreign minister Hubert Védrine argued in 1999 that the United States had gone beyond its superpower status of the twentieth century. "U.S. supremacy today extends to the economy, currency, military areas, lifestyle, language and the products of mass culture that inundate the world, forming thought and fascinating even the enemies of the United States."[2] Or as two American triumphalists put it, "Today's international system is built not around a balance of power but around American hegemony."[3] As global interdependence has increased, many have argued that globalization is simply a disguise for American imperialism. The German newsmagazine *Der Spiegel* reported that "American idols and icons are shaping the world from Katmandu to Kinshasa, from Cairo to Caracas. Globalization wears a 'Made in USA' label."[4]

---

[1] "America's World," *The Economist*, 23 October 1999.
[2] Lara Marlowe, "French Minister Urges Greater UN Role to Counter US Hyperpower," *The Irish Times*, 4 November 1999. In 1998, Védrine coined the term "hyperpower" to describe the United States because "the word 'superpower' seems to me too closely linked to the cold war and military issues." Hubert Védrine with Dominique Moisi, *France in an Age of Globalization* (Washington, DC: Brookings Institution Press, 2001), 2.
[3] Robert Kagan and William Kristol, "The Present Danger," *The National Interest* (Spring 2000).
[4] William Drozdiak, "Even Allies Resent U.S. Dominance," *Washington Post*, 4 November 1997.

JOSEPH S. NYE, JR. is University Distinguished Service Professor and former Dean of Harvard's Kennedy School of Government. His most recent books include *The Powers to Lead, The Future of Power*, and *Presidential Leadership and the Creation of the American Era*.

The United States is undoubtedly the world's number one power, but how long can this situation last, and what should we do with it? Some pundits and scholars argue that U.S. preeminence is simply the result of the collapse of the Soviet Union and that this "unipolar moment" will be brief.[5] American strategy should be to husband strength and engage the world only selectively. Others argue that America's power is so great that it will last for decades, and the unipolar moment can become a unipolar era.[6] Charles Krauthammer argued in early 2001 that "after a decade of Prometheus playing pygmy, the first task of the new administration is to reassert American freedom of action." We should refuse to play "the docile international citizen. . . . The new unilateralism recognizes the uniqueness of the unipolar world we now inhabit and thus marks the real beginning of American post-Cold War foreign policy."[7]

Even before September 2001, this prescription was challenged by many, both liberals and conservatives, who consider themselves realists and consider it almost a law of nature in international politics that if one nation becomes too strong, others will team up to balance its power. In their eyes, America's current predominance is ephemeral.[8] As evidence, they might cite an Indian journalist who urges a strategic triangle linking Russia, India, and China "to provide a counterweight in what now looks like a dangerously unipolar world,"[9] or the president of Venezuela telling a conference of oil producers that "the 21st century should be multipolar, and we all ought to push for the development of such a world."[10] Even friendly sources such as *The Economist* agree that "the one-superpower world will not last. Within the next couple of decades a China with up to $1\frac{1}{2}$ billion people, a strongly growing economy and probably a still authoritarian government will almost certainly be trying to push its interests. . . . Sooner or later some strong and honest man will pull post-Yeltsin Russia together, and another contender for global influence

---

[5] See Charles Krauthammer, "The Unipolar Moment," *Foreign Affairs* (Winter 1990-1991): 23-33; Christopher Lane, "The Unipolar Illusion: Why New Great Powers Will Arise," *International Security* (Spring 1993): 5-51; Charles Kupchan, "After Pax Americana: Benign Power, Regional Integration and the Sources of Stable Multipolarity," *International Security* (Fall 1998).
[6] William Wohlforth, "The Stability of a Unipolar World" in Michael Brown et al., *America's Strategic Choices*, rev. ed. (Cambridge, MA: MIT Press, 2000), 305, 309; also from a liberal perspective, G. John Ikenberry, "Institutions, Strategic Restraint, and the Persistence of American Postwar Order," *International Security* (Winter 1998-99): 43-78.
[7] Charles Krauthammer, "The New Unilateralism," *Washington Post*, 8 June 2001.
[8] Kenneth Waltz, "Globalization and Governance," *Political Science and Politics* (December 1999): 700.
[9] Sunanda K. Datta-Ray, "Will Dream Partnership Become Reality?" *The Straits Times* (Singapore), 25 December 1998.
[10] Hugo Chavez quoted in Larry Rohter, "A Man with Big Ideas, a Small Country . . . and Oil," *New York Times*, 24 September 2000.

will have reappeared."[11] In my view, terrorism notwithstanding, American preponderance will last well into this century—but only if the United States learns to use power wisely.

Predicting the rise and fall of nations is notoriously difficult. In February 1941, publishing magnate Henry Luce boldly proclaimed the "American century." Yet by the 1980s, many analysts thought Luce's vision had run its course, the victim of such culprits as Vietnam, a slowing economy, and imperial overstretch. In 1985, economist Lester Thurow asked why, when Rome had lasted a thousand years as a republic and an empire, we were slipping after only fifty.[12] Polls showed that half the public agreed that the nation was contracting in power and prestige.[13]

The declinists who filled American bestseller lists a decade ago were not the first to go wrong. After Britain lost its American colonies in the eighteenth century, Horace Walpole lamented Britain's reduction to "a miserable little island" as insignificant as Denmark or Sardinia.[14] His prediction was colored by the then current view of colonial commerce and failed to foresee the coming industrial revolution that would give Britain a second century with even greater preeminence. Similarly, the American declinists failed to understand that a "third industrial revolution" was about to give the United States a "second century."[15] The United States has certainly been the leader in the global information revolution.

On the other hand, nothing lasts forever in world politics. A century ago, economic globalization was as high by some measures as it is today. World finance rested on a gold standard, immigration was at unparalleled levels, trade was increasing, and Britain had an empire on which the sun never set. As author William Pfaff put it, "Responsible political and economic scholars in 1900 would undoubtedly have described the twentieth-century prospect as continuing imperial rivalries within a Europe-dominated world, lasting paternalistic tutelage by Europeans of their Asian and African colonies, solid constitutional government in Western Europe, steadily growing prosperity, increasing scientific knowledge turned to human benefit, etc. All would have been wrong."[16] What followed, of

---

[11] "When the Snarling's Over," *The Economist*, 13 March 1999.

[12] Paul Kennedy, *The Rise and Fall of the Great Powers: Economic Change and Military Conflict from 1500–2000* (New York: Random House, 1987); Lester Thurow, *The Zero Sum Solution* (New York: Simon and Schuster, 1985).

[13] Martilla and Kiley, Inc. (Boston, MA), *Americans Talk Security*, no. 6, May 1988, and no. 8, August 1988.

[14] Quoted in Barbara Tuchman, *The March of Folly: From Troy to Vietnam* (New York: Knopf, 1984), 221.

[15] Daniel Bell, *The Coming of Post-Industrial Society: A Venture in Social Forecasting* (New York: Basic Books, 1999 [1973]), new introduction.

[16] William Pfaff, *Barbarian Sentiments: America in the New Century*, rev. ed. (New York: Hill and Wang, 2000), 280.

course, were two world wars, the great social disease of totalitarian fascism and communism, the end of European empires, and the end of Europe as the arbiter of world power. Economic globalization was reversed and did not again reach its 1914 levels until the 1970s. Conceivably, it could happen again.

Can we do better as we enter the twenty-first century? The apocrypha of Yogi Berra warns us not to make predictions, particularly about the future. Yet we have no choice. We walk around with pictures of the future in our heads as a necessary condition of planning our actions. At the national level, we need such pictures to guide policy and tell us how to use our unprecedented power. There is, of course, no single future; there are multiple possible futures, and the quality of our foreign policy can make some more likely than others. When systems involve complex interactions and feedbacks, small causes can have large effects. And when people are involved, human reaction to the prediction itself may make it fail to come true.

We cannot hope to predict the future, but we can draw our pictures carefully so as to avoid some common mistakes.[17] A decade ago, a more careful analysis of American power could have saved us from the mistaken portrait of American decline. More recently, accurate predictions of catastrophic terrorism failed to avert a tragedy that leads some again to foresee decline. It is important to prevent the errors of both declinism and triumphalism. Declinism tends to produce overly cautious behavior that could undercut influence; triumphalism could beget a potentially dangerous absence of restraint, as well as an arrogance that would also squander influence. With careful analysis, the United States can make better decisions about how to protect its people, promote values, and lead toward a better world over the next few decades. I begin this analysis with an examination of the sources of U.S. power.

THE SOURCES OF AMERICAN POWER

We hear a lot about how powerful America has become in recent years, but what do we mean by power? Simply put, power is the ability to effect the outcomes you want and, if necessary, to change the behavior of others to make this happen. For example, NATO's military power reversed Slobodan Milosevic's ethnic cleansing of Kosovo, and the promise of economic aid to Serbia's devastated economy reversed the Serbian government's initial disinclination to hand Milosevic over to the Hague tribunal.

---

[17]On the complexities of projections, see Joseph S. Nye, Jr., "Peering into the Future," *Foreign Affairs* (July-August 1994); see also Robert Jervis, "The Future of World Politics: Will It Resemble the Past?" *International Security* (Winter 1991–1992).

The ability to obtain the outcomes one wants is often associated with the possession of certain resources, and so we commonly use shorthand and define power as possession of relatively large amounts of such elements as population, territory, natural resources, economic strength, military force, and political stability. Power in this sense means holding the high cards in the international poker game. If you show high cards, others are likely to fold their hands. Of course, if you play your hand poorly or fall victim to bluff and deception, you can still lose, or at least fail to get the outcome you want. For example, the United States was the largest power after World War I, but it failed to prevent the rise of Hitler or Pearl Harbor. Converting America's potential power resources into realized power requires well-designed policy and skillful leadership. But it helps to start by holding the high cards.

Traditionally, the test of a great power was "strength for war."[18] War was the ultimate game in which the cards of international politics were played and estimates of relative power were proven. Over the centuries, as technologies evolved, the sources of power have changed. In the agrarian economies of seventeenth- and eighteenth-century Europe, population was a critical power resource because it provided a base for taxes and the recruitment of infantry (who were mostly mercenaries), and this combination of men and money gave the edge to France. But in the nineteenth century, the growing importance of industry benefited first Britain, which ruled the waves with a navy that had no peer, and later Germany, which used efficient administration and railways to transport armies for quick victories on the Continent (though Russia had a larger population and army). By the middle of the twentieth century, with the advent of the nuclear age, the United States and the Soviet Union possessed not only industrial might but nuclear arsenals and intercontinental missiles.

Today the foundations of power have been moving away from the emphasis on military force and conquest. Paradoxically, nuclear weapons were one of the causes. As we know from the history of the cold war, nuclear weapons proved so awesome and destructive that they became muscle bound—too costly to use except, theoretically, in the most extreme circumstances.[19] A second important change was the rise of nationalism, which

---

[18] A. J. Taylor, *The Struggle for Mastery in Europe, 1848–1918* (Oxford, UK: Oxford University Press, 1954), xxix.
[19] Whether this would change with the proliferation of nuclear weapons to more states is hotly debated among theorists. Deterrence should work with most states, but the prospects of accident and loss of control would increase. For my views, see Joseph S. Nye, Jr., *Nuclear Ethics* (New York: Free Press, 1986).

has made it more difficult for empires to rule over awakened populations. In the nineteenth century, a few adventurers conquered most of Africa with a handful of soldiers, and Britain ruled India with a colonial force that was a tiny fraction of the indigenous population. Today, colonial rule is not only widely condemned but far too costly, as both cold war superpowers discovered in Vietnam and Afghanistan. The collapse of the Soviet empire followed the end of European empires by a matter of decades.

A third important cause is societal change inside great powers. Postindustrial societies are focused on welfare rather than glory, and they loathe high casualties except when survival is at stake. This does not mean that they will not use force, even when casualties are expected—witness the 1991 Gulf War or Afghanistan today. But the absence of a warrior ethic in modern democracies means that the use of force requires an elaborate moral justification to ensure popular support (except in cases where survival is at stake). Roughly speaking, there are three types of countries in the world today: poor, weak preindustrial states, which are often the chaotic remnants of collapsed empires; modernizing industrial states such as India or China; and the postindustrial societies that prevail in Europe, North America, and Japan. The use of force is common in the first type of country, still accepted in the second, but less tolerated in the third. In the words of British diplomat Robert Cooper, "A large number of the most powerful states no longer want to fight or to conquer."[20] War remains possible, but it is much less acceptable now than it was a century or even half a century ago.[21]

Finally, for most of today's great powers, the use of force would jeopardize their economic objectives. Even nondemocratic countries that feel fewer popular moral constraints on the use of force have to consider its effects on their economic objectives. As Thomas Friedman has put it, countries are disciplined by an "electronic herd" of investors who control their access to capital in a globalized economy.[22] And Richard Rosecrance writes, "In the past, it was cheaper to seize another state's territory by force than to develop the sophisticated economic and trading apparatus needed to derive benefit from commercial exchange with it."[23] Imperial Japan used the former approach when it created the Greater East Asia

---

[20] Robert Cooper, *The Postmodern State and the World Order* (London: Demos, 2000), 22.
[21] John Mueller, *Retreat from Doomsday: The Obsolescence of Major War* (New York: Basic Books, 1989).
[22] Thomas Friedman, *The Lexus and the Olive Tree: Understanding Globalization* (New York: Farrar, Straus and Giroux, 1999), chap. 6.
[23] Richard N. Rosecrance, *The Rise of the Trading State* (New York: Basic Books, 1986), 16, 160.

Co-prosperity Sphere in the 1930s, but Japan's post-World War II role as a trading state turned out to be far more successful, leading it to become the second largest national economy in the world. It is difficult now to imagine a scenario in which Japan would try to colonize its neighbors, or succeed in doing so.

As mentioned above, none of this is to suggest that military force plays no role in international politics today. For one thing, the information revolution has yet to transform most of the world. Many states are unconstrained by democratic societal forces, as Kuwait learned from its neighbor Iraq, and terrorist groups pay little heed to the normal constraints of liberal societies. Civil wars are rife in many parts of the world where collapsed empires left power vacuums. Moreover, throughout history, the rise of new great powers has been accompanied by anxieties that have sometimes precipitated military crises. In Thucydides' immortal description, the Peloponnesian War in ancient Greece was caused by the rise to power of Athens and the fear it created in Sparta.[24] World War I owed much to the rise of the kaiser's Germany and the fear that it created in Britain.[25] Some foretell a similar dynamic in this century arising from the rise of China and the fear it creates in the United States.

Geoeconomics has not replaced geopolitics, although in the early twenty-first century there has clearly been a blurring of the traditional boundaries between the two. To ignore the role of force and the centrality of security would be like ignoring oxygen. Under normal circumstances, oxygen is plentiful and we pay it little attention. But once those conditions change and we begin to miss it, we can focus on nothing else.[26] Even in those areas where the direct employment of force falls out of use among countries—for instance, within Western Europe or between the United States and Japan—nonstate actors such as terrorists may use force. Moreover, military force can still play an important political role among advanced nations. For example, most countries in East Asia welcome the presence of American troops as an insurance policy against uncertain neighbors. Moreover, deterring threats or ensuring access to a crucial resource such as oil in the Persian Gulf increases America's influence

---

[24]Thucydides, *History of the Peloponnesian War*, trans. Rex Warner (London: Penguin, 1972), book I, chapter 1.
[25]And in turn, as industrialization progressed and railroads were built, Germany feared the rise of Russia.
[26]Henry Kissinger portrays four international systems existing side by side: the West (and Western Hemisphere), marked by democratic peace; Asia, where strategic conflict is possible; the Middle East, marked by religious conflict; and Africa, where civil wars threaten weak postcolonial states. "America at the Apex," *The National Interest* (Summer 2001).

with its allies. Sometimes the linkages may be direct; more often they are present in the back of statesmen's minds. As the Defense Department describes it, one of the missions of American troops based overseas is to "shape the environment."

With that said, economic power *has* become more important than in the past, both because of the relative increase in the costliness of force and because economic objectives loom large in the values of postindustrial societies.[27] In a world of economic globalization, all countries are to some extent dependent on market forces beyond their direct control. When President Clinton was struggling to balance the federal budget in 1993, one of his advisers stated in exasperation that if he were to be reborn, he would like to come back as "the market" because that was clearly the most powerful player.[28] But markets constrain different countries to different degrees. Because the United States constitutes such a large part of the market in trade and finance, it is better placed to set its own terms than are Argentina or Thailand. And if small countries are willing to pay the price of opting out of the market, they can reduce the power that other countries have over them. Thus American economic sanctions have had little effect, for example, on improving human rights in isolated Myanmar. Saddam Hussein's strong preference for his own survival rather than the welfare of the Iraqi people meant that crippling sanctions failed for more than a decade to remove him from power. And economic sanctions may disrupt but not deter nonstate terrorists. But the exceptions prove the rule. Military power remains crucial in certain situations, but it is a mistake to focus too narrowly on the military dimensions of American power.

SOFT POWER

In my view, if the United States wants to remain strong, Americans need also to pay attention to our soft power. What precisely do I mean by soft power? Military power and economic power are both examples of hard command power that can be used to induce others to change their position. Hard power can rest on inducements (carrots) or threats (sticks). But there is also an indirect way to exercise power. A country may obtain the outcomes it wants in world politics because other countries want to follow it, admiring its values, emulating its example, aspiring to its level of prosperity

---

[27] Robert O. Keohane and Joseph S. Nye, Jr., *Power and Interdependence*, 3rd ed. (New York: Longman, 2000), chap. 1.
[28] James Carville quoted in Bob Woodward, *The Agenda: Inside the Clinton White House* (New York: Simon and Schuster, 1994), 302.

and openness. In this sense, it is just as important to set the agenda in world politics and attract others as it is to force them to change through the threat or use of military or economic weapons. This aspect of power—getting others to want what you want—I call soft power.[29] It co-opts people rather than coerces them.

Soft power rests on the ability to set the political agenda in a way that shapes the preferences of others. At the personal level, wise parents know that if they have brought up their children with the right beliefs and values, their power will be greater and will last longer than if they have relied only on spankings, cutting off allowances, or taking away the car keys. Similarly, political leaders and thinkers such as Antonio Gramsci have long understood the power that comes from setting the agenda and determining the framework of a debate. The ability to establish preferences tends to be associated with intangible power resources such as an attractive culture, ideology, and institutions. If I can get you to *want* to do what I want, then I do not have to force you to do what you do *not* want to do. If the United States represents values that others want to follow, it will cost us less to lead. Soft power is not merely the same as influence, though it is one source of influence. After all, I can also influence you by threats or rewards. Soft power is also more than persuasion or the ability to move people by argument. It is the ability to entice and attract. And attraction often leads to acquiescence or imitation.

Soft power arises in large part from our values. These values are expressed in our culture, in the policies we follow inside our country, and in the way we handle ourselves internationally. The government sometimes finds it difficult to control and employ soft power. Like love, it is hard to measure and to handle, and does not touch everyone, but that does not diminish its importance. As Hubert Védrine laments, Americans are so powerful because they can "inspire the dreams and desires of others, thanks to the mastery of global images through film and television and because, for these same reasons, large numbers of students from other countries come to the United States to finish their studies."[30] Soft power is an important reality.

Of course, hard and soft power are related and can reinforce each other. Both are aspects of the ability to achieve our purposes by affecting the

---

[29]For a more detailed discussion, see Joseph S. Nye, Jr., *Bound to Lead: The Changing Nature of American Power* (New York: Basic Books, 1990), chap. 2. This builds on what Peter Bachrach and Morton Baratz called the "second face of power" in "Decisions and Nondecisions: An Analytical Framework," *American Political Science Review* (September 1963): 632–42.
[30]Védrine, *France in an Age of Globalization*, 3.

behavior of others. Sometimes the same power resources can affect the entire spectrum of behavior from coercion to attraction.[31] A country that suffers economic and military decline is likely to lose its ability to shape the international agenda as well as its attractiveness. And some countries may be attracted to others with hard power by the myth of invincibility or inevitability. Both Hitler and Stalin tried to develop such myths. Hard power can also be used to establish empires and institutions that set the agenda for smaller states—witness Soviet rule over the countries of Eastern Europe. But soft power is not simply the reflection of hard power. The Vatican did not lose its soft power when it lost the Papal States in Italy in the nineteenth century. Conversely, the Soviet Union lost much of its soft power after it invaded Hungary and Czechoslovakia, even though its economic and military resources continued to grow. Imperious policies that utilized Soviet hard power actually undercut its soft power. And some countries such as Canada, the Netherlands, and the Scandinavian states have political clout that is greater than their military and economic weight, because of the incorporation of attractive causes such as economic aid or peacekeeping into their definitions of national interest. These are lessons that the unilateralists forget at their and our peril.

Britain in the nineteenth century and America in the second half of the twentieth century enhanced their power by creating liberal international economic rules and institutions that were consistent with the liberal and democratic structures of British and American capitalism—free trade and the gold standard in the case of Britain, the International Monetary Fund, World Trade Organization, and other institutions in the case of the United States. If a country can make its power legitimate in the eyes of others, it will encounter less resistance to its wishes. If its culture and ideology are attractive, others more willingly follow. If it can establish international rules that are consistent with its society, it will be less likely to have to

---

[31]The distinction between hard and soft power is one of degree, both in the nature of the behavior and in the tangibility of the resources. Both are aspects of the ability to achieve one's purposes by affecting the behavior of others. Command power—the ability to change what others do—can rest on coercion or inducement. Co-optive power—the ability to shape what others want—can rest on the attractiveness of one's culture and ideology or the ability to manipulate the agenda of political choices in a manner that makes actors fail to express some preferences because they seem to be too unrealistic. The forms of behavior between command and co-optive power range along a continuum: command power, coercion, inducement, agenda setting, attraction, co-optive power. Soft power resources tend to be associated with co-optive power behavior, whereas hard power resources are usually associated with command behavior. But the relationship is imperfect. For example, countries may be attracted to others with command power by myths of invincibility, and command power may sometimes be used to establish institutions that later become regarded as legitimate. But the general association is strong enough to allow the useful shorthand reference to hard and soft power.

change. If it can help support institutions that encourage other countries to channel or limit their activities in ways it prefers, it may not need as many costly carrots and sticks.

In short, the universality of a country's culture and its ability to establish a set of favorable rules and institutions that govern areas of international activity are critical sources of power. The values of democracy, personal freedom, upward mobility, and openness that are often expressed in American popular culture, higher education, and foreign policy contribute to American power in many areas. In the view of German journalist Josef Joffe, America's soft power "looms even larger than its economic and military assets. U.S. culture, low-brow or high, radiates outward with an intensity last seen in the days of the Roman Empire—but with a novel twist. Rome's and Soviet Russia's cultural sway stopped exactly at their military borders. America's soft power, though, rules over an empire on which the sun never sets."[32]

Of course, soft power is more than just cultural power. The values the U.S. government champions in its behavior at home (for example, democracy), in international institutions (listening to others), and in foreign policy (promoting peace and human rights) also affect the preferences of others. America can attract (or repel) others by the influence of its example. But soft power does not belong to the government in the same degree that hard power does. Some hard power assets (such as armed forces) are strictly governmental, others are inherently national (such as our oil and gas reserves), and many can be transferred to collective control (such as industrial assets that can be mobilized in an emergency). In contrast, many soft power resources are separate from American government and only partly responsive to its purposes. In the Vietnam era, for example, American government policy and popular culture worked at cross-purposes. Today popular U.S. firms or nongovernmental groups develop soft power of their own that may coincide or be at odds with official foreign policy goals. That is all the more reason for the government to make sure that its own actions reinforce rather than undercut American soft power. All these sources of soft power are likely to become increasingly important in the global information age of this new century. And, at the same time, the arrogance, indifference to the opinions of others, and narrow approach to our national interests advocated by the new unilateralists are a sure way to undermine American soft power.

---

[32] Josef Joffe, "Who's Afraid of Mr. Big?" *The National Interest* (Summer 2001): 43.

Power in the global information age is becoming less tangible and less coercive, particularly among the advanced countries, but most of the world does not consist of postindustrial societies, and that limits the transformation of power. Much of Africa and the Middle East remains locked in preindustrial agricultural societies with weak institutions and authoritarian rulers. Other countries, such as China, India, and Brazil, are industrial economies analogous to parts of the West in the mid-twentieth century.[33] In such a variegated world, all three sources of power—military, economic, and soft—remain relevant, although to different degrees in different relationships. However, if current economic and social trends continue, leadership in the information revolution and soft power will become more important in the mix. Table 1 provides a simplified description of the evolution of power resources over the past few centuries.

Power in the twenty-first century will rest on a mix of hard and soft resources. No country is better endowed than the United States in all three dimensions—military, economic, and soft power. Its greatest mistake in such a world would be to fall into one-dimensional analysis and to believe that investing in military power alone will ensure its strength.

BALANCE OR HEGEMONY?

America's power—hard and soft—is only part of the story. How others react to American power is equally important to the question of stability and governance in this global information age. Many realists extol the virtues of the classic nineteenth-century European balance of power, in which constantly shifting coalitions contained the ambitions of any especially aggressive power. They urge the United States to rediscover the virtues of a balance of power at the global level today. Already in the 1970s, Richard Nixon argued that "the only time in the history of the world that we have had any extended periods of peace is when there has been a balance of power. It is when one nation becomes infinitely more powerful in relation to its potential competitors that the danger of war arises."[34] But whether such multipolarity would be good or bad for the United States and for the world is debatable. I am skeptical.

War was the constant companion and crucial instrument of the multipolar balance of power. The classic European balance provided stability in the sense of maintaining the independence of most countries, but there were wars among the great powers for 60 percent of the years since

---

[33]See Cooper, Postmodern State; Bell, *The Coming of Post-Industrial Society*.
[34]Nixon quoted in James Chace and Nicholas X. Rizopoulos, "Towards a New Concert of Nations: An American Perspective," *World Policy Journal* (Fall 1999): 9.

TABLE 1
Leading States and Their Power Resources, 1500–2000

Period	State	Major Resources
Sixteenth century	Spain	Gold bullion, colonial trade, mercenary armies, dynastic ties
Seventeenth century	Netherlands	Trade, capital markets, navy
Eighteenth century	France	Population, rural industry, public administration, army, culture (soft power)
Nineteenth century	Britain	Industry, political cohesion, finance and credit, navy, liberal norms (soft power), island location (easy to defend)
Twentieth century	United States	Economic scale, scientific and technical leadership, location, military forces and alliances, universalistic culture and liberal international regimes (soft power)
Twenty-first century	United States	Technological leadership, military and economic scale, soft power, hub of transnational communications

1500.[35] Rote adherence to the balance of power and multipolarity may prove to be a dangerous approach to global governance in a world where war could turn nuclear.

Many regions of the world and periods in history have seen stability under hegemony—when one power has been preeminent. Margaret Thatcher warned against drifting toward "an Orwellian future of Oceania, Eurasia, and Eastasia—three mercantilist world empires on increasingly hostile terms. . . . In other words, 2095 might look like 1914 played on a somewhat larger stage."[36] Both the Nixon and Thatcher views are too mechanical because they ignore soft power. America is an exception, says Josef Joffe, "because the 'hyperpower' is also the most alluring and seductive society in history. Napoleon had to rely on bayonets to spread France's revolutionary creed. In the American case, Munichers and Muscovites *want* what the avatar of ultra-modernity has to offer."[37]

The term "balance of power" is sometimes used in contradictory ways. The most interesting use of the term is as a predictor about how countries will behave; that is, will they pursue policies that will prevent any other country from developing power that could threaten their independence? By the evidence of history, many believe, the current preponderance of the United States will call forth a countervailing coalition that will eventually limit American power. In the words of the self-styled realist political scientist Kenneth Waltz, "both friends and foes will react as countries always have to threatened or real predominance of one among them: they will work to right the balance. The present condition of international politics is unnatural."[38]

---

[35]Jack S. Levy, *War in the Modern Great Power System, 1495–1975* (Lexington: University Press of Kentucky, 1983), 97.
[36]Margaret Thatcher, "Why America Must Remain Number One," *National Review*, 31 July 1995, 25.
[37]Josef Joffe, "Envy," *The New Republic*, 17 January 2000, 6.
[38]Kenneth Waltz, "Globalization and American Power," *The National Interest* (Spring 2000): 55–56.

In my view, such a mechanical prediction misses the mark. For one thing, countries sometimes react to the rise of a single power by "bandwagoning"—that is, joining the seemingly stronger rather than weaker side—much as Mussolini did when he decided, after several years of hesitation, to ally with Hitler. Proximity to and perceptions of threat also affect the way in which countries react.[39] The United States benefits from its geographical separation from Europe and Asia in that it often appears as a less proximate threat than neighboring countries inside those regions. Indeed, in 1945, the United States was by far the strongest nation on earth, and a mechanical application of balancing theory would have predicted an alliance against it. Instead, Europe and Japan allied with the Americans because the Soviet Union, while weaker in overall power, posed a greater military threat because of its geographical proximity and its lingering revolutionary ambitions. Today, Iraq and Iran both dislike the United States and might be expected to work together to balance American power in the Persian Gulf, but they worry even more about each other. Nationalism can also complicate predictions. For example, if North Korea and South Korea are reunited, they should have a strong incentive to maintain an alliance with a distant power such as the United States in order to balance their two giant neighbors, China and Japan. But intense nationalism resulting in opposition to an American presence could change this if American diplomacy is heavy-handed. Nonstate actors can also have an effect, as witnessed by the way cooperation against terrorists changed some states' behavior after September 2001.

A good case can be made that inequality of power can be a source of peace and stability. No matter how power is measured, some theorists argue, an equal distribution of power among major states has been relatively rare in history, and efforts to maintain a balance have often led to war. On the other hand, inequality of power has often led to peace and stability because there was little point in declaring war on a dominant state. The political scientist Robert Gilpin has argued that "*Pax Britannica* and *Pax Americana*, like the *Pax Romana*, ensured an international system of relative peace and security." And the economist Charles Kindleberger claimed that "for the world economy to be stabilized, there has to be a stabilizer, one stabilizer."[40] Global governance requires a large state to take the lead. But how much and what kind of inequality of power is necessary—

---

[39]Stephen Walt, "Alliance Formation and the Balance of Power," *International Security* (Spring 1985).
[40]Robert Gilpin, *War and Change in World Politics* (New York: Cambridge University Press, 1981), 144–45; Charles Kindleberger, *The World in Depression, 1929–1939* (Berkeley: University of California Press, 1973), 305.

or tolerable—and for how long? If the leading country possesses soft power and behaves in a manner that benefits others, effective countercoalitions may be slow to arise. If, on the other hand, the leading country defines its interests narrowly and uses its weight arrogantly, it increases the incentives for others to coordinate to escape its hegemony.

Some countries chafe under the weight of American power more than others. *Hegemony* is sometimes used as a term of opprobrium by political leaders in Russia, China, the Middle East, France, and others. The term is used less often or less negatively in countries where American soft power is strong. If hegemony means being able to dictate, or at least dominate, the rules and arrangements by which international relations are conducted, as Joshua Goldstein argues, then the United States is hardly a hegemon today.[41] It does have a predominant voice and vote in the International Monetary Fund, but it cannot alone choose the director. It has not been able to prevail over Europe and Japan in the World Trade Organization. It opposed the Land Mines Treaty but could not prevent it from coming into existence. Saddam Hussein remained in power for more than a decade despite American efforts to drive him out. The U.S. opposed Russia's war in Chechnya and civil war in Colombia, but to no avail. If hegemony is defined more modestly as a situation where one country has significantly more power resources or capabilities than others, then it simply signifies American preponderance, not necessarily dominance or control.[42] Even after World War II, when the United States controlled half the world's economic production (because all other countries had been devastated by the war), it was not able to prevail in all of its objectives.[43]

---

[41]Joshua S. Goldstein, *Long Cycles: Prosperity and War in the Modern Age* (New Haven: Yale University Press, 1988), 281.

[42]See Robert O. Keohane, *After Hegemony: Cooperation and Discord in the World Political Economy* (Princeton: Princeton University Press, 1984), 235.

[43]Over the years, a number of scholars have tried to predict the rise and fall of nations by developing a general historical theory of hegemonic transition. Some have tried to generalize from the experience of Portugal, Spain, the Netherlands, France, and Britain. Others have focused more closely on Britain's decline in the twentieth century as a predictor for the fate for the United States. None of these approaches has been successful. Most of the theories have predicted that America would decline long before now. Vague definitions and arbitrary schematizations alert us to the inadequacies of such grand theories. Most try to squeeze history into procrustean theoretical beds by focusing on particular power resources while ignoring others that are equally important. Hegemony can be used as a descriptive term (though it is sometimes fraught with emotional overtones), but grand hegemonic theories are weak in predicting future events. See Immanuel Wallerstein, *The Politics of the World Economy: The States, the Movements, and the Civilizations: Essays* (New York: Cambridge University Press, 1984), 38, 41; George Modelski, "The Long Cycle of Global Politics and the Nation-State," *Comparative Studies in Society and History* (April 1978); George Modelski, *Long Cycles in World Politics* (Seattle: University of Washington Press, 1987). For a detailed discussion, see Nye, *Bound to Lead*, chap. 2.

Pax Britannica in the nineteenth century is often cited as an example of successful hegemony, even though Britain ranked behind the United States and Russia in GNP. Britain was never as superior in productivity to the rest of the world as the United States has been since 1945, but Britain also had a degree of soft power. Victorian culture was influential around the globe, and Britain gained in reputation when it defined its interests in ways that benefited other nations (for example, opening its markets to imports or eradicating piracy). America lacks a global territorial empire like Britain's, but instead possesses a large, continental-scale home economy and has greater soft power. These differences between Britain and America suggest a greater staying power for American hegemony. Political scientist William Wohlforth argues that the United States is so far ahead that potential rivals find it dangerous to invite America's focused enmity, and allied states can feel confident that they can continue to rely on American protection.[44] Thus the usual balancing forces are weakened.

Nonetheless, if American diplomacy is unilateral and arrogant, our preponderance would not prevent other states and nonstate actors from taking actions that complicate American calculations and constrain its freedom of action.[45] For example, some allies may follow the American bandwagon on the largest security issues but form coalitions to balance American behavior in other areas such as trade or the environment. And diplomatic maneuvering short of alliance can have political effects. As William Safire observed when Presidents Vladimir Putin and George W. Bush first met, "Well aware of the weakness of his hand, Putin is emulating Nixon's strategy by playing the China card. Pointedly, just before meeting with Bush, Putin traveled to Shanghai to set up a regional cooperation semi-alliance with Jiang Zemin and some of his Asian fellow travelers."[46] Putin's tactics, according to one reporter, "put Mr. Bush on the defensive, and Mr. Bush was at pains to assert that America is not about to go it alone in international affairs."[47]

Pax Americana is likely to last not only because of unmatched American hard power but also to the extent that the United States "is uniquely capable of engaging in 'strategic restraint,' reassuring partners and facilitating cooperation."[48] The open and pluralistic way in which U.S. foreign

---

[44]Wohlforth, "The Stability of a Unipolar World."
[45]Stephen Walt, "Keeping the World 'Off-Balance': Self-Restraint and US Foreign Policy," *Kennedy School Research Working Paper Series 00-013*, October 2000.
[46]William Safire, "Putin's China Card," *New York Times*, 18 June 2001.
[47]Patrick Tyler, "Bush and Putin Look Each Other in the Eye," *New York Times*, 17 June 2001.
[48]Ikenberry, "Institutions, Strategic Restraint," 47; also Ikenberry, "Getting Hegemony Right," *The National Interest* (Spring 2001): 17-24.

policy is made can often reduce surprises, allow others to have a voice, and contribute to soft power. Moreover, the impact of American preponderance is softened when it is embodied in a web of multilateral institutions that allow others to participate in decisions and that act as a sort of world constitution to limit the capriciousness of American power. That was the lesson the United States learned as it struggled to create an antiterrorist coalition in the wake of the September 2001 attacks. When the society and culture of the hegemon are attractive, the sense of threat and need to balance it are reduced.[49] Whether other countries will unite to balance American power will depend on how the United States behaves as well as the power resources of potential challengers.*

---

[49] Josef Joffe, "How America Does It," *Foreign Affairs* (September-October 1997).
*This article is adapted from *The Paradox of American Power* (New York: Oxford University Press, 2002). It was originally published in *Political Science Quarterly* 117 (Winter 2002–2003): 545–559.

Understanding the Bush Doctrine: Preventive Wars and Regime Change

ROBERT JERVIS

THE INVASION OF IRAQ, ALTHOUGH IMPORTANT IN ITSELF, is even more noteworthy as a manifestation of the Bush doctrine. In a sharp break from the President's pre-September 11 views that saw American leadership, and especially its use of force, restricted to defending narrow and traditional vital interests, he has enunciated a far-reaching program that calls for something very much like an empire.[1]

The doctrine has four elements: a strong belief in the importance of a state's domestic regime in determining its foreign policy and the related judgment that this is an opportune time to transform international politics; the perception of great threats that can be defeated only by new and vigorous policies, most notably preventive war; a willingness to act unilaterally when necessary; and, as both a cause and a summary of these beliefs, an overriding sense that peace and stability require the United States to assert its primacy in world politics. It is, of course, possible that I am exaggerating and that what we are seeing is mostly an elaborate rationale for the overthrow of Saddam Hussein that will have little relevance beyond that. I think the doctrine is real, however. It is quite

---

[1] For somewhat similar analyses, but with quite different evaluations, see James Chace, "Imperial America and the Common Interest," *World Policy* 19 (Spring 2002): 1–9; Charles Krauthammer, "The Unipolar Moment Revisited," *National Interest* 70 (Winter 2002/03): 5–17; Stephen Peter Rosen, "An Empire, If You Can Keep It," ibid 71 (Spring 2003): 51–62; Robert Art, *A Grand Strategy for America* (Ithaca, NY: Cornell University Press, 2003), 87–92.

ROBERT JERVIS is Adlai E. Stevenson Professor of International Politics at Columbia University and author most recently of *Why Intelligence Fails: Lessons from the Iranian Revolution and the Iraq War*.

articulate, and American policy since the end of the military campaign has been consistent with it. Furthermore, there is a tendency for people to act in accord with the explanations they have given for their own behavior, which means that the doctrine could guide behavior even if it were originally a rationalization.[2]

I will describe, explain, and evaluate the doctrine. These three tasks are hard to separate. Evaluation and explanation are particularly and perhaps disturbingly close. To see the doctrine as a response to an unusual external environment may verge on endorsing it, especially for Realists who both oppose the doctrine and see states as rational. In the end, I believe it to be the product of idiosyncratic and structural factors, both a normal reaction to an abnormal situation and a policy that is likely to bring grief to the world and the United States. The United States may be only the latest in a long line of countries that is unable to place sensible limits on its fears and aspirations.[3]

DEMOCRACY AND LIBERALISM

This is not to say that the doctrine is entirely consistent, and one component may not fit well with the rest despite receiving pride of place in the "The National Security Strategy of the U.S.," which starts thusly: "The great struggles of the twentieth century between liberty and totalitarianism ended with a decisive victory for the forces of freedom—and a single sustainable model for national success: freedom, democracy, and free enterprise." The spread of these values opens the path to "make the world not just safer but better," a "path [that] is not America's alone. It is open to all."[4] This taps deep American beliefs and traditions enunciated by Woodrow Wilson and echoed by Bill Clinton, and it is linked to the belief, common among powerful states, that its values are universal and their

---

[2] See Deborah Larson, *Origins of Containment: A Psychological Explanation* (Princeton: Princeton University Press, 1985), which draws on Bem's theory of self-perception. See Daryl Bem, "Self-Perception Theory" in Leonard Berkowitz, ed., *Advances in Experimental Social Psychology*, vol. 6 (New York: Academic Press, 1972), 1-62.

[3] Paul Kennedy, *The Rise and Fall of the Great Powers: Economic Change and Military Conflict from 1500 to 2000* (New York: Random House, 1987); Robert Gilpin, *War and Change in World Politics* (New York: Cambridge University Press, 1981); Geoffrey Parker, *The Grand Strategy of Philip II* (New Haven: Yale University Press, 1998).

[4] White House, "The National Security Strategy of the United States" (Washington, DC: September 2002), i, 1. Bush's West Point speech similarly declared: "Moral truth is the same in every culture, in every time, and in every place.... We are in a conflict between good and evil.... When it comes to the common rights and needs of men and women, there is no clash of civilizations." "Remarks by the President at 2002 Graduation Exercise of the Unites States Military Academy," White House Press Release, 1 June 2002, 3; Paul Allen, *Philip III and Pax Hispanica, 1598-1621: The Failure of Grand Strategy* (New Haven: Yale University Press, 2000).

spread will benefit the entire world. Just as Wilson sought to "teach [the countries of Latin America] to elect good men," so Bush will bring free markets and free elections to countries without them. This agenda horrifies Realists (and perhaps realists).[5] Some mid-level officials think this is window dressing; by contrast, John Gaddis sees it as the heart of the doctrine,[6] a view that is endorsed by other officials.

The administration's argument is that strong measures to spread democracy are needed and will be efficacious. Liberating Iraq will not only produce democracy there, but it will also encourage democracy in the rest of the Middle East. There is no incompatibility between Islam or any other culture and democracy; the example of political pluralism in one country will be emulated. The implicit belief is that democracy can take hold when the artificial obstacles to it are removed. Far from being the product of unusually propitious circumstances, a free and pluralist system is the "natural order" that will prevail unless something special intervenes.[7] Furthermore, more democracies will mean greater stability, peaceful relations with neighbors, and less terrorism, comforting claims that evidence indicates is questionable at best.[8] Would a democratic Iraq be stable? Would an Iraq that reflected the will of its people recognize Israel or renounce all claims to Kuwait? Would a democratic Palestinian state be more willing to live at peace with Israel than an authoritarian one, especially if it did not gain all of the territory lost in 1967? Previous experience also calls into question the links between democracy and free markets, each of which can readily undermine the other. But such doubts do not cloud official pronouncements or even the off-the-record comments of top officials. The United States now appears to have a faith-based foreign policy.

This or any other administration may not act on it. No American government has been willing to sacrifice stability and support of U.S. policy to honor democracy in countries like Algeria, Egypt, Saudi Arabia, and Pakistan.[9] But the current view does parallel Ronald Reagan's policy of not accepting a detente with the Union of Soviet Socialist Republics (USSR) that was limited to arms control and insisting on a larger agenda

---

[5]Thus, Samuel Huntington, who agrees that a state's foreign policy is strongly influenced by its domestic regime, argues that conflict can be reduced only by not pushing Western values on other societies. See his *The Clash of Civilizations and the Remaking of the World Order* (New York: Simon and Schuster, 1996).
[6]John Lewis Gaddis, "Bush's Security Strategy," *Foreign Policy* 133 (November/December 2002): 50–57.
[7]For the concept of natural order, see Stephen Toulmin, *Foresight and Understanding: An Enquiry into the Aims of Science* (Bloomington: Indiana University Press, 1961).
[8]Edward Mansfield and Jack Snyder, *Democratization and War* (Cambridge, MA: MIT Press, forthcoming).
[9]It can be argued that Carter's policy toward the shah's regime in Iran is an exception. There is something to this, but the conflict between his policy and stability is more apparent in retrospect than it was at the time.

that included human rights within the Soviet Union and, thus, implicitly called for a new domestic regime. The Bush administration is heir to this tradition when it declares that any agreement with North Korea would have to address a range a problems in addition to nuclear weapons, including "the abominable way [the North] treats its people."[10] The argument is that, as in Iraq, regime change is necessary because tyrannical governments will always be prone to disregard agreements and coerce their neighbors just as they mistreat their own citizens. Notwithstanding their being Realists in their views about how states influence one another, Bush and his colleagues are Liberals in their beliefs about the sources of foreign policy.

Consistent with liberalism, this perspective is highly optimistic in seeing the possibility of progress. A week after September 11, Bush is reported to have told one of his closest advisers: "We have an opportunity to restructure the world toward freedom, and we have to get it right." He expounded this theme in a formal speech marking the six-month anniversary of the attack: "When the terrorists are disrupted and scattered and discredited,... we will see then that the old and serious disputes can be settled within the bounds of reason, and goodwill, and mutual security. I see a peaceful world beyond the war on terror, and with courage and unity, we are building that world together."[11] In February 2002, the President responded to a reporter's question about the predictable French criticism of his policy by saying that "history has given us a unique opportunity to defend freedom. And we're going to seize the moment, and do it."[12] One month later, he declared, "We understand history has called us into action, and we are not going to miss that opportunity to make the world more peaceful and more free."[13]

The absence of any competing model for organizing societies noted at the start of the National Security document is part of the explanation for the optimism. Another is the expectation of a benign form of domino dynamics, as the replacement of the Iraqi regime is expected to embolden the forces of freedom and deter other potential disturbers of the peace. Before the war, Bush declared that when Saddam is overthrown "other regimes will be given a clear warning that support for terror will not be tolerated. Without this outside support for terrorism, Palestinians who are

---

[10] Quoted in David Sanger, "U.S. to Withdraw From Arms Accord With North Korea," *New York Times*, 20 October 2002.
[11] Quoted in Frank Bruni, "For President, a Mission and a Role in History," ibid. 22 September 2001; "President Thanks World Coalition for Anti-Terrorism Efforts," White House Press Release, 11 March 2002, 3-4; also see "Remarks by the President at 2002 Graduation Exercise," 4-5.
[12] "President Bush, Prime Minister Koizumi Hold Press Conference," White House Press Release, 18 February 2002, 6.
[13] "President, Vice President Discuss the Middle East," White House Press Release, 21 March 2002, 2.

working for reform and long for democracy will be in a better position to choose new leaders—true leaders who strive for peace."[14] After the war, Bush reaffirmed his belief that "a free Iraq can be an example of reform and progress to all the Middle East."[15] Even some analysts like Thomas Friedman, who are skeptical of much of the administration's policy, believe that the demonstration effect of regime change in Iraq can be large and salutary.

The mechanisms by which these effects are expected to occur are not entirely clear. One involves establishing an American reputation for opposing tyranny. But the power of reputation is questioned by the Bush administration's skepticism toward deterrence, which works partly by this means. Another mechanism is the power of example: people will see that tyrants are not invulnerable and that democracy can provide a better life. But seeing one dictator overthrown (not an unusual occurrence) may not have much influence on others. The dynamics within the Soviet bloc in 1989–1991 were a product of special conditions, and while contagion, tipping, and positive feedback do occur, so does negative feedback. We may hope for the former, but it is unreasonable to expect it.

THREAT AND PREVENTIVE WAR

The second pillar of the Bush doctrine is that we live in a time not only of opportunity, but also of great threat posed primarily by terrorists and rogue states. Optimism and pessimism are linked in the belief that if the United States does not make the world better, it will grow more dangerous. As Bush said in his West Point address of 1 June 2002: "Today our enemies see weapons of mass destruction as weapons of choice. For rogue states these weapons are tools of intimidation and military aggression against their neighbors. These weapons may also allow these states to attempt to blackmail the U.S. and our allies to prevent us from deterring or repelling the aggressive behavior of rogue states. Such states also see these weapons as their best means of overcoming the conventional superiority of the U.S."[16]

These threats cannot be contained by deterrence. Terrorists are fanatics, and there is nothing that they value that we can hold at risk; rogues like Iraq are risk-acceptant and accident prone. The heightened sense of vulnerability increases the dissatisfaction with deterrence, but it is

---

[14]Speech to the American Enterprise Institute, 26 February 2003. For a general discussion of the administration's optimism about the effects of overthrowing Saddam on the Middle East, see Philip Gordon, "Bush's Middle East Vision," *Survival* 45 (Spring 2003): 155–165.

[15]Quoted in David Sanger and Thom Shanker, "Bush Says Regime in Iraq is No More; Syria is Penalized," *New York Times*, 16 April 2003.

[16]Also see White House, *National Strategy to Combat Weapons of Mass Destruction* (Washington, DC: December 2002), 1.

noteworthy that this stance taps into the longstanding Republican critique of many American Cold War policies. One wing of the party always sought defense rather than deterrence (or, to be more precise, deterrence by denial instead of deterrence by punishment), and this was reflected in the search for escalation dominance, multiple nuclear options, and defense against ballistic missiles.[17]

Because even defense may not be possible against terrorists or rogues, the United States must be ready to wage preventive wars and to act "against ... emerging threats before they are fully formed," as Bush puts it.[18] Prevention is not a new element in world politics, although Dale Copeland's important treatment exaggerates its previous centrality.[19] Israel launched a preventive strike against the Iraqi nuclear program in 1981; during the Cold War, U.S. officials contemplated attacking the USSR and the Peoples' Republic of China (PRC) before they could develop robust nuclear capabilities.[20] The Monroe doctrine and westward expansion in the nineteenth century stemmed in part from the American desire to prevent any European power from establishing a presence that could menace the United States.

---

[17]It is no accident that the leading theorist of this school of thought, Albert Wohlstetter, trained and sponsored many of the driving figures of the Bush administration, such as Paul Wolfowitz and Richard Perle.

[18]Letter accompanying "National Security Strategy of the United States," ii. Calling this aspect of the doctrine as our policy against Iraq "preemptive," as the Bush administration does, is to do violence to the English language. No one thought that Iraq was about to attack anyone; rather, the argument was that Iraq and perhaps others are terrible menaces that eventually will do the United States great harm and must be dealt with as soon as possible, before the harm has been inflicted and while prophylactic actions can be taken at reasonable cost. For a study of cases, see Robert Litwak, "The New Calculus of Pre-emption," *Survival* 44 (Winter 2002-03): 53–79.

[19]Dale Copeland, *The Origins of Major War* (Ithaca, NY: Cornell University Press, 2000); also see John Mearsheimer, *Tragedy of Great Power Politics* (New York: Norton, 2001). For important conceptual distinctions and propositions, see Jack Levy, "Declining Power and the Preventive Motivation for War," *World Politics* 40 (October 1987): 82–107; for a study that is skeptical of the general prevalence of preventive wars but presents one example, Jack Levy and Joseph Gochal, "Democracy and Preventive War: Israel and the 1996 Sinai Campaign," *Security Studies* 11 (Winter 2001/2): 1–49. On the U.S. experience, see Art, *A Grand Strategy for America*, 181-197. Randall Schweller argues that democratic states fight preventively only under very restrictive circumstances: "Domestic Structure and Preventive War: Are Democracies More Pacific?" *World Politics* 44 (January 1992): 235–269; he notes the unusual nature of the Israeli cases. For the argument that states are generally well served resisting the temptation to fight preventively, see Richard Betts, "Striking First: A History of Thankfully Lost Opportunities," *Ethics and International Affairs* 17 (2003): 17–24. For a review of power transition theory, which in one interpretation is driven by preventive motivation, see Jacek Kugler and Douglas Lemke, *Parity and War: Evaluations and Extensions of The War Ledger* (Ann Arbor: University of Michigan Press, 1996).

[20]Marc Trachtenberg, *History and Strategy* (Princeton: Princeton University Press, 1991), chap. 3; William Burr and Jeffrey Richelson, "Whether to 'Strangle the Baby in the Cradle': The United States and the Chinese Nuclear Program, 1960-64," *International Security* 25 (Winter 2000/01): 54–99. Gregory Mitrovich shows how much of American early Cold War policy was driven by the fear that it could not sustain a prolonged confrontation: *Undermining the Kremlin: America's Strategy to Subvert the Soviet Bloc, 1947-1956* (Ithaca, NY: Cornell University Press, 2000).

The United States was a weak country at that time; now the preventive war doctrine is based on strength and on the associated desire to ensure the maintenance of American dominance. Critics argue that preventive wars are rarely necessary because deterrence can be effective and many threats are exaggerated or can be met with strong but less militarized policies. Libya, for example, once the leading rogue, now seems to be outside of the axis of evil. Otto von Bismarck called preventive wars "suicide for fear of death," and, although the disparity of power between the United States and its adversaries means this is no longer the case, the argument for such wars implies a high degree of confidence that the future will be bleak unless they are undertaken or at least a belief that this world will be worse than the likely one produced by the war.

This policy faces three large obstacles. First, by definition, the relevant information is hard to obtain because it involves predictions about threats that reside sometime in the future. Thus, while in retrospect it is easy to say that the Western allies should have stopped Hitler long before 1939, at the time it was far from clear that he would turn out to be such a menace. No one who reads Neville Chamberlain's speeches can believe that he was a fool. In some cases, a well-placed spy might be able to provide solid evidence that the other had to be stopped, but in many other cases—perhaps including Nazi Germany—even this would not be sufficient, because leaders do not themselves know how they will act in the future. The Bush doctrine implies that the problem is not so difficult, because the state's foreign policy is shaped, if not determined, by its domestic political system. Thus, knowing that North Korea, Iran, and Syria are brutal dictatorships tells us that they will seek to dominate their neighbors, sponsor terrorism, and threaten the United States. But while the generalization that states that oppress their own people will disturb the international system fits many cases, it is far from universal, which means that such short-cuts to the assessment process are fallible. Second and relatedly, even information on capabilities and past behavior may be difficult to come by, as the case of Iraq shows. Saddam's links to terrorists were murky and remain subject to debate, and while much remains unclear, it seems that the United States and Britain not only publicly exaggerated, but also privately overestimated, the extent of his weapons of mass destruction (WMD) program.

Third, unless all challengers are deterred by the exercise of the doctrine in Iraq, preventive war will have to be repeated as other threats reach a similar threshold. Doing so will require sustained domestic, if not international, support, which is made less likely by the first two complications. The very nature of a preventive war means that the evidence is ambiguous and the supporting arguments are subject to rebuttal. If Britain and France had gone to war with Germany before 1939, large segments of the public would have believed that the war was not necessary. If it had gone badly, the public would have wanted to sue for peace; if it had gone well, public opinion would have questioned its wisdom. While it is too early to say how American opinion will view Saddam's overthrow (and opinion is likely to change over time), a degree of skepticism that will inhibit the repetition of this policy seems probable.

National leaders are aware of these difficulties and generally hesitate to take strong actions in the face of such uncertainty. While one common motive for war has been the belief that the situation will deteriorate unless the state acts strongly now, and indeed this kind of fear drives the security dilemma, leaders usually put off decisions if they can. They know that many potential threats will never eventuate or will be made worse by precipitous military action, and they are predisposed to postpone, to await further developments and information, to kick the can down the road. In rejecting this approach in Iraq, if not in North Korea, Bush and his colleagues are behaving unusually, although this does not mean they are wrong.

Part of the reason for their stance is the feeling of vulnerability and the consequent belief that the risks and costs of inaction are unacceptably high. Note one of the few lines that brought applause in Bush's Cincinnati speech of 7 October 2002 and that shows the powerful psychological link between September 11 and the drive to depose Saddam: "We will not live in fear." Taken literally, this makes no sense. Unfortunately, fear is often well founded. What it indicates is an understandable desire for a safer world, despite that fact that the United States did live in fear throughout the Cold War and survived quite well. But if the sentence has little logical meaning, the emotion it embodies is an understandable fear of fear, a drive to gain certainty, an impulse to assert control by acting.[21]

---

[21] A minor illustration of the power of fear was the closing of a New York subway station when a first-year art student taped to the girders and walls thirty-seven black boxes with the word "fear" on them, an unlikely thing for a bomber to do. See Michael Kimmelman, "In New York, Art Is Crime, And Crime Becomes Art," *New York Times*, 18 December 2002. For a study of how people's willingness to sacrifice civil liberties are affected by their fear of a future attack, see Darren Davis and Brian Silver, "Civil Liberties vs. Security: Public Opinion in this Context of the Terrorist Attacks on America" (unpublished manuscript); Leonie Huddy, Stanley Feldman, Charles Taber, and Gallya Lahav, "The Politics of Threat: Cognitive and Affective Reactions to 9/11" (paper presented at the annual meeting of the American Political Science Association, Boston, 29 August–1 September 2002); Leonie Huddy, Stanley Feldman, Theresa Capelos, and Colin Provost, "The Consequences of Terrorism: Disentangling the Effects of Personal and National Threat," *Political Psychology* 23 (September 2002): 485–510. For a general theory of the impact of feelings of vulnerability on policy, see Charles Kupchan, *The Vulnerability of Empire* (Ithaca, NY: Cornell University Press, 1994).

This reading of Bush's statement is consistent with my impression that many people who opposed invading Iraq before September 11, but altered their positions afterwards, had not taken terrorism terribly seriously before September 11, a category that includes George Bush.[22] Those who had studied the subject were, of course, surprised by the timing and method of the attacks, but not that they took place; they changed their beliefs only incrementally. But Bush frequently acknowledges, indeed stresses, that he was shocked by the assault, which greatly increased his feelings of danger and led him to feel that drastically different policies were necessary. As he put it in his Cincinnati speech: "On September 11th, 2001, America felt its vulnerability." It is no accident that this sentence comes between two paragraphs about the need to disarm Iraq. Three months later, in response to an accusation that he always wanted to invade Iraq, Bush replied: "prior to September 11, we were discussing smart sanctions. . . . After September 11, the doctrine of containment just doesn't hold any water. . . . My vision shifted dramatically after September 11, because I now realize the stakes, I realize the world has changed."[23] Secretary of Defense Donald Rumsfeld similarly explained that the United States "did not act in Iraq because dramatic new evidence of Iraq's pursuit of weapons of mass murder. We acted because we saw the existing evidence in a new light, through the prism of our experience on September 11."[24] The claim that some possibilities are unlikely enough to be put aside lost plausibility in face of the obvious retort: "What could be less likely than terrorists flying airplanes into the World Trade Center and the Pentagon?" During the Cold War, Bernard Brodie expressed his exasperation with wild suggestions about military actions the USSR might undertake: "All sorts of notions and propositions are churned out, and often presented for consideration with the prefatory words: 'It is conceivable that. . . .' Such words establish their own truth, for the fact that someone has conceived of whatever proposition follows is enough to establish that it is conceivable. Whether it is worth a second thought, however, is another matter."[25] Worst-case analysis is now hard to dismiss.

The fact that no one can guarantee that an adversary with WMD will not use them means that fear cannot be banished. Although administration

---

[22] According to Robert Woodward, George Tenet believed that "Bush had been the least prepared of all of [the administration leaders] for the terrorist attacks." See *Bush at War* (New York: Simon and Schuster, 2002), 318. Before then, his administration had concentrated on Russia and the PRC.
[23] *New York Times*, 1 February 2003.
[24] Quoted in James Risen, David Sanger, and Thom Shanker, "In Sketchy Data, Trying to Gauge Iraq Threat," ibid., 20 July 2003.
[25] Bernard Brodie, "The Development of Nuclear Strategy," *International Security* 2 (Spring 1978): 83.

officials exaggerated the danger that Saddam posed, they also revealed their true fears when they talked about the possibility that he could use WMD against the United States or its allies. At least some of them may have been insensitive to the magnitude of this possibility; what mattered was its very existence. Psychology plays an important role here because people value certainty and are willing to pay a high price to decrease the probability of a danger from slight to none.[26] Bush's choice of words declaring a formal end to the organized combat in Iraq was telling: "this much is certain: No terrorist network will gain weapons of mass destruction from the Iraqi regime."[27] Concomitantly, people often feel that uncertainty can be best eliminated by taking the initiative. As Bush put it in his letter accompanying the submission of his National Security Strategy, "In the new world we have entered, the only path to peace and security is the path of action." The body of the document declared that "The greater the threat, the greater is the risk of inaction."[28] In the past, a state could let a potential threat grow because it might not turn into a major menace. Now, if one follows this cautious path and the worst case does arise, the price will be prohibitive. Thus, Senator Orrin Hatch dismissed the argument that since the threat from Iraq was not imminent the United States could afford to rely on diplomacy and deterrence by saying, "Imminence becomes murkier in the era of terrorism and weapons of mass destruction."[29] It then makes sense to strike much sooner and more often, even though in some cases doing so will not have been necessary.

UNILATERALISM

The perceived need for preventive wars is linked to the fundamental unilateralism of the Bush doctrine, since it is hard to get a consensus for such strong actions and other states have every reason to let the dominant power carry the full burden.[30] Unilateralism also has deep

---

[26]Daniel Kahneman and Amos Tversky, eds., *Choices, Values, and Frames* (New York: Cambridge University Press, 2000).
[27]"Transcript of President Bush's Remarks on the End of Major Combat in Iraq," *New York Times*, 2 March 2003. (Emphasis added.) He used a similar formulation three months later: "President Meets with Small Business Owners in New Jersey," 16 June 2003, White House Press Release.
[28]"National Security Strategy of the United States," ii, 15; also see "In President's Words: Free People Will Keep the Peace of the World," *New York Times*, 27 February 2003; "Bush's Speech on Iraq: 'Saddam Hussein and His Sons Must Leave," ibid., 18 March 2003; Tony Blair's statement quoted in Emma Daly, "Both Britain and Spain Dismiss Offer On Iraq Missiles," ibid., 1 March 2003.
[29]Quoted in Carl Hulse, "Senate Republicans Back Bush's Iraq Policy, as Democrats Call it Rash and Bullying," ibid., 8 March 2003.
[30]One of those outside the government who helped formulate the Bush doctrine denies that it is unilateralist. See Philip Zelikow, "The Transformation of National Security," *National Interest* 71 (Spring 2003): 24–25.

roots in the non-northeastern parts of the Republican party, was well represented in the Reagan administration, draws on long-standing American political traditions, and was part of Bush's outlook before September 11. Of course, assistance from others was needed in Afghanistan and Iraq. But these should not be mistaken for joint ventures, as the United States did not bend its policy to meet others' preferences. In stressing that the United States is building coalitions in the plural rather than an alliance (the mission determines the coalition, in Rumsfeld's phrase), American leaders have made it clear that they will forego the participation of any particular country rather than compromise.

The seeming exception of policy toward North Korea, in which the United States refuses to negotiate bilaterally and insists that the problem is one for the international community, is actually consistent with this approach. Others were not consulted on the policy and in fact resisted it. The obvious purpose of the American stance was to get others to apply pressure on the adversary. While this is a legitimate aim and, perhaps, the best policy, it is one the United States has selected on its own. Multilateralism here is purely instrumental, a way to avoid giving what the United States regards as a concession to North Korea and a means of further weakening and isolating it, despite others believing this is unwise.

Even before September 11, Bush displayed little willingness to cater to world public opinion or to heed the cries of outrage from European countries as the United States interpreted its interests and the interests of the world in its own way. Thus, the Bush administration walked away from the Kyoto treaty, the International Criminal Court, and the protocol implementing the ban on biological weapons rather than try to work within these frameworks and modify them. The United States also ignored European criticisms of its Middle Eastern policy. On a smaller scale, it forced out the heads of the Organization for the Prohibition of Chemical Weapons and the Intergovernmental Panel on Climate Change. In response to this kind of behavior, European diplomats can only say: "Big partners should consult with smaller partners."[31] The operative word is "should." When in the wake of the overthrow of Saddam, Chirac declares: "We are no longer in an era where one or two countries control the fate of another country," he describes the world as he would like it to be, not as it is.[32]

---

[31]Quoted in Steven Erlanger, "Bush's Move On ABM Pact Gives Pause to Europeans," *New York Times*, 13 December 2001; also see Suzanne Daley, "Many in Europe Voice Worry that U.S. Will Not Consult Them," ibid., 31 January 2002; Erlanger, "Protests, and Friends Too, Await Bush in Europe," ibid., 22 May 2002; Elizabeth Becker, "U.S. Unilateralism Worries Trade Officials," ibid., 17 March 2003.
[32]Quoted in Karen DeYoung, "Chirac Moves To Repair United States Ties," *Washington Post*, 16 April 2003.

The administration has defended each of its actions, but not its general stance. The most principled, persuasive, and perhaps correct defense is built around the difficulty in procuring public goods. As long as leadership is shared, very little will happen because no one actor will be willing to shoulder the costs and the responsibilities. "At this moment in history, if there is a problem, we're expected to deal with it," is how Bush explains it. "We are trying to lead the world," is what one administration official said when the United States blocked language in a UN declaration on child health that might be read as condoning abortion.[33] This is not entirely hypocritical: many of the countries that endorsed the Kyoto protocol had grave reservations but were unwilling to stand up to strongly committed domestic groups.

Real consultation is likely to produce inaction, as was true in 1993, when Clinton called for "lift and strike" in Yugoslavia (that is, lifting the arms embargo against Bosnia and striking Serbian forces). But because he believed in sharing power and was unwilling to move on his own, he sent Secretary of State Warren Christopher to ascertain European views. This multilateral and democratic procedure did not work because the Europeans did not want to be put on the spot; in the face of apparent American indecision, they refused to endorse such a strong policy. If the United States had informed the Europeans rather than consulted them, they probably would have complained, but gone along; what critics call unilateralism often is effective leadership. Could Yasir Arafat have been moved from his central position if the United States had sought consensus rather than staking out its own position? Bush could also argue that just as Reagan's ignoring the sophisticated European counsels to moderate his rhetoric led to the delegitimation of the Soviet system, so his insistence on confronting tyrants has slowly brought others around to his general perspective, if not to his particular policies.

In this context, the strong opposition of allies to overthrowing Saddam was an advantage as well as a disadvantage to Bush. While it exacted domestic costs, complicated the effort to rebuild Iraq, and perhaps fed Saddam's illusion that he could avoid a war, it gave the United States the opportunity to demonstrate that it would override strenuous objections from allies if this was necessary to reach its goals. While this horrified multilateralists, it showed that Bush was serious about his doctrine. When Kofi Annan declared that an American attack without Security Council endorsement "would not be in conformity with the [UN] charter," he may

---

[33] Quoted in Bob Woodward interview with Bush in ibid., 19 November 2002; also see Woodward, *Bush at War*, 281; quoted in Somini Sengupta, "U.N. Forum Stalls on Sex Education and Abortion Rights," *New York Times*, 10 May 2002.

not have realized that for some members of the Bush administration this would be part of the point of the action.[34]

AMERICAN HEGEMONY

The final element of the doctrine, which draws together the others, is the establishment of American hegemony, primacy, or empire.[35] In the Bush doctrine, there are no universal norms or rules governing all states.[36] On the contrary, order can be maintained only if the dominant power behaves quite differently from the others. Thus the administration is not worried that its preventive war doctrine or attacking Iraq without Security Council endorsement will set a precedent for others because the dictates do not bind the United States. Similarly, the United States sees no contradiction between expanding the ambit of nuclear weapons to threaten their employment even if others have not used WMD first on the one hand and a vigorous antiproliferation policy on the other. American security, world stability, and the spread of liberalism require the United States to act in ways others cannot and must not. This is not a double standard, but is what world order requires.

Hegemony is implied when the Nuclear Posture Review talks of dissuading future military competitors. At first glance, this seems to refer to Russia and China. But the point applies to the countries of Western Europe as well, either individually or as a unit. This was clear in the draft defense guidance written by Paul Wolfowitz for Dick Cheney at the end of the first Bush administration and also was implied by President George W. Bush when he declared to the graduating cadets at West Point: "America has, and intends to keep, military strengths beyond challenge—thereby making the destabilizing arms races of other eras pointless, and

---

[34]Patrick Tylor and Felicity Barringer, "Annan Says U.S. Will Violate Charter if It Acts Without Approval," ibid., 11 March 2003.

[35]Paul Schroeder sharply differentiates hegemony from empire, arguing that the former is much more benign and rests on a high degree of consent and respect for diverse interests: "Empire or Hegemony?" address given to the American Historical Association meeting, Chicago, 3 January 2003. I agree that distinctions are needed, but at this point both the terms and the developing American policy are unclear. I have a soft spot in my heart for primacy because it has the fewest connotations. Ten years ago I argued that the United States did not need to seek primacy (at least I was sensible enough to avoid saying whether the United States would be sensible): Jervis, "The Future of World Politics: Will it Resemble the Past?" *International Security* 16 (Winter 1991/92): 39–73; "International Primacy: Is the Game Worth the Candle?" ibid., 17 (Spring 1993): 52–67. For discussions about what an empire means today, whether it necessarily involves territorial control and how it can be maintained, see Rosen, "An Empire if You Can Keep It"; also see Kurth, "Migration and the Dynamics of Empire," *National Interest* 71 (Spring 2003): 5–16; and Anna Simons, "The Death of Conquest," ibid., 41–49.

[36]Only after World War I was lip-service paid to the concept that all states had equal rights. The current United States stance would be familiar to any nineteenth-century diplomat.

limiting rivalries to trade and other pursuits of peace."[37] This would mean not only sustaining such a high level of military spending that no other country or group of countries would be tempted to challenge it, but also using force on behalf of others so they will not need to develop potent military establishments of their own. In an implicit endorsement of hegemonic stability theory, the driving belief is that the world cannot afford to return to traditional multipolar balance of power politics, which would inevitably turn dangerous and destructive.[38]

Although many observers, myself included, were taken by surprise by this turn in American policy, we probably should not have been. It is consistent with standard patterns of international politics and with much previous American behavior in the Cold War. As early as the start of World War II, American leaders understood that the United States would emerge as the prime architect of the new international politics.[39] In the years before the Soviet Union was perceived as a deadly menace, American leaders understood that theirs would be the major role in maintaining peace and prosperity.

Even had the Soviet Union been more benign, instability, power vacuums, and the anticipation of future rivalries would have led the United States to use and increase the enormous power it had developed.[40] The task

---

[37]"Remarks by the President at 2002 Graduation Exercise," 4. The Wolfowitz draft is summarized in stories in the *New York Times*, 8 March and 24 May 1992. Also see Zalmay Khalilzad, *From Containment to Global Leadership? America and the World After the Cold War* (Santa Monica, CA: RAND, 1995); and Robert Kagan and William Kristol, eds., *Present Dangers: Crisis and Opportunity in American Foreign and Defense Policy* (San Francisco: Encounter Books, 2000). This stance gives others incentives to develop asymmetric responses, of which terrorism is only the most obvious example. For possible PRC options, see Thomas Christensen, "Posing Problems Without Catching Up: China's Rise and Challenges for U.S. Security Policy," *International Security* 25 (Spring 2001): 5–40.

[38]It is noteworthy that hegemonic stability theory comes with both a malign and a benign version. See Duncan Snidal, "The Limits of Hegemonic Stability Theory," *International Organization* 25 (Autumn 1985): 579–614; for the applicability of these theories to the pre-Bush post-Cold War world, see Michael Mastanduno, "Preserving the Unipolar Moment: Realist Theories and United States Grand Strategy after the Cold War," *International Security* 21 (Spring 1997): 49–88; see the exchange between Mark Sheetz and Mastanduno in ibid., 22 (Winter 1997/98): 168–174; Ethan Kapstein and Michael Mastanduno, eds., *Unipolar Politics: Realism and State Strategies After the Cold War* (New York: Columbia University Press, 1999); G. John Ikenberry, ed., *America Unrivaled: The Future of the Balance of Power* (Ithaca, NY: Cornell University Press, 2002).

[39]See, for example, David Reynolds, *From Munich to Pearl Harbor: Roosevelt's America and the Origins of the Second World War* (Chicago: Dee, 2001); Warren Kimball, *The Juggler: Franklin Roosevelt as Wartime Statesman* (Princeton: Princeton University Press, 1991).

[40]Melvyn Leffler, *A Preponderance of Power: National Security, the Truman Administration, and the Cold War* (Stanford, CA: Stanford University Press, 1992); Thomas Christensen, *Useful Adversaries: Grand Strategy, Domestic Mobilization, and Sino-American Conflict, 1947–1958* (Princeton: Princeton University Press, 1996); for the domestically imposed limits on this process, see Aaron Friedberg, *In the Shadow of the Garrison State: America's Anti-Statism and Its Cold War Grand Strategy* (Princeton: Princeton University Press, 2000); Michael Hogan, *A Cross of Iron: Harry S. Truman and the Origins of the National Security State, 1945–1954* (New York: Cambridge University Press, 1998).

could not be done by the United States alone, however. The world was not strictly bipolar, especially because the United States sought to limit its defense spending, and the prime target of the conflict was the allegiance of West Europe. The United States knew that allied, and especially European, support was necessary to resist Soviet encroachments. Allies, fearing a return to American isolationism, reciprocally made great efforts to draw the United States in.[41] Although American power was central and consent often was forthcoming only because of veiled (or not so veiled) rewards and threats, on fundamental issues the United States had to take allied interests and views to heart. Thus, Charles Maier exaggerates only slightly when he refers to "consensual American hegemony" within the West.[42] As Europe stabilized and the American deterrent force became concentrated in intercontinental bombers and missiles, the need for allies, although still considerable, diminished. The United States could rebuff Britain and France at Suez in a way that it could not have done five years earlier. Twenty-five years later, Reagan could pay even less heed to allied wishes than Eisenhower had. Of course, the United States could not do everything it wanted. Not only was it restrained by Soviet power, but to go it alone would have alienated domestic opinion, risked policy setbacks, and endangered an international economic system already under great pressure. But the degree to which the United States sought consensus and respected allied desires varied from issue to issue and president to president. Above a significant but limited minimum level, cooperation with allies had become a matter of choice, not necessity.

The required minimum level of cooperation decreased with the end of the Cold War and the emergence of unipolarity. The United States now has a greater share of world power than any state since the beginning of the state system, and it is not likely to lose this position in the foreseeable future.[43]

---

[41]Geir Lunstestad, "Empire by Invitation? The United States and Western Europe, 1945–1952," *Journal of Peace Research* 23 (September 1986): 263–277; James McAllister, *No Exit: America and the German Problem, 1943–1954* (Ithaca, NY: Cornell University Press, 2002).

[42]Charles Maier, *In Search of Stability: Explorations in Historical Political Economy* (New York: Cambridge University Press, 1987), 148. Also see John Lewis Gaddis, *We Now Know: Rethinking Cold War History* (New York: Oxford University Press, 1997); and Thomas Risse-Kappen, *Cooperation Among Democracies: The European Influence on U.S. Foreign Policy* (Princeton: Princeton University Press, 1995).

[43]William Wohlforth, "The Stability of a Unipolar World," *International Security* 24 (Summer 1999): 5–41; see also Kenneth Waltz, "Structural Realism After the Cold War," ibid. 25 (Summer 2000): 5–41. For a dissenting view, see Immanuel Wallerstein, "The Eagle Has Crash Landed," *Foreign Policy* 131 (July/August 2002): 60–68. The well-crafted argument by Robert Kudrle that the United States does not always gets its way even on some important issues is correct, but I think does not contradict the basic structural point: "Hegemony Strikes Out: The U.S. Global Role in Anti-Trust, Tax Evasion, and Illegal Immigration," *International Studies Perspectives* 4 (February 2003): 52–71.

Before the first Bush's presidency, the United States used a mixture of carrots and sticks and pursued sometimes narrower but often broader conceptions of its interest. Clinton, and Bush before him, cultivated allies and worked hard to maintain large coalitions. Most scholars approve of this mode of behavior, seeing it as the best if not the only way for the United States to secure desired behavior from others, minimize the costs to itself, and most smoothly manage a complex and contentious world.[44] But the choice of this approach was indeed a choice, revocable upon the appearance of changed circumstances and a different leader. The structure of world power meant that there was always a possibility that the United States would act on its own.

Until recently, however, it did not seem clear that the United States would in fact behave in a highly unilateral fashion and assert its primacy. The new American stance was precipitated, if not caused by, the interaction between the terrorist attacks and the election of George W. Bush, who brought to the office a more unilateral outlook than his predecessor and his domestic opponents. Bush's response to September 11 may parallel his earlier religious conversion and owe something to his religious beliefs, especially in his propensity to see the struggle as one between good and evil. There is reason to believe that just as his coming to Christ gave meaning to his previously aimless and dissolute personal life, so the war on terrorism has become, not only the defining characteristic of his foreign policy, but also his sacred mission. An associate of the President reports: "I believe the president was sincere, after 9/11, thinking 'This is what I was put on this earth for.'"[45] We can only speculate on what President Al Gore would have done. My estimate is that he would have invaded Afghanistan, but not proceeded against Iraq; nor would he have moved away from treaties and other arrangements over a wide range of issues. To some extent, the current assertion of strong American hegemony may be an accident.

---

[44]See, for example, G. John Ikenberry, "After September 11: America's Grand Strategy and International Order in the Age of Terror," *Survival* 43 (Winter 2001–2002): 19–34; Ikenberry, *After Victory: Institutions, Strategic Restraint, and the Rebuilding of Order After Major War* (Princeton: Princeton University Press, 2000); John Gerard Ruggie, *Winning the Peace: America and the New World Order* (New York: Columbia University Press, 1996); Joseph Nye, *The Paradox of American Power: Why the World's Only Superpower Can't Go It Alone* (New York: Oxford University Press, 2002); John Steinbrunner, *Principles of Global Security* (Washington, DC: Brookings Institution, 2000). More popular treatments are Clyde Prestowitz, *Rogue Nation: American Unilateralism and the Failure of Good Intentions* (New York: Basic Books, 2003); and Michael Hirsh, *At War With Ourselves: Why America Is Squandering Its Chance to Build a Better World* (New York: Oxford University Press, 2003).

[45]Quoted in James Harding, "Conflicting Views From Two Bush Camps," *Financial Times*, 20 March 2003; for a perceptive analysis, see Bruni, "For President, a Mission and a Role in History." Also see Woodward, *Bush at War*, 102, 205, 281.

But it was an accident waiting to happen. To start with, there are structural reasons to have expected a large terrorist attack. Osama Bin Laden had attacked American interests abroad and from early on sought to strike the homeland. His enmity stemmed primarily from the establishment of U.S. bases in Saudi Arabia, which was a product of America's worldwide responsibilities. Ironically, the overthrow of Saddam is likely to permit the United States to reduce its presence in Saudi Arabia, although I doubt if bin Laden expected this result to follow from his attack or that he will now be satisfied. Furthermore, al Qaeda was not the only group targeting the United States; as Richard Betts has argued, terrorism is the obvious weapon of weak actors against the leading state.[46]

Even without terrorism, both internal and structural factors predisposed the United States to assert its dominance. I think structural factors are more important, but it is almost a truism of the history of American foreign relations that the United States rarely if ever engages in deeply cooperative ventures with equals.[47] Unlike the European states who were surrounded by peers, once the United States had established its dominance first over its neighbors and then over the rest of the New World, it had great choice about the terms on which it would work with others. Thus, when the United States intervened in World War I, it insisted that the coalition be called the "Allied and Associated Powers"—that is, it was an associate with freedom of action, not an ally. The structure of the American government, its weak party system, its domestic diversity, and its political traditions, all make sustained cooperation difficult. It would be an exaggeration to say that unilateralism is the American way of foreign policy, but there certainly is a strong pull in this direction.

More importantly, the United States may be acting like a normal state that has gained a position of dominance.[48] There are four facets to this argument. First and most general is the core of the Realist outlook that power is checked most effectively and often only by counterbalancing

---

[46]Richard Betts, "The Soft Underbelly of American Primacy: Tactical Advantages of Terror," *Political Science Quarterly* 117 (Spring 2002): 19–36.

[47]See, for example, Jesse Helms's defense of unilateralism as the only way consistent with American interests and traditions: "American Sovereignty and the UN," *National Interest* 62 (Winter 2000/01): 31–34. For a discussion of historical, sociological, and geographical sources of the moralistic outlook in American foreign policy, see Arnold Wolfers, *Discord and Collaboration* (Baltimore: Johns Hopkins University Press, 1962), chap. 15; and Louis Hartz, *The Liberal Tradition in America* (New York: Harcourt, Brace, 1955), chap. 11. For a discussion of current U.S. policy in terms of its self-image as an exceptional state, see Stanley Hoffmann, "The High and the Mighty," *American Prospect* 13 (January 2003): 28–31.

[48]Thus, it is not entirely surprising that many of the beliefs mustered in support of United States policy toward Iraq parallel those held by European expansionists in earlier eras: Jack Snyder, "Imperial Temptations," *National Interest* 71 (Spring 2003): 29–40.

power. It follows that states that are not subject to external restraints tend to feel few restraints at all. As Edmund Burke put it, in a position endorsed by Hans Morgenthau: "I dread our *own* power and our *own* ambition; I dread our being too much dreaded. It is ridiculous to say that we are not men, and that, as men, we shall never wish to aggrandize ourselves."[49] With this as one of his driving ideas, Kenneth Waltz saw the likelihood of current behavior from the start of the post-Cold War era:

> The powerful state may, and the United States does, think of itself as acting for the sake of peace, justice, and well-being in the world. But these terms will be defined to the liking of the powerful, which may conflict with the preferences and the interests of others. In international politics, overwhelming power repels and leads others to try to balance against it. With benign intent, the United States has behaved, and until its power is brought into a semblance of balance, will continue to behave in ways that annoy and frighten others.[50]

Parts of the Bush doctrine are unique to the circumstances, but it is the exception rather than the rule for states to stay on the path of moderation when others do not force them to do so.[51]

Second, states' definitions of their interests tend to expand as their power does.[52] It then becomes worth pursuing a whole host of objectives that were

---

[49]Quoted in Hans Morgenthau, *Politics Among Nations*, 5th ed. (New York: Knopf, 1978), 169–170. (Emphasis in the original.)

[50]Kenneth Waltz, "America as a Model for the World? A Foreign Policy Perspective," *PS: Political Science and Politics* 24 (December 1991): 69; also see Waltz's discussion of the Gulf War: "A Necessary War?" in Harry Kriesler, ed., *Confrontation in the Gulf* (Berkeley, CA: Institute of International Studies, 1992), 59–65. Charles Krauthammer also expected this kind of behavior, but believed that it will serve the world as well as the American interests. Krauthammer, "The Unipolar Moment," *Foreign Affairs, America and the World, 1990-91* 70 (no. 1, 23–33); also see Krauthammer, "The Unipolar Moment Revisited." For a critical analysis, see Chace, "Imperial America and the Common Interest." As Waltz noted much earlier, even William Fulbright, while decrying the arrogance of American power, said that the United States could and should "lead the world in an effort to change the nature of its politics": quoted in *Theory of International Politics* (Reading, MA: Addison-Wesley, 1979), 201.

[51]Alexander Wendt and, more persuasively, Paul Schroeder, would disagree or at least modify this generalization, arguing that prevailing ideas can and have led to more moderate and consensual behavior: Wendt, *Social Theory of International Politics* (New York: Cambridge University Press, 1999); Schroeder, *The Transformation of European Politics, 1763-1848* (New York: Oxford University Press, 1994); and "Does the History of International Politics Go Anywhere?" in David Wetzel and Theodore Hamerow, eds., *International Politics and German History* (Westport, CT: Praeger, 1997), 15–36. This is a central question of international politics and history that I cannot fully discuss here, but believe that at least the mild statement that unbalanced power is dangerous can easily be sustained.

[52]See, for example, Fareed Zakaria, "Realism and Domestic Politics: A Review Essay," *International Security* 17 (Summer 1992): 177–198; Robert Tucker, "The Radical Critique Assessed" in Tucker, *The Radical Left and American Foreign Policy* (Baltimore: Johns Hopkins University Press, 1971), 69–77, 106–111. For a discussion of alternative possibilities suggested by American history, see Edward Rhodes, "The Imperial Logic of Bush's Liberal Agenda," *Survival* 45 (Spring 2003): 131–154.

out of reach when the state's security was in doubt and all efforts had to be directed to primary objectives. Under the new circumstances, states seek what Arnold Wolfers called "milieu goals."[53] The hope of spreading democracy and liberalism throughout the world has always been an American goal, but the lack of a peer competitor now makes it more realistic—although perhaps not very realistic—to actively strive for it. Seen in this light, the administration's perception that this is a time of great opportunity in the Middle East is the product, not so much of the special circumstances in the region, but of the enormous resources at America's disposal.

More specifically, the quick American victory in Afghanistan probably contributed to the expansion of American goals. Likewise, the easy military victory in Iraq, providing the occupation can be brought to a successful conclusion, will encourage the pursuit of a wider agenda, if not threatening force against other tyrants ("moving down the list," in the current phrase). Bush's initial speech after September 11 declared war on terrorists "with a global reach." This was ambitious, but at least the restriction to these kinds of terrorists meant that many others were not of concern. The modifier was dropped in the wake of Afghanistan, however. Not only did rhetoric shift to seeing terrorism in general as a menace to civilization and "the new totalitarian threat,"[54] but the United States sent first military trainers and then a combat unit to the Philippines to attack guerrillas who posed only a minimal threat to Americans and who have no significant links to al Qaeda. Furthermore, at least up until a point, the exercise of power can increase power as well as interests. I do not think that the desire to control a large supply of oil was significant motivation for the Iraqi war, but it will give the United States an additional instrument of influence.

A third structural explanation for American behavior is that increased relative power brings with it new fears. The reasons are both objective and subjective. As Wolfers notes in his classic essay on "National Security as Ambiguous Symbol," the latter can diverge from the former.[55] In one manifestation of this, as major threats disappear, people psychologically elevate ones that were previously seen as quite manageable.[56] People now

---

[53] Wolfers, *Discord and Collaboration*, chap. 5.
[54] "President Thanks World Coalition for Anti-Terrorism Efforts"; David Sanger, "In Reichstag, Bush Condemns Terror as New Despotism," *New York Times*, 24 May 2002. Also see "Remarks by President at 2002 Graduation Exercise." The question of how broad the target should be was debated within the administration from the start, with Bush initially insisting on a focus on al Qaeda: Woodward, *Bush at War*.
[55] Wolfers, *Discord and Collaboration*, chap. 10.
[56] John Mueller, "The Catastrophe Quota: Trouble after the Cold War," *Journal of Conflict Resolution* 38 (September 1994): 355–375; also see Frederick Hartmann, *The Conservation of Enemies: A Study in Enmity* (Westport, CT: Greenwood Press, 1982).

seem to be as worried as they were during the height of the Cold War despite the fact that a terrorist or rogue attack, even with WMD, could cause only a small fraction of a possible World War III's devastation. But there is more to it than psychology. A dominant state acquires an enormous stake in the world order, and interests spread throughout the globe. Most countries are primarily concerned with what happens in their immediate neighborhoods; the world is the hegemon's neighborhood, and it is not only hubris that leads it to be concerned with anything that happens anywhere. The result is a fusion of narrow and broad self-interest. At a point when most analysts were worried about the decline of American power, not its excesses, Waltz noted that for the United States, "like some earlier great powers. . . . the interest of the country in security came to be identified with the maintenance of a certain world order. For countries at the top, this is predictable behavior. . . . Once a state's interests reach a certain extent, they become self-reinforcing."[57]

The historian John S. Galbraith explored the related dynamic of the "turbulent frontier" that produced the unintended expansion of colonialism. As a European power gained an enclave in Africa or Asia, usually along the coast or river, it also gained an unpacified boundary that had to be policed. This led to further expansion of influence and often of settlement, and this in turn produced a new area that had to be protected and a new zone of threat.[58] There were few natural limits to this process. There are not likely to be many now. The wars in Afghanistan and Iraq have led to the establishment of U.S. bases and security commitments in central Asia, an area previously beyond reach. It is not hard to imagine how the United States could be drawn further into politics in the region and to find itself using force to oppose terrorist or guerrilla movements that arise there, perhaps in part in reaction to the American presence. The same dynamic could play out in Colombia.

The fourth facet can be seen as a broader conception of the previous point. As Realists stress, even states that find the status quo acceptable have to worry about the future.[59] The more an actor sees the current situation as satisfactory, the more it will expect the future to be worse.

---

[57]Waltz, *Theory of International Politics*, 200.
[58]John S. Galbraith, "The 'Turbulent Frontier' as a Factor in British Expansion," *Comparative Studies in Society and History* 2 (January 1960): 34–48; *Reluctant Empire: British Policy on the South African Frontier, 1834–1854* (Berkeley: University of California Press, 1963). Also see Ronald Robinson and John Gallager with Alice Denny, *Africa and the Victorians: The Official Mind of Imperialism* (London: Macmillan, 1961). A related imperial dynamic that is likely to recur is that turning a previously recalcitrant state into a client usually weakens it internally and requires further intervention.
[59]See esp., Copeland, *Origins of Major War*; Mearsheimer, *Tragedy of Great Power Politics*.

Psychology plays a role here too: prospect theory argues that actors are prone to accept great risks when they believe they will suffer losses unless they act boldly. The adoption of a preventive war doctrine may be a mistake, especially if taken too far, but is not foreign to normal state behavior. It appeals to states that have a valued position to maintain. However secure states are, only rarely can they be secure enough, and if they are currently very powerful, they will have strong reasons to act now to prevent a deterioration that could allow others to harm them in the future.[60]

All this means that under the Bush doctrine the United States is not a status quo power. Its motives may not be selfish, but the combination of power, fear, and perceived opportunity leads it to seek to reshape world politics and the societies of many of its members. This tracks with and extends traditional ideas in American foreign relations held by both liberals and conservatives who saw the United States as a revolutionary country. As the first modern democracy, the United States was founded on principles of equality, progress, and a government subordinate to civil society that, while initially being uniquely American, had universal applicability. Because a state's foreign policy is inseparable from its domestic regime, a safe and peaceful world required the spread of these arrangements.[61] Under current conditions of terrorism and WMD, tyrannical governments pose too much of a potential if not actual danger to be tolerated. The world cannot stand still. Without strong American intervention, the international environment will become more menacing to America and its values, but strong action can increase its security and produce a better world. In a process akin to the deep security dilemma,[62] in order to protect itself, the United States is impelled to act in a way that will increase, or at least bring to the surface, conflicts with others. Even if the prevailing situation is satisfactory, it cannot be maintained by purely defensive measures. Making the world safe for American democracy is

---

[60] Waltz (*Theory of International Politics*) sees this behavior as often self-defeating; Mearsheimer (*Tragedy of Great Power Politics*) implies that it is not; Copeland's position is somewhere in between.

[61] George W. Bush would endorse Wilson's claim that America's goal must be "the destruction of every arbitrary power anywhere in the world that can separately, secretly, and of its single choice disturb the peace of the world" just as he would join Clinton in calling for "the spread of his revolt [i.e., the American revolution], this liberation, to the great stage of the world itself!" "An Address at Mount Vernon," 4 July 1918, in Arthur Link et al., eds., *The Papers of Woodrow Wilson*, vol. 48, *May 13–July 17, 1918* (Princeton: Princeton University Press, 1985), 516–517.

[62] Robert Jervis, "Was the Cold War a Security Dilemma?" *Journal of Cold War History* 3 (Winter 2001): 36–60; also see Paul Roe, "Former Yugoslavia: The Security Dilemma That Never Was?" *European Journal of International Relations* 6 (September 2000): 373–393. The current combination of fear and hope that produces offensive actions for defensive motives resembles the combination that produced the pursuit of preponderance in the aftermath of World War II.

believed to require that dictatorial regimes be banished, or at least kept from weapons of mass destruction. Although not mentioned in the pronouncements, the Bush doctrine is made possible by the existence of a security community among the world's most powerful and developed states—the United States, Western Europe, and Japan.[63] The lack of fears of war among these countries allows the United States to focus on other dangers and to pursue other goals. Furthermore, the development of the security community gives the United States a position that it now wants to preserve.

HEGEMONY, IRAQ, AND EUROPE

This perspective on the Bush doctrine helps explain international disagreements about Iraq. Most accounts of the French opposition stress its preoccupation with glory and its traditional jealousy and disdain for the United States. Europe's resistance to the war is attributed to the peaceful world view produced by its success in overcoming historical rivalries and creating a law-governed society, summarized by the phrase "Americans are from Mars, the Europeans are from Venus."[64] Also frequently mentioned is the European aversion to the crude and bullying American style: "Bush is just a cowboy." There is something to these positions, but are Europeans really so averse to force and wedded to law? When faced with domestic terrorism, Germany and other European countries did not hesitate to employ unrestrained state power that John Ashcroft would envy, and their current treatment of minorities, especially Muslims, does not strike these populations as liberal. The French continue to intervene in Africa unilaterally, disregarded legal rulings to drop their ban on British beef, and join other European states in playing as fast and loose with trade regulations as does the United States. Most European states favored the war in Kosovo and supported the United States in Afghanistan; had they been attacked on September 11, they might not have maintained their aversion to the use of force.

Even more glaringly, the claims for a deep cultural divide overlook the fundamental difference between how Europe and the United States are placed in the international system. The fact that the latter is hegemonic has three implications. First, only the United States has the power to do anything about problems like Iraq; the others have incentives to ride

---

[63] Robert Jervis, "Theories of War in an Era of Leading Power Peace," *American Political Science Review* 96 (March 2003): 1–14.
[64] The best known statement of this position is Robert Kagan, *Of Paradise and Power: America and Europe in the New World Order* (New York: Knopf, 2003).

free. Second, the large European states have every reason to be concerned about American hegemony and sufficient resources to seek to constrain it. This is not traditional power balancing, which is driven by security fears; the French are not afraid of an American attack, and the German worry is that the United States will withdraw too many of its troops. But they do fear that a world dominated by the United States would be one in which their values and interests would be served only at American sufferance. It is hardly surprising that an April 2002 poll showed that overwhelming majorities within many European countries felt that American policy toward Iraq and the Middle East in general was based "mainly on its own interests."[65] The National Security Advisor, Condoleezza Rice, has forgotten her knowledge of basic international politics when she expresses her shock at discovering that "there were times that it appeared that American power was seen [by France and Germany] to be more dangerous than, perhaps, Saddam Hussein."[66] The United States may be correct that American dominance serves Europe and the world, but we should not be startled when others beg to differ. The United States probably is as benign a hegemon as the world has ever seen. Its large domestic market, relatively tolerant values, domestic diversity, and geographic isolation all are helpful. But a hegemon it remains, and by that very fact it must make others uneasy.

Third, the Europeans' stress on the need to go through the Security Council shows less their abstract attachment to law and world governance than their appreciation of power. France especially, but also Russia and China (two countries that are not from Venus), will gain enormously if they can establish the principle that large-scale force can be used only with the approval of the Council, of which they are permanent members. Security Council membership is one of the major resources at these countries' disposal. The statement of a Russian leader that "if someone tries to wage war on their own account . . . without an international mandate, it means all the world is confusion and a wild jungle"[67] would carry more moral weight if Russia did not have a veto in the mandate-granting body. If the Council were not central, French influence would be much diminished.

The United Kingdom does not readily fit this picture, of course. Structure always leaves room for choice, and Tony Blair told Parliament on 24 September 2002 that "it is an article of faith with me that the American relationship and our ability to partner [with] America in these difficult

---

[65] Adam Clymer, "European Poll Faults U.S. for its Policy in the Mid East," *New York Times*, 19 April 2002.
[66] Quoted in David Sanger, "Witness to Auschwitz Evil, Bush Draws a Lesson," ibid., 1 June 2003.
[67] Quoted in John Tagliabue, "France and Russia Ready to Use Veto Against Iraq War," ibid., 6 March 2003.

issues is of fundamental importance, not just to this country but to the wider world." Blair's personal views may be part of the explanation, but this has been the British stance ever since World War II, which resisted becoming too much a part of Europe and sought to maintain a major role in the world through supporting rather than opposing the United States. But only one ally can seek to have a "special relationship" with the hegemon, and Britain's having taken this role makes it harder for others to emulate it.

Structure also explains why many of the smaller European countries chose to support the United States in Iraq despite hostile public opinion. The dominance they fear most is not American, but Franco-German. The United States is more powerful, but France and Germany are closer and more likely to menace them.[68] Seeking a distant protector is a standard practice in international politics. That France and Germany resented the resulting opposition is no more surprising than the American dismissal of "old Europe," with the resulting parallel that while France and Germany bitterly decried the American effort to hustle them into line, they disparaged and bullied the East European states that sided with the United States—quite un-Venusian behavior.

CONCLUSION

Where we will go from here depends in part on unpredictable events such as economic shocks, the course of reconstruction in Iraq, the targets and success of future terrorist attacks, and the characteristics of the leaders that arise through diverse domestic processes. The war against Saddam, however, already marks out the path on which the United States is embarked and illuminates the links between preventive war and hegemony, which was much of the reason for the opposition at home and abroad. Bush's goals are extraordinarily ambitious, involving remaking not only international politics but recalcitrant societies as well, which is seen as an end in itself and a means to American security. For better or (and?) for worse, the United States has set itself tasks that prudent states would shun. As a result, it will be infringing on what adversaries, if not allies, see as their vital interests. Coercion and especially deterrence may be insufficient for these tasks because these instruments share with traditional diplomacy the desire to minimize conflict by limiting one's own claims to interests that others can afford to respect. States that seek more need to be highly

---

[68]This is a version of Stephen Walt's argument that states balance against threat, not power: *The Origins of Alliances* (Ithaca, NY: Cornell University Press, 1987).

assertive if not aggressive, which provides additional reasons to question the goals themselves. The beliefs of Bush and his colleagues that Saddam's regime would have been an unacceptable menace to American interests if it had been allowed to obtain nuclear weapons not only tell us about their fears for the limits of United States influence that might have been imposed, but also speak volumes about the expansive definition of United States interests that they hold.[69]

The war is hard to understand if the only objective was to disarm Saddam or even to remove him from power. Even had the inflated estimates of his WMD capability been accurate, the danger was simply too remote to justify the effort. But if changing the Iraqi regime was expected to bring democracy and stability to the Middle East, discourage tyrants and energize reformers throughout the world, and demonstrate the American willingness to provide a high degree of what it considers world order whether others like it or not, then as part of a larger project, the war makes sense. Those who find both the hopes and the fears excessive if not delusional agree with the great British statesman Lord Salisbury when he tried to bring some perspective to the Eastern Crisis of 1877–1878: "It has generally been acknowledged to be madness to go to war for an idea, but if anything is more unsatisfactory, it is to go to war against a nightmare."[70]

We can only speculate about the crucial question of whether the Bush doctrine will work. Contrary to the common impression, democracies, especially the United States, do not find it easy to sustain a clear line of policy when the external environment is not compelling. Domestic priorities ordinarily loom large, and few Americans think of their country as having an imperial mission. Wilsonianism may provide a substitute for the older European ideologies of a *mission civilisatrice* and the white man's burden, but since it rests on the assumption that its role will not only be noble but also popular, I am skeptical that it will endure if it meets much indigenous opposition from those who are supposed to benefit from it. Significant casualties will surely be corrosive, and when the going gets tough I think the United States will draw back.

Furthermore, while the United States is the strongest country in the world, its power is still subject to two familiar limitations: it is harder to build than to destroy, and success depends on others' decisions because

---

[69] I have discussed how Bush's policy toward Iraq does and does not fit with deterrence thinking in "The Confrontation Between Iraq and the United States: Implications for the Theory and Practice of Deterrence," *European Journal of International Relations* 9 (June 2003): 315–337.
[70] Quoted in R. W. Seton-Watson, *Disraeli, Gladstone, and the Eastern Question* (New York: Norton, 1972), 222.

their cooperation is necessary for the state to reach its goals. Of course, American military capability is not to be ignored, and I doubt whether countries like Iran, Syria, and North Korea will ignore it. They may well reason as Bush expects them to and limit their WMD programs and support for terrorism, if not reform domestically. But the prospects for long-run compliance are less bright. Although a frontal assault on American interests is perhaps unlikely, highly motivated adversaries will not give up the quest to advance their interests as they see them. The war in Iraq has increased the risks of their pursuing nuclear weapons, but it has also increased their incentives to do so. Amid the debate about what these weapons can accomplish, everyone agrees that they can deter invasion, which makes them very attractive to states who fear they might be in the American gun sights. Both Waltz's argument that proliferation will produce stability and the contrary and more common claim that it would make the world more dangerous imply that the spread of nuclear weapons will reduce American influence because others will have less need of its security guarantees and will be able to fend off its threats to their vital interests.[71] The American attempt to minimize the ability of others to resist U.S. pressures is the mark of a country bent, not on maintaining the status quo, but on fashioning a new and better order.

Obviously, U.S. military capabilities matter less in relations with allies and probably with Russia. From them the United States wants wholehearted cooperation on issues such as sharing highly sensitive information on terrorism, rebuilding failed states, preventing proliferation, and, perhaps most importantly, managing the international economy. There is little danger or hope that Europe will form a united counterweight to the United States and try to thwart it by active opposition, let alone the use of force. But political resistance is quite possible and, even more than with adversaries, the fate of the American design for world order lies in the hands of its allies.[72] Although the United States governs many of the incentives that Europe and potential supporters face, what it needs from them cannot be coerced. It is possible that they will see themselves better

---

[71] Kenneth Waltz, *The Spread of Nuclear Weapons: More May Be Better* (London: IISS, Adelphi Paper No. 171, 1981); Scott Sagan and Kenneth Waltz, *The Spread of Nuclear Weapons: A Debate Renewed* (New York: Norton, 2003). For a range of views, see Marc Trachtenberg, "Waltzing to Armageddon?" *National Interest* 69 (Fall 2002): 144–155; Eric Herring, ed., *Preventing the Use of Weapons of Mass Destruction*, special issue of *Journal of Strategic Studies* 23 (March 2000); T. V. Paul, Richard Harknett, and James Wirtz, eds., *The Absolute Weapon Revisited: Nuclear Arms and the Emerging International Order* (Ann Arbor: University of Michigan Press, 1998).

[72] For a discussion of possible forms of nonviolent opposition, see Robert Pape, "Soft Balancing Against the United States" (unpublished paper, University of Chicago, 2003).

off with the United States as an assertive hegemon, allowing them to gain the benefits of world order while being spared the costs, and they may conclude that any challenge would fail or bring with it dangerous rivalry. Without the war in Iraq, I doubt that the spring of 2003 would have seen the degree of cooperation that the United States obtained from Europe in combatting the Iranian nuclear program and from Japan and the PRC in containing North Korea.

But I suspect that much will depend on the allies' answers to several questions: Can the American domestic political system sustain the Bush doctrine over the long run? Will the United States be open to allied influence and values? Will it put pressure on Israel as well as on the Arabs to reach a settlement? More generally, will it seek to advance the broad interests of the diverse countries and people in the world, or will it exploit its power for its own narrower political, economic, and social interests? Bush's world gives little place for other states—even democracies—except as members of a supporting cast. Conflating broader with narrower interests and believing that one has a monopoly on wisdom are obvious ways that a hegemon can come to be seen as tyrannical.[73] Woodrow Wilson said that both nationalism and internationalism called for the United States to join the League of Nations: "The greatest nationalist is the man who wants his nation to be the greatest nation, and the greatest nation is the nation which penetrates to the heart of its duty and mission among the nations of the world. With every flash of insight into the great politics of mankind, the nation that has that vision is elevated to a place of influence and power which it cannot get by arms."[74] Wilson surely meant what he said, but his great certainty that he knew what was best for the world was troubling. In the presidential campaign, Bush said that the United States needed a "more humble foreign policy."[75] But its objectives and conceptions make the Bush doctrine quite the opposite. Avoiding this imperial temptation will be the greatest challenge that the United States faces.*

---

[73] See David Calleo, *The German Problem Reconsidered: Germany and the World Order, 1870 to the Present* (New York: Cambridge University Press, 1978) for a summary of relevant laboratory experiments; see Robert Goodin, "How Amoral *Is* Hegemon," *Perspectives on Politics* 1 (March 2003): 123–126.

[74] "A Luncheon Address to the St. Louis Chamber of Commerce," 5 September 1919 in Arthur Link et al., eds., *The Papers of Woodrow Wilson*, vol. 63, *September 4–November 5, 1919* (Princeton: Princeton University Press, 1990), 33.

[75] Quoted in David Sanger, "A New View of Where America Fits in the World," *New York Times*, 18 February 2001.

*I am grateful for comments from Robert Art, Richard Betts, Jim Caraley, Dale Copeland, Peter Gourevitch, Chaim Kaufmann, Robert Lieber, Marc Trachtenberg, and Kenneth Waltz. This article was originally published in *Political Science Quarterly* 118 (Fall 2003): 365–388.

Globalization as a Security Strategy: Power and Vulnerability in the "China Model"

ANDREW J. NATHAN
ANDREW SCOBELL

FOREIGN ECONOMIC POLICY IS A KEY ELEMENT of any country's security policy.[1] For China, autarky in the Mao Zedong years was a response to American containment and isolation and to perceived Soviet unreliability as an ally. Mao believed that he could resist pressure from both superpowers only by putting his country on the path of self-reliant development.[2] The policy worked in the sense that neither superpower could blackmail China economically or gain access to try to subvert the loyalty of Chinese elites or the public. Meanwhile, at tremendous cost to his people, Mao was able to develop a basic industrial economy with surpluses squeezed from agriculture. He sustained a large if backward military and developed a nuclear capability sufficient to deter a Soviet or American attack.

---

[1]Classic statements include David A. Baldwin, *Economic Statecraft* (Princeton, NJ: Princeton University Press, 1985); Paul Kennedy, *The Rise and Fall of Great Powers: Economic Change and Military Conflict from 1500 to 2000* (New York: Vintage Books, 1987); Robert Gilpin, *Global Political Economy: Understanding the International Economic Order* (Princeton, NJ: Princeton University Press, 2000); Robert O. Keohane and Joseph S. Nye, *Power and Interdependence: World Politics in Transition* (Boston, MA: Little, Brown, 1977).
[2]Alexander V. Pantsov with Steven I. Levine, *Mao: The Real Story* (New York: Simon & Schuster, 2012), chaps. 29, 30.

ANDREW J. NATHAN is the Class of 1919 Professor of Political Science at Columbia University. ANDREW SCOBELL is Senior Political Scientist at the RAND Corporation and adjunct professor of Asian Studies at Georgetown University's Edmund A. Walsh School of Foreign Service.

Deng Xiaoping, who came to power two years after Mao's death, sought a different balance of security gains and losses in a different orientation to the world economy. He abandoned autarky because the depressed living standards and rigid political repression that were required for self-reliant development had themselves become threats to the survival of the regime.[3] Deng's policy of "reform and opening"—the revolution (or some said counterrevolution) that made rapid economic growth possible—led to the phenomenal "rise of China," which saw the country's gross domestic product (GDP) shoot up at an average annual rate of 9.6 percent starting in 1978 to reach $6 trillion in 2010. This surge in economic power gave China the resources, starting in the 1990s, to make itself into a modern military power, to begin exercising soft power, and to influence negotiations in various international regimes.

But the "China model" of fast-paced growth was not a one-sided good for Beijing. The strategic choices that had to be taken to make the boom happen also entailed significant sacrifices for China's security. Growth was achieved by means of a deep engagement in the global economy that made China more vulnerable to pressures and influences from the outside world than it had ever been before. By moving from autarky to interdependence, China increased not only its power over the destinies of others, but also the power of others over its own destiny.

In this sense, the engagement policy pursued by the United States since 1972 achieved its key strategic goal of tying China's interests to the interests of the U.S.-created global order. Although China is in many respects dissatisfied with its level of economic, political, and military security and seeks to improve them, it has acquired too large a stake in the stability of the world order and the prosperity of the West to believe it can serve its own interests by frontally challenging the existing world order.

GAINS AND LOSSES TO THE TURN OF THE CENTURY

Usually viewed as an obvious choice and an unalloyed triumph, Beijing's embrace of globalization was, in fact, halting, costly, and ambivalent, embracing a set of dilemmas as troubling as the equal and opposite dilemmas entailed in Maoist autarky.[4] Chinese leaders did not follow a blueprint but, as Deng put it, "crossed the river by feeling the stones." As

---

[3] Ezra F. Vogel, *Deng Xiaoping and the Transformation of China* (Cambridge, MA: The Belknap Press of Harvard University Press, 2011), chaps. 6, 7.

[4] A similar process is described in David W.P. Elliott, *Changing Worlds: Vietnam's Transition from Cold War to Globalization* (New York: Oxford University Press, 2012).

each step of reform produced positive results, Chinese leaders reluctantly yielded to pressure from advisers and foreign partners to do more.

Even before Mao's death, Deng, then serving as Deputy Premier, had advocated a limited opening in trade policy. Deng's rivals denounced his ideas as currying favor with the capitalist world, promoting old-fashioned arts and crafts in preference to modern industry, and selling off national resources and sovereignty. Their denunciations were one of the factors in Deng's fall from power in 1975. Coming back to power after Mao's death, Deng pushed ahead by spreading the right to import and export foreign commodities from about a dozen specialized central government–owned corporations to what eventually became thousands of trading companies belonging to central government ministries, provincial governments, and government-owned enterprises. Foreign trade almost quadrupled from 10 percent of GDP in 1978 to 38 percent of GDP in 2001.

In the area of foreign investment, Deng initially sought only to accelerate the growth of exports by inserting capital and expertise into the export sector of the state-owned economy. In 1979, China adopted the Joint Venture Law, which limited foreign ownership to less than half the value of any enterprise. The government tried at first to limit foreign investment to four small special economic zones. In 1984, it extended incentives to 14 coastal cities and the island of Hainan; in 1988, it opened the entire coastal region from Liaoning in the north to Guangdong in the south to foreign investment; and in the 1990s, it removed virtually all remaining regional and sectoral restrictions.

China also began to accept foreign aid in 1978, breaking with its tradition of being solely an aid donor (although a small one) and accepting assistance from the United Nations Development Program (UNDP). In 1980, it rejoined the International Monetary Fund (IMF) and the World Bank and accepted aid from both; and in 1986, it joined the Asian Development Bank. By 2001, China had received a grand total of almost $40 billion in Overseas Development Assistance (ODA) from a host of multilateral organizations, such as the World Bank, the UNDP, other UN agencies, and a variety of countries, such as Japan and Canada.

These steps to engage with the world economy turned out to have come at a good time. The long historical process of globalization took another leap forward in the mid-1980s. Between 1980 and 2007, global GDP increased by an average of 3.1 percent a year. World trade quintupled during the same period from $4 trillion to $27.5 trillion. Having entered the waters, China was carried along on the current: Chinese trade grew thirty-fold from $25.8 billion in 1984 to $762 billion in 2005. By 2004, 30.8 percent of China's industrial output was produced by factories with foreign investment. The linkage and demonstration effects of foreign trade and investment on Chinese suppliers, consumers, and competitors led to higher quality performance across the economy. Through foreign partnerships, Chinese firms gained new technology, learned new management practices, and gained access to world markets. Even though growth was unequal, it was widespread. Every part of the country and every social class had a share. The number of Chinese below the official poverty line dropped from 250 million in 1978 to 25 million by 2005.[5]

But to gain these benefits, Chinese leaders had to compromise China's autonomy more than they had anticipated would be necessary. Opening the door to foreign trade and investment required changes in the regulatory environment and support systems for foreign economic interactions. From 1979 to 2000, China adopted hundreds of laws and regulations to govern foreign economic relations. It established specialized courts and other dispute resolution mechanisms. Visa restrictions had to be eased to cultivate the nascent tourist industry and to allow foreign businesspersons to visit easily. The flow of foreign visitors increased from 1.8 million in 1979 to 83.4 million in 2000 and kept growing after that. To accommodate them, the number of hotel rooms soared, with a massive shift from Soviet-style hotels to those meeting Western standards. Similar foreigner-friendly changes were made in banking, communications, and transportation.

By the late 1990s, foreign officials were monitoring Chinese tariffs, import quotas, certification requirements, factory hygiene, financial services, and retail networks. Moody's and Standard and Poor's passed judgment on China's credit worthiness. U.S. Customs, Food and Drug Administration, and Commerce Department officials showed up to inspect Chinese factories. Foreign lawyers pointed out enforcement failures and suggested revisions in laws and regulations. China had to introduce unfamiliar institutions, such as stock markets, brokerage firms, risk funds, commodities futures markets, and consulting firms. China had even found it necessary to amend its constitution in 1982 to include a commitment to protect "the lawful rights and interests" of foreign investors.

Moreover, each step toward prosperity made China's economic health more dependent than before on the health of foreign markets, especially those in the United States, which was China's largest export market until

---

[5]Many of the economic data used here and elsewhere follow Barry Naughton, *The Chinese Economy: Transitions and Growth* (Boston, MA: MIT Press, 2007).

2007, and the EU, which subsequently became the largest market. China's prosperity was tied to the health of the American dollar and the euro, which were the main currencies in which China, like other countries, conducted its foreign trade and kept its foreign exchange reserves.

Most risky from a security standpoint were the deep effects that the opening exerted on society and culture. Between 1978 and 2003, China dispatched more than 700,000 students to study at institutions of higher education abroad, mostly in the United States, in an effort to rapidly acquire advanced technology. Fewer than 25 percent of these students returned upon graduation, and those who did often carried ideas that undermined China's official ideology. Western-educated and -oriented economists, bankers, lawyers, and traders gained a growing voice in shaping policies. Young people lost faith in old values, and, according to conservative Chinese critics, came to think that "even the moon is brighter in the West." Christianity took off and spread among the population, including tens of millions who participated in illegal "house churches" that local officials often tolerated because it would have been too disruptive to try to close them down. Corruption increased, and many observers rightly or wrongly attributed the increase to "foreign flies coming in the open window." In the eyes of Chinese conservatives, the 1989 democracy movement was a devil's brew of contradictory Western impacts: on the one hand, it was sparked by public opposition to inflation, and corruption associated with the open-door policy, and on the other, it expressed a pro-Western democratic and individualist ethos and was cheered on and even given some material support by people in Hong Kong and the West.

Not only did the open policy confront domestic opposition, it also engendered a wide range of conflicts with foreign partners. Trading partners accused Beijing of protectionism and dumping (exporting products at below cost). The advanced industrial countries pushed China to accept quotas on the exports of textiles and other products and to honor foreign standards of hygiene, packaging, labeling, and the environmental friendliness of goods destined for export. As the central government made concession after concession to outside demands, policy on the ground lagged behind due to local protectionism, corruption, and an inadequate legal system.[6] China's failure to fulfill its commitments generated new waves of conflict with other countries.

---

[6]Martin K. Dimitrov, *Piracy and the State: The Politics of Intellectual Property Rights in China* (New York: Cambridge University Press, 2009).

GETTING OUT BY GETTING DEEPER IN: JOINING THE WTO

Fuller engagement in the globalized economic system was the only path of escape from the dynamic of constant domestic criticism and international friction that marked the first two decades of the open-door policy.[7] Such deepening of engagement required China to seek membership in the World Trade Organization (WTO). WTO membership would bind the hands of conservative domestic opponents of globalization and put the country's tempestuous economic relations with the rest of the world on a rule-bound basis that would be relatively insulated from foreign political pressure. But WTO membership could achieve these results only by entrenching China more deeply than ever in interdependence with its trading partners and by binding it more tightly in a complicated system of mutual commitments with its international partners.

WTO accession negotiations are inherently demanding. An applicant for membership has to reach agreement bilaterally with each current member (there were 90 members when China first applied, 142 by the time it had finished its talks) and then give the same benefits to all members ("most-favored-nation treatment"). All the concessions are made by the applicant, with each bilateral agreement providing the starting point for more demands by the next negotiating partner.

Negotiators were especially tough on China because it was the biggest nonmarket economy ever to try to join the organization. The core issues were how large a cost the rest of the world would pay to help China plunge more deeply into world markets and how rapidly China would lower its barriers to imports and foreign investments in exchange for enhanced access to WTO members' markets. The issues were politically toxic in both China and the West, and the negotiations dragged on for 15 years. The U.S.–China agreement was finally signed in 1999; after cleaning up remaining matters with several other members, China signed an accession agreement in November 2001 and entered the WTO in December 2001.

The accession agreement was more than 800 pages long, with thousands of specific commitments covering virtually all aspects of the economy. Under its provisions, China undertook to make sweeping changes in its economic policies, lowering tariffs, removing many nontariff barriers to imports, abolishing export subsidies, providing access to the Chinese market for foreign products on the same terms as domestic products ("national treatment"), improving legal protection for intellectual property,

---

[7]Much of the material in this section derives from Scott Harold, "Freeing Trade: Negotiating Domestic and International Obstacles on China's Long Road to the GATT/WTO 1971–2001" (Ph.D. diss., Columbia University, 2007).

and allowing foreign-invested enterprises to enter hitherto-banned sensitive sectors, including distribution, franchising, transport, telecom value-added services, banking and financial services, insurance, securities, legal and accounting services, construction, and education. The government had to repeal thousands of WTO-inconsistent laws and regulations and reform the courts, legal system, banking system, and relevant administrative agencies. These changes made China's economy one of the most open in the world.

Merely to negotiate these commitments, not to mention to implement them, China found it necessary to create and restructure numerous government agencies and hire or train thousands of specialized bureaucrats, thus changing the DNA of its own government institutions. Moreover, to satisfy suspicious U.S. negotiators, China had to agree to a transitional review mechanism, under which China, alone among WTO members, was to be reviewed annually for eight years for its compliance with the accession agreement. In exchange for meeting its commitments to liberalize its economy, China is scheduled to receive "full market economy status" in 2016, which will immunize it from certain kinds of trade disputes. Meanwhile, however, using the WTO dispute resolution mechanism, the United States and other trading partners have frequently sued China for dumping and have often won.

HOLDING SOMETHING BACK: THE "CHINA MODEL"
However, Beijing did not give everything away by joining the WTO. Instead of being forced to make a transition to a fully Western-style economy, Chinese policymakers created a distinctive state-directed yet marketized model that maintained key elements of self-control. The post-WTO "China model" drew strength from global trade and investment without compromising the primary role of the domestic market in its economic growth; benefited from but was not dominated by the surging private and foreign-invested sectors; and, above all, used market mechanisms to promote efficiency without undermining the state's ability to rule the economy's commanding heights.

To be sure, the new Chinese economy was in some ways a privatized market economy like those of the West. Private capitalists, including foreigners, could invest in most sectors. Private enterprises grew faster than state enterprises in the 1990s and 2000s. Prices of most goods were set by market mechanisms. Yet the state remained dominant to a far greater degree than in the West. The government continued to own all land, both rural and urban; to manage directly the energy industry, water supply, banking, and railway transportation; and to control those former state enterprises that had nominally been privatized via the Party's assignment of top managers,[8] the presence of Party committees, and government direction of bank credit. A thousand or so of the largest state-owned enterprises were turned into integrated "national champions" that dominated strategic sectors such as energy, telecoms, heavy industry, defense industry, mining, media, banking, and transport.[9] By 2010, 42 Chinese companies were listed in the *Fortune* Global 500, and a majority of them were more than 50 percent state-owned. Direct and indirect policy levers gave the government the major voice in determining the prices of land, labor, housing, energy, and credit. Although agriculture had been privatized, the state continued to influence the prices of agricultural products through land use controls, subsidies, and barriers to imports, among other measures.

The Chinese currency, the renminbi, was not easily convertible into foreign currencies. For trade purposes, it could be converted by anyone (on the current account), but for investments (the capital account), which are longer term and involve greater quantities of money, the currency could be exchanged only by qualified investors for certain types of investments. The exchange rate floated within a narrow band whose limits were set by the government through its buying and selling of foreign exchange, all of which it held in its own hands. The limit on free conversion of money on the capital account served as a powerful barrier to international speculation in the renminbi, which might otherwise have forced the government to allow its value to go up faster than policymakers wanted it to.

Although WTO membership opened the Chinese economy to foreign enterprises, domestic companies—aided by the economy's size and complexity, by cheap loans from government banks, and by some cheating on WTO rules—continued to dominate the domestic market. Meanwhile, under a "going-out" policy initiated soon after WTO entry, the government used the reciprocal opening of other economies to prod Chinese enterprises to compete in the global marketplace, helping them to succeed with credit from state-owned banks.

Nor did WTO membership make China dependent on foreign trade for its growth. To be sure, China's foreign trade ratio (foreign trade as a percentage of GDP) was high for a large continental economy, around 51.9 percent in 2008. Yet China ranked only 19th in foreign trade ratio in 2008,

---

[8]Richard MacGregor, *The Party: The Secret World of China's Communist Rulers* (New York: HarperCollins, 2010).
[9]Vikram Nehru, Aart Kraay, and Xiaoqing Yu, *China 2020: Development Challenges in the New Century* (Washington, DC: World Bank, 1997), 29–30.

below Indonesia (54.5 percent) and not far above France (51.8 percent). Moreover, foreign trade consists of both imports and exports. Chinese exports consist mainly of products assembled by Chinese workers for foreign brand names from imported components. Chinese policymakers in the mid-1980s dubbed this strategy "two heads outside" (*liangtou zaiwai*) because both the source of components and the market for products were outside China. In such a global supply chain, profits attributable to engineering and design, brand value, and marketing are captured by the foreign owner of the brand name; profits attributable to the manufacture of high-value components go to external manufacturers (often elsewhere in Asia); and the yield to the Chinese economy is limited to the cost of labor for assembly.[10] Yet the full value of the exported product shows up in China's trade statistics.

In all, therefore, Chinese growth was less "export driven" than was the case with the so-called Asian tigers in the 1950s through the 1970s, in the sense that it did not depend on running a consistent trade surplus. Indeed, on a global basis, China's imports and exports were close to balanced for most of the open-door period, generating large surpluses only after 2005. During this time, the growing surplus with the United States (and smaller surpluses with other rich countries, especially in Europe) was balanced in most years by deficits with countries from which China purchased components, raw materials, and energy. Even after China began to run a net surplus of exports over imports, the contribution of net exports to the GDP did not exceed a couple of percentage points, often less.[11] The main drivers of growth were rising productivity and efficiency, infrastructure investment, and domestic demand generated by a more-affluent population. When foreign markets went into recession in 2008, China's domestic market was sufficiently large—with the aid of a substantial government stimulus package—to avoid a corresponding slump in the rate of growth.

In all these ways, China found a way to throw itself into the surging currents of globalization without handing control over its destiny to outside actors. Although many noncompetitive firms went out of business, their disappearance improved the economy's efficiency, and the firms that

---

[10]The datum is from Dong Tao, a Credit Suisse economist, quoted in David Barboza, "Some Assembly Needed: China as Asia Factory," *The New York Times*, 9 February 2006, accessed at http://www.nytimes.com/2006/02/09/business/worldbusiness/09asia.html, 8 August 2008. Another report said the value of exports to the Chinese economy was as little as 20 percent of the face value of the exported products; see David D. Hale and Lyric Hughes Hale, "Reconsidering Revaluation: The Wrong Approach to the U.S.–China Trade Imbalance," *Foreign Affairs* 87 (January–February 2008): 57–66.

[11]Information provided by Daniel H. Rosen, Rhodium Group, personal communication, 19 March 2013.

remained were stronger than before. Instead of globalization fostering domestic instability, as many observers expected, the regime drew strength from prosperity. The government used surging budgetary resources to start building a social welfare net that blunted domestic dissent. And it used its growing international respectability to cultivate its people's national pride, which strengthened its hold on power.

ECONOMIC POLICY: POWER POLITICS BY OTHER MEANS

China's importance as a trade and investment partner altered its strategic situation for the better.[12] By 2010, China ranked as the number two trading country in the world and was an important economic partner to all of the world's major powers. It was no longer conceivable that the West would unite to isolate China as it did in the era of containment. The post-Tiananmen sanctions were the last sanctions to be imposed on China, despite continuing human rights abuses and numerous economic disputes. Constituencies in the West that favored putting pressure on China—the human rights and labor movements, manufacturers crushed by Chinese competition, victims of copyright and patent infringement—found themselves politically checkmated by constituencies having a positive economic stake in relations with China—the financial industry, importers, firms with factories in China, and others. Strong business lobbies emerged in the United States and Europe that worked to stabilize relations with Beijing. Trade threats lost their credibility.[13]

Economic ties smoothed China's relations around its periphery. In Hong Kong, the business community supported retrocession to Chinese control in 1997, believing that economic ties with the mainland would do more for Hong Kong than would political reforms. In Taiwan, cross-strait trade and investment weakened support for independence. Trade and investment prospects contributed to South Korea's shift of diplomatic recognition from Taipei to Beijing in 1992. In the 2000s, Australia put new emphasis on good relations with China as its prosperity became increasingly tied to Chinese ore and energy purchases and mining investments. China's rise as a manufacturing assembly center for the more-advanced Asian economies created the first period of Asian economic integration in history, supporting China's assurance strategy in

---

[12]The subhead for this section borrows a phrase from Jonathan Holslag, "China's Regional Dilemma: An Inquiry Into the Limits of China's Economic and Military Power" (Ph.D. diss., Vrije Universiteit Brussel, 2011).

[13]Ka Zeng, *Trade Threats, Trade Wars: Bargaining, Retaliation, and American Coercive Diplomacy* (Ann Arbor: University of Michigan Press, 2004).

the region.[14] China's need for raw materials made it a key customer and hence a key diplomatic partner of many countries in Africa, Latin America, and the Middle East.

Economic ties opened the way to strategic access. Governments welcomed China to build roads, pipelines, ports, and railways, extending China's transport network deep into Vietnam, Burma, Nepal, Sri Lanka, Pakistan, Turkmenistan, Uzbekistan, Kazakhstan, and Mongolia. Such projects not only eased access to energy imports and opened China's hinterland to cross-border trade but helped tie neighboring economies more closely to China's and, in some cases, created logistical facilities with potential military use.[15]

Robust development gave China enough money to make the transition from foreign aid recipient to donor and lender. In 1982 the government established a Department of Foreign Aid in the Ministry of Foreign Economic Relations and Trade (later renamed the Ministry of Commerce). In the 1990s, it established three banks with international responsibilities —the China Development Bank, the China Agricultural Development Bank, and the China Exim Bank, the latter charged to create a program of concessional loans abroad. China does not publish official figures on foreign aid, but one scholar estimates that its ODA jumped from $500 million in 1996 to more than $3 billion by 2007.[16]

FUNDING MILITARY MODERNIZATION

The economic boom made possible a series of annual increases in China's military budget starting in 1989. The officially announced defense budget has risen in double digits virtually every year since 1990. Most analysts believe that an accurate estimate of total defense spending on a comparable basis to other countries' defense budgets would be double the official figure. In 2009, for example, according to a U.S. Department of Defense estimate, the official level of the Chinese defense budget expressed in U.S. dollars was about $70 billion, and the actual total of military-related spending was about $150 billion.[17]

---

[14]Hideo Ohashi, "China's Regional Trade and Investment Profile" in David Shambaugh, ed., *Power Shift: China and Asia's New Dynamics* (Berkeley: University of California Press, 2005), 71–95; Deng Ziliang and Zheng Yongnian, "China Reshapes the World Economy" in Wang Gungwu and Zheng Yongnian, eds., *China and the New International Order* (London: Routledge, 2008), 127–148.
[15]Jonathan Holslag, "China's Roads to Influence," *Asian Survey* 50 (July–August 2010): 641–662.
[16]Deborah Brautigam, *The Dragon's Gift: The Real Story of China in Africa* (New York: Oxford University Press, 2009), 179.
[17]*Military and Security Developments Involving the People's Republic of China, 2010* (Washington, DC: Office of the Secretary of Defense, 2010), 42–43.

Top priority has been given to building up the People's Liberation Army (PLA) Navy. Starting in the 1990s, China's shipbuilding complex began to produce a dozen new classes of ocean-going vessels with advanced weapon systems, including four types of submarines, five types of guided-missile destroyers, and three types of guided-missile frigates, and to convert an imported aircraft carrier for Chinese use. The acquisitions enabled the Navy to make the initial transition from a coastal defense force to an ocean-going, or blue water, force. Besides expanding its surface fleet, the PLA Navy has enhanced its submarine force with advanced weapons and sensors. A large new naval base on Hainan Island completed in the late 2000s signaled Beijing's intent to continue a robust submarine program and a commitment to defend its claims in the South China Sea.

The PLA Air Force engaged in a wholesale modernization of its inventory. It retired some 70 percent of its air fleet between 1990 and 2010, amounting to approximately 3,500 aircraft, and acquired several hundred advanced fighter planes. In addition, China has worked hard to improve its air defenses, by acquiring one of the world's largest surface-to-air missile forces and enhancing its system for detecting attacks, including the use of a small number of airborne early-warning and control aircraft.

The ground forces also acquired new hardware. Notable additions included third-generation Type-99 main battle tanks, which are gradually being introduced to group armies throughout China, as well as armored personnel carriers and infantry fighting vehicles. New generations of artillery and multiple rocket launchers are also being introduced.

The Second Artillery is in charge of China's ballistic missile forces, which include both nuclear and conventional warheads. The greatest expansion has taken place in China's arsenal of short-range ballistic missiles, which numbered about 1,200 by 2011. By virtue of sheer numbers, improved accuracy, and greater mobility, these conventionally armed rockets pose significant challenges to Taiwan and potentially also to countries around China's periphery.

Globalization reduced the effectiveness of rules and regulations used by the West to limit the flow of sensitive technologies to the People's Republic of China (PRC).[18] A mix of technology transfer through access to foreign commercial technology, technical assistance from Russia and Israel, espionage, and domestic research and development allowed

---

[18] Carla Hills and Dennis Blair, chairs, *U.S.-China Relations: An Affirmative Agenda, a Responsible Course*, Task Force Report (New York: Council on Foreign Relations, April 2007), 47–54.

China to attain near world levels in aerospace, information technology, telecommunications, and ship building. In 2008, the government created a civilian entity called the State Administration for Science, Technology, and Industry for National Defense (SASTIND) to handle research, testing, development, and evaluation of new military systems. SASTIND oversees a military–industrial complex of 10 large defense–industrial corporations that employ at least 2.5 million civilian workers.[19] Although indigenous military production capabilities have improved significantly in recent decades, it will still be necessary for China to continue to import some types of full systems and many component systems for the foreseeable future.

SOFT-POWER PAYOFFS

China's growing economic clout also brought Beijing a surge of soft power—the ability to exert influence beyond what a country wields through the use of force and money because of the appeal of its cultural values, its ideas, and the perceived success of its way of doing things.[20] When China's GDP passed Japan's in 2010 to make it the world's second-largest economy, China's leaders—and its financial officials—became global superstars, welcomed everywhere. Two symbols encapsulated the country's surging prestige: the incomprehensibly huge number affixed to its foreign exchange reserves, which passed the $2 trillion mark in 2005 and kept growing, and the eye- and ear-bursting opening ceremony of the 2008 Beijing Olympics—a grand enactment of vigor, vastness, and vaunting ambition.

Chinese foreign relations experts in the early 2000s had formed the consensus that soft power was a necessary part of comprehensive national power. It would reduce the fear of China's rise and create a more-welcoming environment for other forms of Chinese influence. They believed the core of China's soft power should be its culture—including traditional art, literature, philosophy, and the Chinese language—together with its contemporary image as a peace-loving nation standing for

---

[19]Tai Ming Cheung, *Fortifying China: The Struggle to Build a Modern Defense Economy* (Ithaca, NY: Cornell University Press, 2009); Evan Feigenbaum, *China's Techno-Warriors: National Security and Strategic Competition from the Nuclear to the Information Age* (Stanford, CA: Stanford University Press, 2003).
[20]Joseph S. Nye, Jr., *Soft Power: The Means to Success in World Politics* (New York: PublicAffairs, 2004); Joshua Kurlantzick, *China's Charm Offensive: How China's Soft Power Is Transforming the World* (New Haven, CT: Yale University Press, 2007); David M. Lampton, *The Three Faces of Chinese Power: Might, Money, and Minds* (Berkeley: University of California Press, 2008).

harmony at home and abroad.[21] Hu Jintao made this policy official in his report to the Seventeenth Party Congress in 2007: "In the present era, culture has become a ... factor of growing significance in the competition in overall national strength.... We must ... enhance culture as part of the soft power of our country."[22] The Central Committee reinforced the point in 2011 with a lengthy, formal decision on "deepening reform of the cultural system."[23]

The Chinese Foreign Ministry funded "China Year" exhibitions and activities in various countries. China sent cultural artifacts on loan to museums around the world. In 2005, Beijing permitted selected treasures from the Forbidden City to be displayed in London. Some of the famous terra cotta warriors normally displayed near the tomb of Emperor Qin Shihuang visited the British Museum and other locales in 2007–2010. Starting in 2004, the Ministry of Education began establishing Confucius Institutes in collaboration with foreign universities and other institutions to teach Chinese language and culture, partly with the help of teachers sent from China on temporary assignment. Reviled in Mao's China as backward and feudal, Confucius was now seen to personify Chinese values of harmony, community, and deference. Within a few years, there were some 300 such institutes in 60 countries on five continents, including more than two dozen in the United States, mostly at universities.

Chinese media moved into foreign markets under the combined leadership of the State Council Information Office and the Foreign Ministry's new Office of Public Diplomacy. Long-established publications such as *China Daily*, *Beijing Review*, and *China Pictorial*, as well as similar publications in other foreign languages, became glossy and professional. China Central Television, Xinhua TV, and China Radio

---

[21] Bonnie S. Glaser and Melissa E. Murphy, "Soft Power With Chinese Characteristics: The Ongoing Debate," in Carola McGiffert, ed., *Chinese Soft Power and Its Implications for the United States: Competition and Cooperation in the Developing World* (Washington, DC: Center for Strategic and International Studies, 2009), 10–26, accessed at http://csis.org/files/media/csis/pubs/090305_mcgiffert_chinesesoftpower_web.pdf, 9 December 2010; Joel Wuthnow, "The Concept of Soft Power in China's Strategic Discourse," *Issues & Studies* 44 (June 2008): 1–28.

[22] Hu Jintao, *Hold High the Great Banner of Socialism with Chinese Characteristics and Strive for New Victories in Building a Moderately Prosperous Society in All Respects: Report to the Seventeenth National Congress of the Communist Party of China* (15 October 2007), accessed at http://news.xinhuanet.com/english/2007-10/24/content_6938749_6.htm, 10 December 2010.

[23] "Zhonggong zhongyang guanyu shenhua wenhua tizhi gaige tuidong shehuizhuyi wenhua dafazhan dafanrong ruogan zhongda wenti de jueding" (Decision of the CCP Central Committee on Some Important Questions Concerning Deepening the Reform of the Cultural System and Promoting the Great Development and Great Flourishing of Socialist Culture), 18 October 2011, accessed at http://economy.caijing.com.cn/2011-10-26/110933747.html, 22 January 2012; an official English translation was not available at the time this document was consulted.

International broadcast to the world in many languages. The official Xinhua News Agency established an office in New York City's Times Square to compete with the traditional wire services to supply news to global media. The quality of Chinese journalism was upgraded as media workers were increasingly trained at professional journalism programs in Chinese universities. Under the rubric of e-government, many agencies at the central and provincial levels and even some at lower levels established English-language Web sites alongside their Chinese-language sites. All Chinese media were still government or Party owned and had to follow directives from the CCP's propaganda department, but their look and content were modernized, and they were increasingly accepted worldwide as reliable sources of information.[24]

China's universities sought international standing and connections. In 2003, Shanghai Jiaotong University began ranking 1,200 universities worldwide on an annual basis. The rankings gained widespread attention and spotlighted China's massive investment in its top schools. In the first year of rankings, the best Chinese universities (Peking and Tsinghua) stood tied with four dozen others around the world in ranks 201–250. By the time the 2010 rankings were announced, these two schools had risen to the 151–200 level, and five other Chinese institutions had joined the (expanded) tier of 201–300. As conditions in academia improved, foreign-trained Chinese PhDs returned in large numbers to teach. Chinese institutions welcomed more than 100,000 foreign students a year to study the Chinese language or to take academic degrees, the majority from Asia and Africa. Foreign schools set up joint programs on Chinese campuses. The China Scholarship Council, under the Ministry of Education, began to send a couple of thousand PhD students abroad each year to study for one or two semesters before returning home to teach, thus increasing the cosmopolitan character of Chinese academia.

But global engagement also made China more vulnerable to pressure from other countries' soft power. The public's enhanced exposure to foreign ideas of freedom, democracy, and rule of law undermined the Chinese Communist Party's (CCP) ideological authority. Even as human rights conditions in China improved, so did the flow of information to the outside world about abuses. As a result, Chinese diplomats were drawn into a long battle to confront and deflect international pressure on human rights issues.

---

[24]Anne-Marie Brady, *Marketing Dictatorship: Propaganda and Thought Work in Contemporary China* (Lanham, MD: Rowman and Littlefield, 2007).

COMPLIANCE AND INFLUENCE IN INTERNATIONAL REGIMES

China's entry into the world system caused it to become an active member of virtually all the international regimes in existence—a massive change in posture from the Mao period, when the PRC was a member of almost no international organizations except those that formed part of the socialist camp.[25] China subjected itself to the strictures of these regimes but also gained a voice in their future evolution.

Until 1971, the China seat in the UN was held by the rival Republic of China regime on Taiwan headed by Chiang Kai-shek instead of by the PRC. After the PRC regained that seat, it began to join other international organizations connected to the UN, such as the World Health Organization (WHO) and the Food and Agriculture Organization. It started to take an active role in UN bodies related to human rights. It regained the China seat in bodies such as the World Bank, the IMF, the WTO, the Asian Development Bank, the International Olympic Committee, and many others.

Once the PRC joined an international regime, it complied with its rules about as much as any other member. Even when it came to the international human rights regime, China attended the necessary meetings and filed the necessary reports on time, even if its actions at home contravened what international nongovernmental organizations (NGOs) claimed was the covenants' real intent.[26]

China's compliance often involved disputes with other members over the meaning of the rules, as when China, using the WTO dispute resolution mechanism, sued the United States over the meaning of the term *dumping*, or when China differed with the United States over the legitimate ambit of authority for the UN Security Council to intervene in the internal affairs of states such as Serbia or Iraq in pursuit of what the UN Charter defines as "international peace and security."

One of the most dramatic shifts came in China's participation in the global nonproliferation regime. Under Mao, China rejected all international limits on proliferation of missiles, nuclear weapons, and other weapons of mass destruction, arguing that such restrictions aimed only to consolidate the two superpowers' hegemony. Starting in the mid-1980s and accelerating during the 1990s, China acceded to a host of treaties—

---

[25]Elizabeth Economy and Michel Oksenberg, eds., *China Joins the World: Progress and Prospects* (New York: Council on Foreign Relations, 1999).
[26]Rosemary Foot, *Rights Beyond Borders: The Global Community and the Struggle Over Human Rights in China* (Oxford: Oxford University Press, 2000); Ann Kent, *China, the United Nations, and Human Rights* (Philadelphia: University of Pennsylvania Press, 1999).

including the Biological Weapons Convention (1984), the Nuclear Non-Proliferation Treaty (1992), the Chemical Weapons Convention (1993), and the Comprehensive Test Ban Treaty (1996)—and it joined a long list of additional agreements, institutions, and committees. Through its diplomatic activity, China tried to prevent or roll back the nuclear weapons programs of North Korea and Iran. It announced its support for the idea of nuclear-free zones and for treaties that had been proposed to ban the circulation of fissile materials, to ban the first use of nuclear weapons, to ban the development of antiballistic missiles, and to ban an arms race in outer space. Although the motives for joining different parts of the arms control and nonproliferation regime varied, in general the shift reflected Beijing's judgment that China's security was better served by political stability than by instability in the world regions where it had growing economic interests, like the Middle East and, of course, Asia.[27]

China was not blindly compliant, and as its power increased—and its diplomats' sophistication about each regime's rules grew—it sought to become not only a rule follower, but a rule shaper. For example, as a WTO member, China gained an influential voice in shaping changes in the global trade regime. In the Doha Round of trade talks from 2001 to 2008, China and other large developing countries clashed with the United States and Western Europe over measures to safeguard poor third-world farmers against possible surges in imports of agricultural commodities from rich countries. This conflict led to the collapse of this round of trade liberalization talks. Even though the WTO project of setting universal rules for world trade through multilateral negotiations was set back by this collapse—some said that the project could go no further in the foreseeable future—China continued to pursue ways to open up trade further through agreements with single partners (for example, Chile, Australia, and Thailand) and groups of partners (for example, Association of Southeast Asian Nations [ASEAN], whose free-trade agreement with China came into effect in 2010). Such agreements had little measurable impact on trade volumes, but they sent a message about multipolarity and third-world cooperation that was consistent with overall Chinese diplomatic strategy. In international climate talks, China joined with other developing countries in arguing that the advanced countries should bear the main burden of reducing greenhouse gas emissions and should help pay for

---

[27]Other factors included American lobbying and China's "social learning" from other states. Evan S. Medeiros, *Reluctant Restraint: The Evolution of China's Nonproliferation Policies and Practices, 1980-2004* (Stanford, CA: Stanford University Press, 2007); Alastair Iain Johnston, *Social States: China in International Relations, 1980-2000* (Princeton, NJ: Princeton University Press, 2008).

developing countries' policy adjustments. China's behavior as a rule-shaper was no different from that of other powers, all of whom use their seats at various tables to pursue their own interests.[28]

For China, as for other states, participation in international regimes has been a mixed blessing. It has involved a yielding of autonomy to the shared community of states, to independent international bureaucrats, and even to an ill-defined international public opinion influenced by NGOs and other private actors. Yet to fail to participate would be to forego many of the benefits that globalization offers.

SHARED VULNERABILITY IN THE GLOBAL ECONOMY

Alongside gains to China's power, the deep immersion in globalization has also posed a new set of challenges to China's security, as it has to all countries that are deeply engaged with it: the risk that countries will harm each other, intentionally or unintentionally, in the course of trying to manage their own economies. By the time China joined the WTO, the globalized economy was larger and more-interdependent than anyone—in China and probably elsewhere—had ever foreseen it would become. International trade as a percentage of world GDP had gone from 38.5 percent in 1980 to 54 percent in 2005; international investment as a percentage of world GDP went from 0.5 percent to 2.3 percent. Global flows of this magnitude created historically novel pressures on job markets, commodity prices, and foreign exchange markets, among other domains. In politics, they generated demands for protectionism and, with respect to China in particular, the fear of a "China threat" to the economic welfare of other economies. While producing a new level of mutual vulnerability, intensified globalization made it harder than ever to figure out how to apportion responsibility for solving systemic problems. China faced these challenges with distinctive strengths rooted in its economic and political system, but also with specific weaknesses arising from its position in the world economy.

First, globalization linked job markets across borders. Even though workers could not travel freely to find jobs, many types of jobs could be transferred more easily than before to places where they could be done at good quality for low cost. From 1985 through 2004, Chinese township and village enterprises created an estimated 3.5 million new manufacturing jobs per year, filling them mostly with workers who were no longer

---

[28]Ann Kent, *Beyond Compliance: China, International Organizations, and Global Security* (Stanford, CA: Stanford University Press, 2007); Rosemary Foot and Andrew Walter, *China, the United States, and Global Order* (New York: Cambridge University Press, 2011).

needed for farm labor as the agricultural economy became more efficient and partly with the 20 million or more new workers entering the job market each year.[29] These workers started out in the 1980s producing clothing, toys, shoes, bicycles, lamps, and power tools. They moved up the technological ladder in the 1990s to produce computers, household appliances, specialty steel, automobiles, and ships. Chinese manufacturers then set their sights on higher-tech global markets, including airplanes, electric and luxury cars, electronics, pharmaceuticals, and environmental technologies.

The rise in Chinese jobs manufacturing for export did not automatically mean a decline in jobs elsewhere. For one thing, as the global economy grew, manufacturing was increasing not only in China but in other countries as well. Second, the rise of living standards in China generated new jobs in China's trade partners in agriculture (to supply China with meat, soy beans, apples, and so on), manufacturing (to supply China with parts for assembly), high-tech industry (to sell China airplanes, power stations, precision machine tools, and medical instruments, among other products), intellectual property (movies, music, software, and so on), and services (including legal and financial services). Because of this dynamic, U.S. exports to China increased every year after 2001 even as its trade deficit with China also increased. Third, job markets were changing in other countries through their own internal processes of development independent of whatever was happening in China. In wealthy countries, advances in technology caused productivity to increase, so fewer workers were needed to produce more goods, and workers tended to shift from manufacturing to the service sector. In developing countries, job markets also changed constantly as economies changed.

Yet certain jobs did migrate to China. Most of them had been lost by the West long ago when wage increases made it uneconomical to manufacture low-price products. Such jobs were moving from other Asian economies or countries such as Mexico to take advantage of China's low wages and increasingly reliable quality, creating pressure on other developing economies to find new competitive advantages against not only China, but other rivals. Direct loss of jobs from the advanced countries to China were statistically small, yet they were politically visible.

Despite these complexities, China's size and rate of growth made it the natural focus of blame for job losses in the West. There were no "made

---

[29]The number of jobs created by township and village enterprises is taken from Naughton, *The Chinese Economy*, 286, fig. 12.2; the number of new entrants into the workforce is calculated using Naughton, *The Chinese Economy*, 175, table 7.3.

in India" labels on software or "made in Brazil" labels on aircraft for consumers to see, but they saw "made in China" labels on shoes, radios, toys, clothing, and products that in many cases were not really made but only assembled in China. In the United States, Europe, and Japan, labor and industry groups demanded more antidumping investigations directed at China than at any other country. Labor rights groups exposed violations in Chinese factories producing for export. The Chinese government tried to manage the political backlash by sourcing imports in a wide range of electoral districts all across the United States and Europe and by arguing that its low-priced, good-quality goods enhanced living standards in the West. In the developing world, China sought to position itself as an economic good neighbor. But none of this stemmed the hostility to globalization in general, and to China in particular, produced by the worldwide acceleration of job shifts.

Second, the rise of globalization meant increased mutual vulnerability in commodity markets. By 2010, China was one of the world's top consumers—and in many cases one of the top importers—of many strategic commodities, including oil, food grains, wool, cotton, rubber, copper, lead, zinc, tin, nickel, aluminia, and rare earths.[30] As global demand surged with global growth, supply interruptions or demand surges produced bumps in the market, when prices rose and supplies proved harder to get. To avoid short-term inflationary effects, the government subsidized the domestic prices of gasoline, electricity, transportation, and fertilizers, among other items. Not only did the subsidies drain the government's coffers, but they promoted wasteful use of commodities, leaving a legacy of financial and environmental damage.

For the longer term, Chinese policymakers tried to guard against commodity shortages in several ways. Under the rubric of "grain security," they tried to keep grain imports at 5 percent of consumption by promulgating policies to preserve arable land, raise per-hectare productivity, and use tax relief and subsidies to encourage peasant farmers to produce food grains alongside the more-profitable specialty crops. Under the heading of "energy security," they promoted more efficient use of energy; invested in domestic oil and coal production, hydropower, nuclear, solar, and wind energy; and sought to lock in "equity oil" abroad so that they could count on supplies even in times of global shortage. They purchased shares in copper, iron, and cobalt mines abroad. They placed restrictions

---

[30]David Hale, "China's Growing Appetites," *The National Interest* (Summer 2004): 137–147.

on the export of rare earths to preserve supplies for domestic production of electronic products, batteries, and solar panels.

In the face of rapid growth, however, such policies could only slow, not stop, the erosion of commodity security. Expanding factories, roads, airports, and housing chewed up arable land. Water was too scarce to provide the intensive irrigation that green-revolution strains of rice and wheat needed to supply higher outputs per acre. The population was not only growing in size, but changing its diet. As people used their new wealth to buy more eggs, meat, farmed fish, and beer, it took more grain to meet each person's needs. New factories, cars, and airplanes required more hydrocarbon energy than Chinese coal mines and oilfields plus Chinese-owned overseas sources could supply.

Dramatic increases in Chinese demand were often seen elsewhere in alarmist terms as the main factor disrupting world market stability. The actual effects varied by commodity. In petroleum, for example, greater Chinese demand contributed to rising prices for crude oil, but, at least during the period 1995–2004, global production also increased, which softened the effect on prices. In 2004, China accounted for only 8 percent of world consumption, whereas the United States guzzled 25 percent of the world's petroleum output. By contrast, the price of a product such as wood pulp (the key input for paper) remained basically constant despite growing Chinese demand during the same 10-year period. In the case of ferrous scrap metal (important in the making of steel), dramatic price increases occurred during the same period, pushed to some extent by China, but also by rising demand in other steel-producing countries such as South Korea and Turkey.

People worried that China's demographic size and the speed of its economic growth (along with the rise of India and some other countries), beyond their impact on prices, had finally brought the earth close to the long-discussed limits of its carrying capacity.[31] Ideas such as a global "limit to growth" and "peak oil" (the danger of oil supplies running out) threatened Chinese security by giving rise to pressure on Beijing to rein in the rising living standards that were crucial to the regime's domestic stability.

A third area of interdependent vulnerability in the global economy involved the management of currency and foreign exchange. For domestic firms to buy and sell from foreign firms, they had to use dollars, euros, yen, or a small number of other international reserve currencies. As China's

---

[31] Lester R. Brown, *Who Will Feed China? Wake-Up Call for a Small Planet* (New York: Norton, 1995).

trade went into a global surplus around 2005, Chinese accounts accumulated large quantities of these currencies. Because most global trade is conducted in dollars, most of this surplus came in the form of dollars. (Only a small fraction of China's foreign trade has so far been conducted on a "currency swap" basis with the use of the Chinese yuan and another nonreserve currency such as the Brazilian real.) In the face of this situation, the government had to make two policy decisions: how to treat the exchange rate between Chinese and foreign currencies and how to deal with the foreign exchange reserve generated by the trade surplus.

The government chose to keep control over both the exchange rate and the management of foreign exchange reserves. The People's Bank of China set the exchange rates between the Chinese yuan and the global reserve currencies, and the State Administration of Foreign Exchange managed the reserves. The chief reason to sustain government control of these functions was to prevent changes in the value of foreign currencies from causing inflation in the domestic economy and hence affecting Chinese citizens' welfare and political loyalty. A second reason was to maintain exchange rates at levels favorable to the promotion of Chinese exports. A third was to manage foreign exchange reserves in such a way as to ease political relations with influential officials in Washington and other foreign capitals—for example, by purchasing U.S. Treasury bonds to help the U.S. government manage its fiscal deficits.

But such policies were rife with pitfalls both economic and political. On the economic side, a low yuan-to-dollar (or yen-to-euro) exchange rate promoted exports at the cost of shifting benefits from Chinese to Western consumers. In effect, by virtue of government-controlled exchange rates, Chinese workers accepted lower wages to subsidize higher living standards for Western consumers. Artificially low yuan values also helped create overinvestment, waste, inflows of speculative capital, stock market and real estate bubbles, and inflationary pressures—all of which required government responses to try to manage and smooth them out.

Likewise, conservative management of foreign exchange reserves saddled the Chinese economy with low (sometimes even negative) returns on huge investments. In 2011, China held the equivalent of $3.2 trillion in foreign exchange reserves—more than any other country. Although the makeup of these reserves was a secret, most experts estimated that about 70 percent of the money was held in dollar-denominated assets during the 2000s, even though the value of the dollar was declining in relationship to other reserve currencies. In 2007, China set up a sovereign wealth fund, the China Investment Corporation, to invest a fraction of the reserves more aggressively for better returns, but the corporation's initial investments performed badly. The total amount of the reserves was in any case too large for a large share of it to be managed aggressively. Nor could China convert large amounts of its dollars to other currencies without driving down the value of its dollar stake even further while also harming the economic health of one of its chief markets and raising the prices of Chinese products in that market. Through its holdings of U.S. dollars, therefore, China's economic health was to some extent held hostage to the wisdom of financial managers in Washington—a wisdom in which China had little faith after the economic crisis that started in the United States in 2008.

Exchange rate controls and foreign exchange reserve management became added counts in the "China threat" discourse centered in but not limited to Washington. Partly in response to pressure from Washington and partly in order to move toward its own long-term goal of making the renminbi an international exchange currency, Beijing in 2005 launched a "managed float" of exchange rates. The yuan rose in value from 8.27 to the dollar in 2005 to 6.36 in 2011, an increase of 23 percent. But the revaluation had no discernible effect on the U.S.–China trade balance, and the slow, irregular pace of the increase failed to mollify critics, who intermittently threatened trade sanctions if China did not move faster toward a market-determined exchange rate.

MUTUAL VULNERABILITY IN OTHER GLOBAL SYSTEMS

The logic of mutual vulnerability extended beyond the economy to encompass other interconnected spheres of life—most importantly, the environment, public health, and new information technology. Here, too, the new logic applied: even though countries are more likely to hurt one another inadvertently than on purpose, such harms could be serious, and they are increasingly likely because global systems are too complex to control.

Mutual vulnerability in the natural environment is one example of this logic. China is one of the most polluted countries in the world. To a large extent, the pollution is caused by China's production for consumers abroad. There is also much pollution from dumping of electronic waste that has come back to China after outliving its usefulness in the West. In this way, participation in the global economy imposes heavy economic and health costs on the Chinese people.[32] In turn, some of China's behaviors hurt the environment for people abroad. Poisons dumped by Chinese factories into

---

[32]Jonathan Watts, *When a Billion Chinese Jump: How China Will Save Mankind—or Destroy It* (New York: Scribner, 2010).

the Songhua River have more than once reached downstream populations in the Russian Far East. River and ocean dumping have polluted the waters off the Chinese coast and pushed Chinese fisherman farther into the surrounding seas to compete with boats from other countries. Because of prevailing winds, emissions from Chinese factories have reached Korea and Japan as acid rain and "yellow dust." Soot as far away as Los Angeles has occasionally been chemically traced to Chinese factories. If a nuclear accident on the scale of Japan's 2011 Fukushima reactor disaster were to occur somewhere on the Chinese coast, it might deliver radiation to more people in Japan, Korea, and Taiwan—depending on which Chinese reactor was involved—than in China itself. Farther away, demand created by China's economic growth contributes indirectly to forest depletion, water pollution, and habitat destruction in Southeast Asia, Africa, and Latin America.

It is in China's long-term interest to help solve such environmental problems. They often arise from inefficiencies, the improvement of which will bring benefits to all. As jobs in polluting industries are lost, new jobs can be created in remediation and green industry. But that kind of transition is painful and expensive and can hurt vocal constituencies. As in other countries, in China, the enforcement of environmental regulations lags behind policy commitments, and there is always the question of who bears the cost. Whereas foreign critics claim that China uses backward environmental standards to subsidize exports and compete for jobs unfairly, the Chinese criticize the use of environmental protection standards by developed countries to erect barriers to Chinese imports.

The grand example of mutual vulnerability in the environment is climate change, because the movements of the earth's atmosphere mix everyone's pollution together and bring its baneful effects to bear indiscriminately. Burning 2.6 tons of coal per person per year as of 2009, China has become the number one contributor to the production of carbon dioxide and other greenhouse gases. But coal remains the only way to meet a large fraction of China's soaring energy needs. A wholesale switch to renewable sources is not an option. China is developing nuclear power, but nuclear plants are expensive and slow, require sophisticated safety equipment, and pose environmental risks of their own. Major hydropower projects such as the Three Gorges Dam entail habitat damage and population displacements and have proven internationally controversial. Any increase in oil and gas use makes China more dependent on international sources of supply, and these fuels carry their own environmental problems, which will worsen as Beijing implements its commitment to develop the domestic automobile industry to supply China's emerging middle class with private cars.

Beijing has shown a willingness to recognize its shared interest in the global commons and to cooperate with evolving world standards. It created the National Environmental Protection Administration (upgraded to a ministry in 2008), as well as local environmental protection agencies, and signed a number of international environmental agreements. The government is phasing out the household use of charcoal briquettes for cooking and heating and requires state-owned factories to burn coal more efficiently and install emissions-scrubbing equipment. But China has drawn the line at slowing its pace of development to ameliorate pollution problems that the Chinese argue were created by the developed world. It took the position at the 2009 Copenhagen climate negotiations that China would not take extra measures to slow emissions unless the developed countries drastically slowed their own emissions and gave major aid to China and other developing countries to help cover the cost of emissions cuts there.[33]

China and other countries are also mutually vulnerable in the area of public health. HIV/AIDS came into China from outside. Now there are three epidemics, two of which are linked to cross-border transmission—intravenous drug use along the Burma border and sex work along the east coast (the third epidemic is the blood transfusion epidemic in Henan, which is gradually diminishing as the blood purchase stations are banned and the victims die). No disease that originated in China has so far spread to the rest of the world in a major way. But the spread of severe acute respiratory syndrome (2002) and avian flu (2003) from China to neighboring countries put the world on notice that China might produce disease vectors that would travel quickly under modern conditions to the rest of the world. As a result, international health organizations such as the WHO began to pressure the Chinese authorities to share information more quickly and accurately than they had done in the past, thus leading to another loss—however beneficial in the long run—to China's accustomed autonomy.

A third example of mutual vulnerability lies in the Internet and other forms of new information technology. The Internet took off in China around the mid-1990s and reached some 500 million users in its first decade. Between 2000 and 2009, cell phone subscriptions increased from 7 per 100 persons to 56, with escalating use of texting and the Chinese

---

[33] Foot and Walter, *China, the United States, and Global Order*, chap. 5.

equivalent of Twitter. The government promoted the use of information technology as a focus of economic growth but also invested major resources in a multilayered control system, popularly known as the Great Firewall, to prevent information from destabilizing domestic politics. In 2009, the government shut down the Internet in Xinjiang for six months to prevent the spread of antigovernment ideas among the restive population. In 2011, the authorities worked hard to control the spread of information about unrest in the Middle East and the use of the Internet and cell phones to call for a peaceful "Jasmine revolution." The Internet also served as a channel for threats projected outward from China to other users. For example, the Pentagon, Google, and numerous other institutions and individual users outside China reported hacking and phishing attempts and virus attacks emanating from China. It was unclear when the hackers were private persons and when they were Chinese government institutions.

THE CHINA THREAT UNDER CONDITIONS OF GLOBALIZATION

If—a big if—China's economic growth continues for another decade or two at the rate it has sustained in the past three decades, the country will possess the resources to build up its military further and acquire bases overseas, and it may feel the need to use force to protect its expanding interests. Technological diffusion might erode the U.S. lead in military and information technology, so that even if the United States continues to modernize its military, China might be able to close the gap.[34] The renminbi might replace the dollar as the largest international reserve currency. Chinese culture and values might achieve global influence along with Chinese products. If the United States were to resist these trends, the two countries might go to war.[35]

But such a vision of China's rise as an unalloyed threat to Western interests is based on a one-sided understanding of China's place in the global system. Although immersion in globalization has indeed increased China's economic, military, and soft power, it has also rendered China more interdependent and vulnerable. Both trends will intensify as China's

---

[34] But for an argument that this is unlikely, see Michael Beckley, "China's Century? Why America's Edge Will Endure," *International Security* 36 (Winter 2011/12): 41–78.

[35] Aaron L. Friedberg, *A Contest for Supremacy: China, America, and the Struggle for Mastery in Asia* (New York: Norton, 2011); Martin Jacques, *When China Rules the World: The Rise of the Middle Kingdom and the End of the Western World* (London: Allen Lane, 2009); John J. Mearsheimer, *The Tragedy of Great Power Politics* (New York: Norton, 2001); Arvind Subramanian, *Eclipse: Living in the Shadow of China's Economic Dominance* (Washington, DC: Peterson Institute for International Economics, 2011).

economy grows. Although economic growth has produced frictions in China's relations with the United States and its allies, common interests have prevented these frictions from developing into direct economic, political, or military conflicts in the period since China embarked on its immersion in globalization.

The richer China becomes, the greater will be its stake in the security of the sea lanes, the stability of the world trade and financial regimes, nonproliferation, the control of global climate change, and cooperation in public health. If and when it becomes the world's largest economy, its prosperity will continue to be tied up with that of the United States, Europe, and Japan. Of course the reverse is also true: Western prosperity and security will be tied to the welfare of China. Barring a collapse of some unpredictable kind in the international system as a whole, China and its rivals will continue to find themselves hostage to each other's welfare. Globalization poses new kinds of security risks not only to China but to all participants in the global system. But there are too many benefits in the system for any of its members to opt out.*

---

*This article is adapted from *China's Search for Security* by Andrew J. Nathan and Andrew Scobell (New York: Columbia University Press, 2012). It was originally published in *Political Science Quarterly* 128 (Fall 2013): 427–454.

Creating a Disaster: NATO's Open Door Policy

ROBERT J. ART

THE UNITED STATES AND ITS NATO ALLIES have gotten themselves into a real pickle. With their decision to enlarge NATO by taking in Poland, Hungary, and the Czech Republic, they have created three predicaments. Each is serious, none is easy to solve, and all require resolution.

The first predicament is: Where does enlargement stop? Who gets to join NATO and who does not? The weightiest members of the alliance have not determined in their own minds how many new members to take in. Yet, they have set in motion a process that is producing its own political momentum toward an ever-growing membership. Stopping expansion after one or two limited rounds, after all, will inevitably draw new lines in Europe, as those who do not want to be left out so potently argue. In response, NATO has declared that it is not in the business of drawing new such lines: "no more Yaltas" is the refrain now heard. Consequently, NATO has declared an open door membership policy: it will consider applications from any country that can meet the requirements for joining. If pursued to its logical end, this policy will convert NATO from an effective military alliance of limited membership into an entity of great size but with unclear function and effectiveness—perhaps an Organization for Security and Co-operation in Europe (OSCE) with real military muscle, or perhaps another OSCE-like talk shop (see the third predicament below).

The second predicament is: How large can a NATO-without-Russia become before the West more or less permanently alienates Russia?

ROBERT J. ART is Christian A. Herter Professor of International Relations at Brandeis University and Director of MIT's Seminar XXI Program.

Membership may indeed be open to all who qualify, but in practice neither Russian nor Ukrainian entry is in the cards for a long time. Taking in Ukraine without also inducting Russia is the quickest way to alienate Russia, because Russians across the political spectrum consider Ukraine to be part of Russia. Incorporating some of Mother Russia into NATO would justifiably give rise within Russia to fears of encirclement by, and exclusion from, the West. The same can be said for inducting the three Baltic states into NATO—Latvia, Lithuania, and Estonia. These, like Ukraine, were formerly part of the Soviet Union, not a part of the Soviet empire in Eastern Europe, like Poland, Hungary, and the Czech Republic. Taking Russia into NATO could well destroy American and allied support for the alliance. Unless the terms of NATO are changed, Russia's membership in NATO means that the United States is committed to defend it against all potential attackers, a large undertaking that not even the sole remaining superpower—and certainly not the United States Senate, as well as many of its allies—will blithely undertake. Thus, if Russia and Ukraine are ever to join NATO, they will be near the end, not the middle, of the queue.

Not to worry, we are told by the proponents of enlargement. NATO can expand without alienating Russia and endangering Ukraine. The special deals cut with these two—the Founding Act with Russia and the NATO-Ukraine Charter—will square the circle. Both states will be kept organically out of NATO but intimately tied to it.[1] As a result, Ukraine will feel more secure and Russia will have sway in NATO councils but without a veto over its actions. In Russia's case, in addition, Polish-Hungarian-Czech membership is said to be to Russia's advantage. Its western borders are made more secure and its own transition to democracy enhanced by having those three states solidly democratic and in NATO. By this line of reasoning, NATO can grow quite large, still exclude Russia, yet not alienate it.

The third predicament is: What will happen to NATO if it takes in a whole lot of new members? There are a slew of potential candidates: Lithuania, Latvia, and Estonia are banging at the door and Secretary of State Madeleine Albright promised they would not be excluded; Slovenia, Bulgaria, and Romania have indicated their desire to join, but have been told to wait for the next round of expansion; Austria, Finland, Sweden, Ukraine, and potentially Macedonia, Albania, and Bosnia, none of which

---

[1]The agreement between NATO and Russia, entitled "Founding Act on Mutual Relations, Cooperation, and Security Between NATO and the Russian Federation," was signed in Paris on 27 May 1997. The text can be found in *Arms Control Today* 27 (May 1997): 21–24. The "Charter on a Distinctive Partnership between the North Atlantic Treaty Organization and Ukraine" was signed in Madrid on 9 July 1997. The text can be found in *NATO Review* 4 (July-August 1997): 5–6 of the special insert.

currently seeks membership but might well should all the previous states get in; and finally, the former republics of the Soviet Union, all of whom are members of the OSCE, Europe's only pan-European-Central Asian, quasi-security institution. Can NATO take in all, most, or many of these states and still retain sufficient political cohesion and military readiness to be effective? Or will expansion beyond a certain point render it ineffective?

Not to worry, we are told. New members will not subtract from, but add to, NATO's effectiveness. First, NATO has expanded before without diluting itself. Originally comprised of twelve states when it was founded in 1949, NATO grew to sixteen members by the end of the cold war, adding Greece and Turkey in 1952, West Germany in 1955, and Spain in 1982. If done properly and carefully, therefore, growth in size need not detract from NATO's functioning, as previous enlargements demonstrate. Second, states will be permitted to join only when they can meet NATO's military requirements. NATO will not be reduced to new members' standards; rather they will be brought up to NATO standards, thereby maintaining NATO's military effectiveness. Third, NATO's political cohesion will remain intact, because only democratic states will be permitted to join. Democracies are like-minded in their approach to security issues, and this will guarantee the consensus necessary to act when action is required. Fourth, NATO cannot stand still because conditions in Europe are changing. If NATO is to survive, it must adapt itself to the new security challenges. Defense of member territory is no longer the sole directive for NATO; now it must address instability within and among the newly-created states of Europe. This requires crisis prevention, peacekeeping, and peacemaking—missions that NATO has already begun to undertake. Fifth, new members will help NATO with its new tasks. A bigger alliance will be a more effective alliance, better at combatting instability, either because NATO permanently pacifies areas by incorporating them into its fold or because a bigger NATO has more resources and better geographic position from which to operate out of area. According to this line of reasoning, bigger is both necessary and better.

How big should NATO become? How much bigger can it get without provoking Russia? Will it get so big that it will choke on its own engorged membership? These are the predicaments that the yellow-brick-road of enlargement has created. All three are inextricably entangled; hence none can be solved in isolation from the others. All, moreover, require resolution, because the stakes are so high. NATO is the institutional repository for America's military ties to Europe, but it is also the keystone of America's global military role. If NATO is somehow gutted, the United States will likely withdraw militarily from Europe, revert to isolationism, or both—results not in Europe's, America's, or the world's best interests.

OPEN DOOR MEMBERSHIP—A BAD SOLUTION

In their carefully reasoned and provocative article, Bruce Russett and Allan Stam address all three predicaments.[2] They tackle the second head on and argue that NATO enlargement will not only alienate Russia, but might also well drive it into China's arms, creating a formidable Sino-Russian alliance hostile to Western interests. To avoid either outcome, they prescribe inducting Russia into NATO in the next expansion, so long as Russia in their words "remains reasonably democratic."[3] They also argue that China should ultimately become a NATO member, because this is an effective way to avoid war with it and to manage its peaceful transition to superpower status. Russett and Stam also provide an explicit answer to the first predicament, taking the logical position that if Russia and China can join, why not any other state that qualifies. Hence their prescription: "NATO should expand to include anyone who meets the criteria. . . ."[4]

Their answer to the third predicament is also clear. To the question, "Can NATO remain effective if it becomes quite large?" their answer appears to be "yes." As best I can figure it, their ultimate vision for NATO is that it transmutes itself by successive enlargements into a pan-Eurasian security organization of democratic states (or PESODS, my acronym) in which the United States, Canada, and Japan will also be members. Should this happen, PESODS will become either the military arm of, or an "essential supplement to," the United Nations.[5] If this vision comes to pass, then: "Ultimately, a great security management system might come to include all but the rogue states. In a sense, that would be the end of international political history."[6] A noble vision: a pan-continental NATO abolishes international politics as we have known it!

Noble as this vision for NATO may appear, I judge it to be profoundly misguided. The Russett-Stam prescription for open door membership, which is also rhetorically NATO's, is unwise. It makes a bad policy even worse, and I oppose it for three reasons.

First, it is not necessary to take Russia into NATO in order to avoid its estrangement, and especially to avert the danger Russett and Stam seem to

---

[2]Bruce Russett and Allan C. Stam, "Courting Disaster: An Expanded NATO vs. Russia and China," *Political Science Quarterly* 113 (Fall 1998): 361–382.
[3]Ibid., 362.
[4]Ibid., 382.
[5]Ibid.
[6]Ibid., 380.

fear so much—an anti-Western Russian-Chinese alliance. The levers to avoid Russia's complete alienation from the West are more effective than Russett and Stam apparently think; Russia's incentives not to sever its ties to the West are greater than they believe; and the incentives for China to enter such an alliance are weaker than they presume.

Second, it is risky to convert NATO into PESODS. To do so will replace an alliance that works well with something that is not likely to work nearly as well, if at all. Russett and Stam are too cavalier with their assumptions that PESODS can be made to work effectively and that the United States will readily support something that so vastly expands its military commitments.

Third, there is a better way to deal with Russia's alienation: construct a viable, modern-day Concert of Europe. To work, such a concert requires that the United States take seriously the Founding Act between Russia and NATO and that it severely limit any expansion of NATO beyond the current round. If properly executed, this alternative is preferable to open door membership, because it will preserve both the West's ties to Russia and NATO's effectiveness.

For these reasons, I find the open door policy unnecessary and risky, and I believe there is a better way to manage, even if not solve, the predicaments created by enlargement.

THE LIMITS OF RUSSIAN-CHINESE COOPERATION

Has the current round of NATO enlargement already totally estranged Russia from the West? Will another round drive it headlong into alliance with China? The answers are not self-evident. In fact, there are three good reasons to believe that the current round, and even another limited round, will neither alienate Russia completely nor inevitably produce a hostile Russian-Chinese alliance. First, Russia cannot afford to cut its ties with the West; second, it does not need a military alliance with China to protect itself; and third, China's interests dictate against entry into an alliance aimed at the United States.

Russia's Need for the West

To begin with, Russia needs the West. If it is to become a full capitalistic democracy in a reasonable period of time and with as little pain as the situation permits, Russia requires the West's help—financial resources, technical and technological know-how, and markets for Russia's raw materials and finished goods. A good case can be made that the West has not given enough financial assistance to help Russia make the transition from authoritarian communism to democratic capitalism, even though it has transferred at least $60 billion to Russia since 1992.[7] Valid though this case may be, it is a far cry from a situation in which the West gives Russia no help at all. That, however, would be the likely result of Russia's entry into a hostile alliance with China; and the consequent cessation of Western assistance would severely, if not catastrophically, harm Russia's economy. Russia's need for the West's assistance, therefore, constrains how much further beyond rapprochement it can go with China. While Russia has complained bitterly about NATO's enlargement, it has not taken steps that would irrevocably break its ties with the West. Russia's anti-enlargement rhetoric has far surpassed the concrete steps taken to counter it.[8]

Russia's Nuclear Security
Russia's security does not rest on great power alliances. It does not need China to protect itself against an enlarged NATO or against any other great power. After all, Russia is a nuclear power, the next most formidable nuclear power in the world after the United States, and nuclear-armed states are rarely subject to massive attack by others. Russia's conventional forces may collectively constitute a basket case, but its nuclear force remains strong enough to deter attack or invasion from any great power. Thus, the prime incentive for Russia to enter into a military alliance with China—the need to protect itself against attack—is absent.[9]

Russett and Stam implicitly recognize this logic when they tell us why China should not fear a NATO that has inducted Russia into its fold. They argue: "As for potential Chinese fears, the Chinese have their deterrents

---

[7] From 1992-1996, the West committed through various sources over $40 billion in aid, and in 1998 it put together an emergency package of another $22 billion in aid from the International Monetary Fund (IMF) to deal with the financial fallout Russia experienced from the Asian crisis. See Coit D. Blacker, "Russia and the West" in Michael Mandelbaum, ed., *The New Russian Foreign Policy* (New York: Council on Foreign Relations, 1998), 172; and Press Briefing by Stanley Fischer, first deputy managing director of the IMF, 13 July 1998 at http://www.imf.org/external/np/tr/1998/tr 980713.htm.

[8] As one example of the rhetoric, President Boris Yeltsin, according to the Associated Press, said on 6 May 1997: "We shall do everything to minimize the consequences of NATO expansion for Russia's security. We shall continue to deepen integration within the Commonwealth of Independent States, especially with Belarus. We shall strengthen cooperation with neighboring countries, first of all with China." Quoted in Stanley Kober, "Russia's Search for Identity" in Ted Galen Carpenter and Barbara Conry, eds., *NATO Enlargement: Illusions and Reality* (Washington, DC: Cato Institute, 1998), 136.

[9] William Wohlforth puts the matter well: "Officially and unofficially, Russians see no direct military threats for at least the next decade.... No power is thought to have interests that could lead to the direct use of force against Russian territory.... All sides—government and opposition, democrats and nationalists—agree that the probability of any direct security threat to Russia now or in the near future is low or nonexistent. The main threats are internal to Russia and the Commonwealth of Independent States and reflect uncontrolled processes or unintended consequences.... While politicians cannot resist the allure of nationalist great-power rhetoric, military and national security officials have dramatically lowered their threat assessments since 1992." See William Wohlforth, "Redefining Security: Russia's Intellectual Adjustment to Decline," *Harvard International Review* 29 (Winter 1996/1997): 59-60.

against Russian or Western aggression. An invasion and occupation of China's vast territory and population is unimaginable, particularly by a NATO limited to a defense orientation."[10] But if this logic is good for China facing a NATO with Russia in it, why is it not equally valid for Russia facing NATO with Poland, Hungary, and the Czech Republic in it? Is Russia, too, not a "vast territory?" Does Russia not have its deterrents against "Western aggression?" Is NATO not as "limited to a defense orientation" with three Central European states in it as it would be with Russia in it? What, in sum, does a military alliance with China add to Russia's homeland security? The answer: very little. Therefore, as long as Russia maintains a second strike nuclear deterrent, it will be secure against any significant external attack.

To take this position, however, is not to dismiss the adverse political effects that enlargement has had on Russian-Western relations. The West has done itself no good by going through with a decision that is unpopular across the entire spectrum of Russian political opinion and that has complicated the life of pro-Western reformers who want to tie Russia closer to the West.[11] Except for those on the extreme right, Russians do not believe that the present enlargement threatens their territory.[12] What they fear from enlargement is exclusion from the West, not attack by NATO. The European Union and NATO are two of the West's most important institutions, and membership in them rightly signifies full participation in Western affairs. Russians can therefore view their inability to join either as meaning that they are not considered worthy of full participation in the Western world.[13] This sense of exclusion is a serious issue. It is not serious enough to create a Sino-Russian alliance, but it is serious enough to complicate American foreign policy in many other ways unless countermeasures are taken. I offer one in the last section of this article.

---

[10] Russett and Stam, "Courting Disaster," 368.
[11] Resentment against enlargement is not simply an elite affair. In a poll conducted before the enlargement agreement was signed, 51 percent of Russians polled saw NATO expansion as a serious threat and only 14 percent disagreed with that premise. See Susan Eisenhower, "The Perils of Victory" in Carpenter and Conry, *NATO Enlargement*, 114.
[12] Again, Wohlforth puts the point well: ". . . The overwhelming majority of Russia's policy elite sees NATO expansion as detrimental to Russia's security interests and as evidence of a policy failure of major proportions. Only the most committed of Westernizers can view NATO expansion with equanimity. However, even strident opponents of the move do not see it as motivated by any immediate designs on Russia, and their opinions vary on the actual significance of the security threat it implies." See Wohlforth, "Redefining Security," 59.
[13] As one Russian scholar, Irina Zhinkina, put it: "How come that the new Russia, which has discarded its former ideology, remembered God, sworn loyalty to the new ideals of democracy and fallen into the embrace of its recent 'probable adversaries' is not accepted [*sic*] to Western civilization. What else must it do?" Quoted in Kober, "Russia's Search for Identity," 135-136.

China's Independent Foreign Policy

China is not likely to join Russia in an alliance directed against the United States solely because NATO gets bigger. Therefore, even if I am wrong and Russia decides to woo China ardently, a military alliance between the two is still not likely to be consummated. It takes two to make an alliance, and China's current and foreseeable interests strongly militate against it, particularly as long as the United States continues to play its cards more wisely in East Asia than it has so far in Europe. Thus, even if Russia comes to want such an alliance, China in all likelihood would reject it. A look at the factors behind the rapprochement between Russia and China will help explain why.

The current rapprochement is a normalization of relations, not a strategic partnership aimed at the United States.[14] Russia and China have cooperated with one another since the end of the cold war for three main reasons. First is the mutual desire to settle their long-standing border conflict in the Far East. Second is a shared approach toward Central Asia—having the borders of the new Central Asian states stable and secure, limiting ethnic separatism and their support of cross-border independence movements, and combatting the perceived Islamic fundamentalist threat from the south. Last are the mutually beneficial gains that are realized from China's purchases of Russian arms. A fourth factor—the desire to counter America's predominance—has played a part, but only a bit part, in the cooperation the two states have forged to date.

The drive to normalize their relations predates the collapse of the Soviet Union. Mikhail Gorbachev began the normalization process in the mid-1980s as part of his "new thinking" in foreign policy. He matched the goal of ending the cold war in the West with sustained efforts to end the long-standing Sino-Soviet conflict in the East. Tentative agreement on the eastern Sino-Soviet border was reached in 1987 and the Gorbachev-Deng Xiaoping summit in May 1989 formally ended the Sino-Soviet

---

[14] Good overviews of the current Sino-Russian rapprochement are: Jennifer Anderson, *The Limits of Sino-Russian Strategic Partnership*, Adelphi Paper 315 (London: International Institute of Strategic Studies, 1997); Andrew J. Nathan and Robert S. Ross, *The Great Wall and the Empty Fortress: China's Search for Security* (New York: W.W. Norton, 1997), chap. 3; Stephen J. Blank and Alvin Z. Rubinstein, eds., *Imperial Decline: Russia's Changing Role in Asia* (Durham, NC: Duke University Press, 1997), 40–126; Sherman Garnett, "Slow Dance: The Evolution of Sino-Russian Relations," *Harvard International Review* 28 (Winter 1996/97): 28–35; Sherman Garnett, "The Russian Far East as a Factor in Russian-Chinese Relations," *SAIS Review* 16 (1996): 1–19; J. Richard Walsh, "China and the New Geopolitics of Central Asia" and Hung P. Nguyen, "Russia and China: The Genesis of an Eastern Rapallo" both in *Asian Survey* 33 (March 1993): 272–284 and 285–302; and Robert Legvold, "Russia and the Strategic Quadrangle" and David M. Lampton, "China and the Strategic Quadrangle" both in Michael Mandelbaum, ed., *The Strategic Quadrangle: Russia, China, Japan, and the United States in East Asia* (New York: Council on Foreign Relations, 1995), 16–62 and 63–107.

conflict. Throughout the 1990s, Boris Yeltsin continued Gorbachev's normalization policy, partly out of Russia's general weakness, partly out of the central government's concern for the vulnerability of its far eastern provinces, which it could no longer wall off from outside influences as the Soviet government did, and partly out of a desire to reduce Russia's military burden. China was open to these overtures, partly because of its desire to reduce its military burden on the northern border, partly to engage in profitable commerce with Russia's far eastern provinces, and partly from its general desire to maintain stable relations with both Russia and the United States so as to be hostage to neither.[15] Each government felt another powerful pressure to settle their border dispute: the concern each has about center-periphery relations. Both governments are worried about the potential erosion of their control over their respective provinces and regions. The last thing each wants is turmoil along the shared border. For all these reasons, both have had strong incentives to settle the matter.

Over the last six years, China and Russia have reached two important agreements: one demarcating the border between them in the Far East and another demilitarizing it one hundred kilometers on either side.[16] To date, the border issue has not been completely solved, but now it is only a minor irritant in Sino-Russian relations.

In Central Asia, Russia and China have reached a modus vivendi based on an overlap of interests. Both states have favored secure and stable borders for the five new states born from the Soviet Union's disintegration. Russia is concerned about the threat that Islamic fundamentalism from the South could have on its own considerable Muslim population, and it is also determined to keep the region within its sphere of influence. China is concerned about its hold over its western province of Xinjiang and, therefore, worries about the threat posed by the Uighurs living in Kazakhstan who favor a Xinjiang independence movement. The Uighurs are the largest ethnic group in Xinjiang. China is also concerned about Islamic fundamentalism in general. China has accepted for the time being Russia's political-military predominance in the region, and in return it has benefited from Russia's efforts to create stable borders and control cross-border independence movements along the periphery of the former Soviet Union.

---

[15]See Nathan and Ross, *Great Wall*, chap. 3, for a good overview of Sino-Soviet and Sino-Russian relations since 1950.
[16]For details on the agreements and their negotiating history, as well as the issues still outstanding, see Anderson, *Limits of Sino-Russian Strategic Partnership*, chap. 2.

China's purchases of Russian arms help modernize China's military, which is badly in need of modernization. But they also help Russia's military-industrial complex, which cannot survive, much less produce the next generation of military equipment, on the orders of the Russian military alone. As a consequence, transfers of technology and equipment began in 1992, and since then Russia has sold to China advanced electronics, air-to-air and surface-to-air missiles, armored fighting vehicles, T-72 tanks, and Su-27 fighters. Russia is now China's largest source of modern arms, providing nearly 70 percent of China's arms imports in 1996.[17] All these considerations have led to a rapprochement in Sino-Russian relations that was much overdue.

Underneath the cooperation in these areas, however, are conflicts, latent and real, and mutual wariness. Russia's provision of advanced military equipment to China is a two-edged sword, especially since China seeks transfers of technology so that it can produce its own advanced weapons. China is a rising power; Russia is a declining one. Arming a rising power only hastens its rise. Russians in the Far East worry about the huge demographic asymmetry between them and the Chinese contiguous to them. There are eight million Russians in the Russian Far East and 120 million Chinese nearby, giving rise in those Russian provinces to fears of Sinicization of the Russian Far East through cross-border trade and illegal immigration. China is becoming an economic competitor to Russia in Central Asia, seeking to revive the old silk road and looking to tap into the huge Caspian energy reserves. China has become Kazakhstan's second most important export market. It is on the verge of surpassing Russia as the dominant supplier of light-industrial products to the whole region, and it has joined with Western and Japanese companies in exploring pipeline construction out of the Caspian area. The states of Central Asia, seeking to free themselves of Russian predominance, welcome the Chinese (and the Western and Japanese) presence. These considerations are not sufficient to break the current cooperation between Russia and China, but neither are they so weak as to provide no resistance against the signing of a firm military alliance between the two.[18]

Concern about "American hegemonism" has played little, if any, role in the Sino-Russian normalization. The border agreements reached by the

---

[17]Garnett, "Slow Dance," 30–31; and Anderson, *Limits of Sino-Russian Strategic Partnership*, 36.

[18]On these matters, see Garnett, "The Russian Far East"; Nathan and Ross, *Great Wall*, 48–55; Peter Pavilions and Richard Giragosian, "The Great Game: Pipeline Politics in Central Asia," *Harvard International Review* 28 (Winter 1996/97): 24–27 and 62–65; and Stephen J. Blank, "Energy, Economics and Security in Central Asia: Russia and Its Rivals, " *Central Asian Survey* 14 (1995): 373–406.

two states tackled problems that needed tackling. The Central Asian modus vivendi and the arms purchases satisfied the interests of the two powers, independent of their concerns about the United States. Normalization would have occurred in the absence of these concerns, and the best proof available is that it began before the Soviet Union disintegrated and left the United States as the world's dominant power. It was Gorbachev's drive to end the Sino-Soviet conflict, not America's emergence as the sole superpower, that jump-started Sino-Russian normalization, that obviated China's need to cooperate with the United States against Soviet hegemonism, and that made possible (although not inevitable) the current Sino-Russian rapprochement.

Does this mean that in the 1990s Russia and China have had no concerns at all about America's singular superpower status? Clearly not. Both share such concerns, and the two proclaimed a strategic partnership in April 1996. Russian foreign policy took a less Western and more balanced turn in late 1994, after the United States declared that it intended to expand NATO. Under Foreign Minister Yevgeny M. Primakov, who took over in January 1996, Russia has tried to create counterweights to the United States by cultivating ties with China, India, and Iran.[19] Practically overnight in April 1996, China agreed to a strategic partnership, in part because of the after-effects of the Taiwan Straits standoff in March 1996 and the reaffirmation of the U.S.–Japan treaty in April. Clearly, America's actions in Europe and East Asia have had something to do with the creation of a Sino-Russian strategic partnership.

For our purposes, however, the important point about this partnership is not its existence, but its meaning. Russia and China view it differently. Russia makes it out to be much more important than does China, and Russia has been the suitor in trying to move the relationship beyond normalization to something more potent. China has been resistant. Jennifer Anderson, a close observer of Sino-Russian relations, makes this clear:

> China's leaders have been far more cautious [about the strategic partnership], repeatedly playing down elements of the relationship and placing it in the context of longer-standing traditions of adherence to the Five Principles of Peaceful Coexistence and aversion to bloc or alliance politics. Jiang's agreement to upgrade links from "constructive" to "strategic" partnership on 24-hours' notice, rather than seeking agreement from other Chinese leaders, appears to confirm that no significant departure from China's foreign-policy stance of independence and pragmatism has taken place. . . . Although Jiang has agreed to describe relations as a "strategic

---

[19]See Blacker, "Russia and the West," 178–188.

partnership," China has often backed away from Russian definitions of what this actually means. . . . Jiang described links with the US as a "strategic partnership" after a trip there in October 1997.[20]

Russia and China differ in how far each is prepared to go in offsetting American power. China wants Russian arms, stable borders, and secure peripheries; but it is wary of Russia's attempt to make more of their cooperation than that. Although Russia wants strategic partnership, China stops at normalization.

Unless current conditions change dramatically, there are four good reasons why China will not allow the current rapprochement to transmute into a military alliance directed against the United States. First, China needs American investment and especially access to America's market to help it modernize. China has a favorable balance of trade with the United States that is second only to Japan's and that often runs neck and neck with it on a monthly basis. No country takes as many Chinese goods as does the United States, and no other country, especially Russia, is placed to do so, should the United States severely restrict China's access to its market. China will not sacrifice its access to America's market simply because Russia wants an alliance with it. Just as is the case for Russia, therefore, China's need for the American market and American investment puts limits on how closely it will cooperate militarily with Russia against the United States.

Second, China no more wants to be under Russia's thumb than under America's. China's goal is an independent foreign policy. It will use Russia to offset the United States, the United States to offset Russia, and both to offset Japan, when circumstances require it. The drive to be independent is powerful in China, especially given its experience with Western, Russian, and Japanese colonialism.

Third, China does not need an alliance with Russia to secure itself against the United States. China, like Russia, is a nuclear power, not as powerful as either Russia or the United States, but a nuclear power nonetheless. Just as Russia does not need China to secure itself against an American-led NATO invasion, so China does not need Russia to secure itself against an American invasion.

Fourth, China's attitude toward a military alliance with Russia will be determined by what happens in Asia, not in Europe. It stretches credulity to believe that China will sign a full-blown, anti-American military alliance with Russia because NATO takes in Slovenia, Romania, Bulgaria, and even the Baltic states and Ukraine. China may consider itself a global power, but

---

[20] Anderson, *Limits of Sino-Russian Strategic Partnership*, 24.

its vital interests and core security concerns lie in Asia, not in Europe. Therefore, what the United States does in Asia, particularly in northeast, east, and southeast Asia, not what it does in Western and Central Europe, will govern how closely China moves towards military cooperation with Russia.

This, then, is the key. It is in America's, not Russia's hands to determine whether China moves from a vague, if not meaningless strategic partnership with Russia into an anti-American military alliance. The United States could bring a military alliance about by pursuing a stupid policy in East Asia. It could, for example, support independence for Taiwan, which it does not. It could move American troops up close to the Yalu when Korea unites, which it should not. It could push the Japanese to patrol aggressively close to Chinese waters, which it dare not. Short of this sort of bungling by the United States, Russia and China will cooperate when their interests dictate, but that cooperation will remain short of a firm and hostile military alliance directed against the United States and its allies.

China is the rising power; Russia, the declining one. As the declining power, Russia needs China more than China needs Russia. The only way China will need Russia as much as Russia appears to need China is if the United States takes steps to drive it into Russia's waiting arms. Therefore, the United States should make certain that it does not commit the blunders in Asia to produce such an outcome.

PESODS AND THE DESTRUCTION OF NATO

The second reason to oppose the open door membership policy is that it will destroy NATO and replace it with something that will work far less well to keep Eurasia stable. If PESODS ever does emerge, it will be too unwieldy to be effective. NATO is too valuable to sacrifice on the altar of what is essentially a putative collective security organization.

PESODS's problem is one of size and scale. When an alliance expands to the number of states and territorial scope that Russett and Stam contemplate for NATO, it will then take on many of the fatal defects that plague a collective security organization (CSO).[21] In all fairness, Russett and Stam do not call their ultimate vision for NATO "collective security," but the functions that they appear to attribute to it make PESODS look pretty much like a CSO. In analyzing what alliances such as NATO do, they state: "Any defensive alliance serves two purposes. The first is to prevent an external

---

[21]Good analyses of why collective security organizations do not work can be found in Hans J. Morgenthau, *Politics Among Nations: The Struggle for Power and Peace*, 3rd ed. (New York: Knopf, 1964), 412–418; Inis L. Claude, Jr., *Power and International Relations* (New York: Random House, 1962), chap. 5; Josef Joffe, "Collective Security and the Future of Europe," *Survival* 34 (Spring 1992): 36–51; and John J. Mearsheimer, "The False Promise of International Institutions," *International Security* 19 (Winter 1994/95): 26–37.

power from trying to alter the international territorial status quo. The second is to prevent any of the member states from wishing to do the same."[22] An alliance is directed primarily against the first contingency and is concluded by states that usually have a specific enemy or enemies in mind. If the alliance is working, however, it will also deal effectively with the second contingency as well, as Russett and Stam point out, even though there is no formal alliance obligation to do so. After all, to deter or defeat an attack against the alliance, its members must be united, not fighting amongst themselves.[23]

By contrast, a genuine CSO is designed to deal explicitly with aggression from both external powers and CSO members. The contracting parties enter a CSO with no specific aggressor state in mind, or to put the point differently, with all potential aggressor states in mind. A CSO's central goal is to deter attack upon any of its members; but if deterrence for some reason fails, it will defend that member. If a CSO works as intended, however, defensive operations should not have to be mounted because attacks will not occur. Deterrence will be highly effective because all potential aggressors know that punishment of aggression will be certain, swift, and overwhelming. It is the automaticity of punishment that is designed to dissuade aggressors from attacking. Hence if a CSO works, aggression and war within its domain will not happen.

Alliances are more qualified than genuine CSOs in the degree to which they bind their member states to render military aid to the victims of aggression. Alliances qualify their commitments either by retaining national control over the decision to use force, or by clearly specifying the exact circumstances under which military aid shall be rendered, or by doing both.[24] What an alliance gives up in certainty of response, however,

---

[22] Russett and Stam, "Courting Disaster," 380.

[23] NATO performed both these functions throughout the cold war. It was an alliance directed against the Soviet Union, but it also prevented conflict among its members, the Greek-Turkish dispute over Cyprus notwithstanding. Through NATO the United States placed a substantial fraction of its cold war military machine in Western Europe, concentrated it in West Germany, and thereby reassured Germany's allies that it would not revert to its aggressive past. "Keeping Russia out, Germany down, and the United States in" was how these two (or three) functions were usually described.

[24] In the Washington Treaty that created NATO, the signatories did not formally qualify the enemy against whom the alliance was directed, although all knew it was the Soviet Union. The treaty did, however, retain for the member states the right of national control over the use of force, thereby rendering military assistance not automatic, but contingent upon national decision. This was the price to be paid in order to get the Washington Treaty through the United States Senate. The text of the treaty makes the point clear. By Article 5, "the Parties agree that an armed attack against one or more of them in Europe or North America shall be considered an attack against them all." By Article 11, however, the members provided a safety catch: "This Treaty shall be ratified and *its provisions carried out by the Parties in accordance with their respective constitutional processes*." (Emphasis added.) The Washington Treaty text can be found in NATO Office of Information and Press, *NATO Handbook* (Brussels, 1995), 231–235.

should be more than compensated for by the strength and intensity of the interest its member states have in preventing a specific aggressor from attacking them. By narrowing its scope (the range of aggressions it seeks to prevent), an alliance thereby strengthens its deterrent power. If it works well, an alliance should be as effective at deterring specific potential aggressors as a genuine CSO is in deterring all potential aggressors.

These foregoing differences between traditional military alliances and genuine CSOs begin to narrow as a defensive alliance grows in size. As it increases the number of members and the geographic scope of operations, the alliance gradually loses its restrictive character and begins to take on the attributes of a CSO. More states and greater territorial coverage mean more contingencies to guard against. The eventual result is that member states have pledged military assistance to prevent circumstances that are more and more remote from their central interests. When the alliance becomes quite large, then the member states are put in the position of guaranteeing practically everyone against practically everything. If the alliance becomes all inclusive for a particular region, it transmutes into a regional CSO.

Because of the eventual size contemplated for PESODS, we can legitimately consider it a regional CSO that covers most of Eurasia, Japan, and North America. The problem with PESODS, however, is that it will be too large to work as Russett and Stam intend. There are three reasons why.

First, PESODS's large size will inhibit the development of the necessary consensus for action. Russett and Stam miss the point when they argue: "the bigger the alliance becomes, the less is the burden on any single state and the greater the security provided."[25] The correct statement would be: "the bigger the alliance becomes, the more difficult it is to develop consensus for military action, and the less secure all states will then feel."[26] States are not likely to honor their commitments to aid one another with force if the possible range of both geographical action and military contingencies is so large that they in effect are guaranteeing everyone against everything. States have never been prepared to give such open-ended guarantees in the past. Why should we expect them to do so now?

For those who argue that democracies will operate differently and achieve the consensus necessary to act, go study the record on Bosnia. The Western Europeans were at loggerheads with one another and with

---

[25] Russett and Stam, "Courting Disaster," 381.
[26] For the argument that collective action problems will prevent even the NATO of present size from engaging in peacekeeping and peacemaking operations, see Joseph Lepgold, "NATO's Post-Cold War Collective Action Problem," *International Security* 23 (Summer 1998): 78–107.

the United States over what to do in Bosnia, and they all were at loggerheads with Russia. Had the United States not seized the leadership role in 1995, NATO would never have undertaken the air strikes against the Serbs in the summer of 1995 that helped bring the Bosnian war to an end. At the time, America's French and British allies were opposing any NATO military actions that could threaten the lives of their peacekeepers who were operating under United Nations auspices in Bosnia. Furthermore, had Russia then been a member of NATO, the alliance would never have launched these air strikes. Russia was opposing the air strikes because it consistently favored the Serbs over the Bosnian Muslims. Roughly the same pattern—allied dissensus and Russia's Serbian bias—has been repeated in the tragedy now taking place in Kosovo.

The first lesson of the Bosnian case is, therefore, this—democratic states find it hard to achieve consensus on taking military action when their own immediate security is not at stake. Just because democracies can agree not to fight with one another does not mean they will invariably agree to fight together in alliance against outsiders. Peacelike in their relations toward one another, there is no guarantee they will be warlike in unison toward others.

The second useful lesson has to do with the role that dominant actors play in security organizations. The United States was essential to produce effective NATO military action. America's ability to dominate NATO wrested the air strikes from the alliance. Without the United States, NATO would not have acted as decisively as it eventually did. There is thus an important point here: if American power is diluted because a large number of states are added to NATO, especially powerful ones like Russia, then effective action will be that much harder for the leader to produce.[27] The Bosnian case demonstrates how essential a dominant actor is in order to get effective military action out of a security organization, whether it be an alliance or a CSO.

The third lesson has to do with the ability of powerful actors to concert their actions. Bosnia lies in an area of the Balkans that both Russia and the United States claim to be within their sphere of influence. The area is thus a shared sphere, and the United States and Russia each had to take the interests of the other into account. The United States had the upper

---

[27]Adding Russia to NATO is not popular with the European members of NATO. David Yost, a close observer of European security affairs, cites German Defense Minister Volker Ruhe's views, made clear in September 1994, as representative of European views on adding Russia: "Russia cannot be integrated, neither [sic] into the European Union nor into NATO.... If Russia were to become a member of NATO it would blow NATO apart.... It would be like the United Nations of Europe—it wouldn't work." Quoted in David S. Yost, "The New NATO and Collective Security," *Survival* 40 (Summer 1998): 139.

hand because it dominated NATO, because British and French troops were already on the ground, and because Russia was militarily weak. The United States was therefore able to get more of what it wanted than Russia could, but it still did not get all that it wanted because Russia retained the ability to thwart NATO action by sending military supplies to the Serbs if NATO went too far. Imagine how PESODS would operate in those parts of Eurasia that even a democratic Russia would consider its exclusive sphere, and then add to that picture a Russia that is much more powerful militarily than it now is, because some day in the future it will be.

The second reason why PESODS will not work is that when consensus on action becomes difficult or impossible to achieve, then the signatories' pledge of military assistance becomes problematic. When that happens, the member states will no longer be able to count on each other if they are attacked. That is fatal to a security organization, whether it be an alliance or a CSO, because their raison d'être is the guarantee of military assistance. The military guarantee cannot be a sometimes affair. If it is perceived as such, then the member states will put little or no trust in the security organization, and one of two things, or both, will happen. Either the member states will fend for themselves, or they will seek out those few states upon whom they can rely. If the former occurs, the alliance or CSO collapses; if the latter, a new alliance is in effect formed. Both fates would likely befall PESODS.

The third reason why PESODS will not work has to do with the interests of the United States. As argued above, for an alliance or a CSO to work, the strongest military power (there always is one) must back the organization. For PESODS, under current and foreseeable circumstances, that power is the United States. The problem is that the United States will not back PESODS fully. How can we expect the United States to agree to make or fulfill military promises that guarantee, in effect, all qualifying states in Eurasia? Americans may not presently know the difference between Slovakia, Slovenia, and Slavonia, but if they find their young men and women dying in any of those places in significant numbers, they will quickly consult the map and wonder why their leaders have put them in harm's way in such places. Because America's leaders know this will happen, they will not send them there in the first place. Bosnia sold in Peoria, partly because the fighting stopped before Americans were sent in and partly because the Balkans are right next door to Western Europe. Bosnia like actions further afield will not sell so well. Imagine an American president going on national television to try to convince the American people that if PESODS is to have credibility, then the United States must help defend

Russia against a Chinese attack to reclaim Bolshoy Ussuriisk and Tarabarov—two islands at the confluence of the Amur and Ussuri rivers, which were left out of the 1991 border agreement between Russia and China.

The bottom line is that a security entity of the size and scale that Russett and Stam envision will founder on the same shoals as did the League of Nations and the United Nations. Neither of these were set up as genuine collective security organizations, because their member states did not want them to be. They refused to yield the right of national decision on the use of force to either organization, and instead retained national control.[28] This had the effect of making these two institutions imperfect CSOs, thereby rendering the use of force problematic in both. As a consequence, the combined track record of the League and the United Nations for collective security enforcement (punishment of aggression) is poor. Of the thirty-two interstate wars between 1922 and 1991, the League and the United Nations attempted collective enforcement only three times. The first—League action against Italy in 1936—was a disaster. The next two—UN action in Korea in 1950 and UN action in the Gulf in 1991—were American-led and American-run affairs.[29] Three attempts out of thirty-two, with one failure and two questionable collective actions, is not a decisive endorsement for collective security.

Exactly the same fate will befall NATO if it is made too large. Its military guarantee, which is the heart of the alliance, will be effectively diluted. Either the member states will formally water it down as NATO enlarges, or they will not honor their military guarantee when their interests dictate ignoring it. Security will no longer be a collective but a divisible enterprise; and at that point, PESODS will be effectively neutered, and NATO will have been destroyed.

A CONCERT OF EUROPE—THE BETTER ALTERNATIVE

There is a better way to deal with the predicaments created by NATO's first round of post-cold war enlargement. It is to limit severely any further expansion and to take seriously the Founding Act. The first step is the prerequisite to the second. If both are taken, there is the chance to create a viable Concert of Europe. To be sure, this will be an imperfect

---

[28] On this point, See Morgenthau, *Politics among Nations*, 298–311.
[29] The first action effectively destroyed the League. The second took place only because the Soviet Union happened to boycott the Security Council meeting on the day that the action was voted. The third was another American-run affair, which the UN essentially delegated to the United States and its NATO-Arab allies. The thirty-two interstate wars for these seventy years can be found in "Correlates of War Project: International and Civil War Data, 1816–1992" (ICPR 9905), Inter-University Consortium for Political and Social Research, Ann Arbor, Michigan, April 1994.

arrangement, but it is the best option that we have to create a workable security structure for all of Europe.[30]

NATO's expansion must be limited and, preferably, stopped, if Russia's cooperation is to be secured. No European-wide structure will succeed if in the process of creating it, Russia is estranged or, worse yet, made an implacable enemy. Yet that is exactly what the United States and its allies risk if they next induct the Baltic states or Ukraine into NATO. According to Anatol Lieven, an experienced correspondent for the *Financial Times* in Moscow and Central Europe, Boris Yeltsin is on record as stating that if NATO takes in any of the former Soviet republics, that will be cause for abrogating the Founding Act and will lead to a complete breakdown of Russia's relations with the West.[31] The same result is nearly as likely if many more states are inducted but Russia continues to be excluded. The larger NATO grows without Russia, the more apparent it becomes that Russia is being discriminated against. Thus, if the Founding Act is to be used as the institutional hook to draw Russia into a cooperative security arrangement with the West, then it is the height of stupidity to take steps that would cause Russia to abrogate it.

If further expansion of NATO without Russia risks alienating it, then the West faces two choices. Either it closes the barn door for a long time after taking in Poland, Hungary, and the Czech Republic, or it makes a second round of expansion, if political expediency requires another one sometime soon, as innocuous as possible by taking in only a few states and only those that are noncontroversial, such as Slovenia, Austria, and Sweden. The states of Europe that lie in the contested zone—such as Finland, the Baltic republics, Ukraine, Bulgaria, Romania, Bosnia, Macedonia—must understand that they have no God-given right to NATO membership. Furthermore, they must be made to understand that NATO expansion beyond a certain size risks bringing on two scenarios: the one they fear most—a Russia hostile to them; and the one they think about least but which is equally bad for them—an ineffective NATO. If these nonmember states cannot, for understandable historic reasons,

---

[30]Some may argue that Europe does not need such a structure. Others may argue that if it does, the United States need not be part of it. Still others may argue that the West does not need to take Russia's concerns into account. I do not think that Russett and Stam hold to any of these views, and neither do I. Our differences, therefore, center on the means to attain the end I believe we three share—to keep Europe as stable, peaceful, prosperous, and democratic as possible. For my veiws on the role of the United States in European affairs, see Robert J. Art, "Why Western Europe Needs the United States and NATO," *Political Science Quarterly* 111 (Spring 1996): 1–39; and on Eurasia in general, Robert J. Art, *Selective Engagement: An American Grand Strategy* (forthcoming), chaps. 2 and 7.
[31]Anatol Lieven, "The NATO-Russia Accord: An Illusory Solution" in Carpenter and Conry, *NATO Enlargement*, 144.

comprehend these two dangers, then the United States together with its Western allies must make the facts of Realpolitik life clear to them, instead of catering to their historic nightmares and pandering to America's manifold European ethnic groups, as has been the case to date. These states must be made to understand that their security is better off with a viable NATO that they cannot join than with one that is not viable but to which they belong. The latter will do them no good whatsoever, but there is always the chance that the former can do them some good.[32] An alliance that works well is better than a CSO that works poorly or not at all.

The second step in creating a workable concert is to integrate Russia more fully into the deliberations of the other European great powers. The mechanism to do this has been set up: it is called the Founding Act. Now what is required is to make certain that it is treated seriously. The West should not view the Act as a sop to sell the first round of expansion to Russian public opinion, but instead should make it the institutional centerpiece of Russian-Western consultation and cooperation on security matters of common concern. The OSCE cannot serve this function. It is too large. With fifty-three member states, almost all of whom have equal say in any dispute, consensus on action is too difficult to produce. This is not to denigrate the OSCE. It has performed many useful functions since the cold war ended, such as preventive diplomacy and election monitoring, but concertation of the great powers for the use of force is not one of them. Instead, the West should attempt to institutionalize NATO-Russian security cooperation through systematic use of the Founding Act. This is possible because NATO contains all the great powers of Europe; the United States is still its acknowledged political-military leader and can use its leadership to help forge consensus; and NATO is still small enough and the habits of consultation strong enough that concertation of Western action is possible. What now has to happen is to bring Europe's other remaining great power—Russia—into this consultative Western process without destroying it.

To achieve this goal, the West should view the NATO-Russian accord as an attempt to construct the twenty-first-century equivalent of the

---

[32]Through its Partnership for Peace program (PFP), NATO has made a vague commitment to PFP members: "NATO will consult with any active participant in the Partnership if that Partner perceives a direct threat to its territorial integrity, political independence or security." This is not a defense pledge, but neither is it meaningless. It leaves the door open for NATO to decide whether it wants to aid a state under duress or attack. See Yost, "The New NATO," 144.

nineteenth-century Concert of Europe.³³ The defining characteristic of the first concert was the agreement among the European great powers not to take unilateral advantage of unstable situations in order to improve their positions vis-à-vis one another. Instead, they all agreed to concert their actions so as to attain the shared goal of preserving the peace. The concertation of action took place in formal conferences that met periodically, at least in the early years of the Concert. Extensive consultation, the reaching of a consensus on action, and joint action were the modus operandi of the first concert.³⁴

In its rhetoric and provisions, the Founding Act makes the same commitment to concerting action between NATO and Russia: "the shared objective of NATO and Russia is to identify and pursue as many opportunities for joint action as possible." The basis for joint action is "their shared commitment to build a stable, peaceful and undivided Europe, whole and free, to the benefit of all its peoples." The goals are defined as "inclusive peace in the Euro-Atlantic area" based on the "principles of democracy and cooperative security." The Act devises a mechanism to bring all this about: "the Permanent Joint Council will be the principal venue of consultation between NATO and Russia in times of crisis or for any other situation affecting peace and stability" and its activities "will be built upon the principles of reciprocity and transparency." Finally, there is an implicit recognition of spheres of influence and an explicit injunction against giving Russia a veto power over NATO deliberations: "The consultations will not extend to internal matters of either NATO, NATO member States or Russia," and "Provisions of this Act do not provide NATO or Russia, in any way, with a right of veto over the actions of the other ... nor do they infringe upon or restrict the rights of NATO or Russia to independent decision-making and action."³⁵ Thus, the intent to foster a European great power concert based on NATO-Russian cooperation is imbedded in the Founding Act. What remains is to implement it.

---

³³My proposal for a modern day Concert parallels in some respects that of Charles A. Kupchan and Clifford A. Kupchan. They want to institutionalize great power concertation in the OSCE, effectively turning it into a formal collective security system by creating a security council of the five great powers. I do not think this is politically feasible, because forty-eight smaller powers of Europe and Central Asia will resist it. I also believe that collective security will not work for the reasons set forth earlier. My proposal, which is NATO's at least on paper, keeps cooperation looser and does not promise what cannot be delivered. For the details of what the revamped OSCE would look like, see Charles A. Kupchan and Clifford A. Kupchan, "Concerts, Collective Security, and the Future of Europe," *International Security* 16 (Summer 1991): 151–160. For a solution that closely parallels mine, see Yost, "The New NATO."

³⁴A good overview of the first Concert of Europe is found in Robert Jervis, "From Balance to Concert: A Study of International Security Cooperation," *World Politics* 38 (October 1985): 58–79.

³⁵Quotes are from the text of the Preamble and Sections 1–3 of the Founding Act, found in *Arms Control Today*, 21–23.

This would-be modern day concert may not achieve the same degree of coordination that the earlier one did. In spite of a lot of fuzzy rhetoric about it, we must remember that the first concert was, after all, a mechanism devised by the monarchs and aristocrats of the great powers to preserve their dynastic necks and their privileged lives. Their purpose in devising a concert of monarchies was to prevent interstate war so as to suppress revolution, because they had learned the hard way from the Revolutionary and Napoleonic era (1792–1815) that war brought revolution. Their concert worked so well for so long because the horrors of the 1792–1815 period were seared into their collective heads.

Can the twenty-first-century version of the European concert work as smoothly for as long? No one can answer the question with certainty now. It depends on a host of important factors—the course of events in Russia, the nature and extent of American leadership, the evolution of the European Union, and the political cohesion of NATO, to name but a few. Concerts, just like alliances, however, work best when consensus among the concerting powers or allies is high. Consensus depends in good part on a preexisting set of common interests among states, which are usually produced by a conjunction of historical events and powerful underlying international conditions. This was certainly the case for the nineteenth-century concert, which was born out of the maelstrom of nearly twenty-five years of continuous great power war. But concerts do not come into existence solely because of shared underlying interests, even though this is the most important factor in their creation. Leadership and institutions can play a role in helping to forge the sense of shared interests. This was true of Europe's first concert; it is equally valid for the present putative one.

CONCLUSION

Three final points need to be made. First, building the modern concert with Russia through the Founding Act requires that Russian interests and perspectives will have to be taken into account. This does not mean giving Russia a veto over NATO's decisions as some have argued, but it does mean taking its views seriously and making compromises when deemed necessary. Any attempt at a European-wide security structure, whether fashioned from PESODS, the present day OSCE, or the Founding Act, will have to take into account the interests of its weightiest members; otherwise it will not work. Concerts mean that great powers act collectively when they can agree to do so; and when they cannot, they act separately. NATO and Russia should act together when they can agree to do so; they will act separately when they cannot. Second, the attempt to fashion the twenty-first-century Concert of Europe out of the Founding Act may well fail. In that case, NATO remains to provide security for Western Europe and the hope of protection for the areas of Europe that do not belong to it. Should Russia turn aggressive, NATO can always expand to protect those areas it wants to protect, or give military equipment and advice and even send combat forces to those areas it chooses to protect but not incorporate. This is a fall-back position should the Concert attempt fail and Russia turn nasty.

Third, what should be patently clear is that no concert based on the Founding Act will come into existence unless NATO remains viable. Because of the American guarantee to its members' security, NATO provides important reassurance to its members, helps stabilize relations among all but one of Europe's great powers (and arguably helps stabilize relations with Russia, too), creates transparency and integrated military planning, and promotes common political-military approaches to crises. No other security institution in Europe does all these things, and in my view no other one that analysts may devise or that currently exists will do so for the foreseeable future. These are the reasons why NATO is so valuable to any European-wide security structure. Whatever it ultimately looks like, such a structure must be grafted onto NATO, not NATO absorbed into it.

In sum, at this time, there is a window of opportunity in Europe for concert construction. The United States should seize it, exercise leadership, and use the Founding Act as the vehicle to build the second Concert of Europe.*

---

*I thank Jim Caraley and Stephen Van Evera for their helpful comments; Tom Christensen for allowing me to pick his brains on China's foreign policy; and Loren Cass for his indefatigable research assistance. This article was originally published in *Political Science Quarterly* 113 (Fall 1998): 383–403.

The Role of Villain:
Iran and U.S. Foreign Policy

PAUL R. PILLAR

THE ISLAMIC REPUBLIC OF IRAN HAS BECOME, in two senses, an extraordinary preoccupation of the United States. One sense is that Iran is the subject of a strikingly large proportion of discourse about U.S. foreign policy. American pundits and politicians repeatedly mention Iran, usually with specific reference to its nuclear program, as among the biggest threats the United States faces. Republican nominee Mitt Romney, when asked in the last presidential debate of the 2012 campaign what was the single greatest future threat to U.S. national security, replied "a nuclear Iran."[1] For politicians of both major U.S. political parties, expressions of concern about Iran and of the need to confront it have become a required catechism. The U.S. Congress has spent much time on such expressions and on imposing with lopsided votes ever broader economic sanctions on Iran. Frequent and evidently serious references are made to launching a military attack against Iran, even though such an attack—an act of aggression—would probably mean a war with heavy costs and damage to U.S. interests and probably would stimulate the very development of an Iranian nuclear weapon that it ostensibly would be designed to preclude.[2]

The other extraordinary aspect of this preoccupation is that it is divorced from the actual extent of any threat that Iran poses to U.S.

---

[1]"Transcript of the Third Presidential Debate," 22 October 2012, accessed at http://www.nytimes.com/2012/10/22/us/politics/transcript-of-the-third-presidential-debate-in-boca-raton-fla.html?pagewanted= all&_r=0, 30 December 2012.
[2]The Iran Project, *Weighing Benefits and Costs of Military Action Against Iran*, accessed at http://www.wilsoncenter.org/sites/default/files/IranReport_091112_FINAL.pdf, 30 December 2012.

PAUL R. PILLAR is nonresident senior fellow at the Center for Security Studies, Georgetown University. His most recent book is *Why America Misunderstands the World: National Experience and Roots of Misperception*.

interests. The Islamic Republic, as a matter of capabilities as well as intentions, does not endanger those interests to a degree that corresponds to the intense focus that the subject receives in American debate. The principal sources of the preoccupation are instead to be found in history, politics, and customary American ways of perceiving adversaries.

AN EXAGGERATED DANGER

One of the most-obvious indications of the disconnect between rhetoric and reality on this subject—and specifically on the core concern of a feared Iranian nuclear weapon—is that the Iranian regime, as assessed by the U.S. intelligence community, has not even decided to build such a weapon.[3] The Iranians are interested in nuclear weapons, and some of their past work belies their public assertions that only non-military purposes have entered the thinking about their nuclear program. They have good reasons, however, not to have decided to cross the nuclear weapons threshold and instead to let any future decision about building a bomb be a response to the policies of the West and especially of the United States. The prospect of reaching economically and politically beneficial agreements with the West is a reason never to build a bomb, which any such agreements would rule out. Conversely, if armed hostilities appear more likely, this would be an incentive to try to develop a nuclear weapon, because of its presumed deterrent value.

American alarm about Iran's nuclear program seldom considers the long record that this program, which began in the 1970s under the Shah, has of slow progress, evidently due to technical problems and insufficient Iranian knowledge.[4] Previous Western assessments have overestimated how quickly Iran could become able to build a nuclear weapon.[5] A similar observation can be made about Iran's work, and estimates about that work, on delivery systems and, specifically, ballistic missiles, notwithstanding cooperation for many years between Iran and North Korea on missiles and other defense matters.[6] An Iranian missile with intercontinental range now seems at least several years away, if it ever materializes at all.

---

[3] James Risen and Mark Mazzetti, "U.S. Spies See No Iran Moves to Build Bomb," *The New York Times*, 25 February 2012.
[4] On the technical and knowledge deficiencies of the Iranian program, see the comments of former international nuclear inspector Olli Heinonen in Yossi Melman, "Behind the scenes of UN nuclear inspection of Iran," *Haaretz*, 22 October 2010, accessed at http://www.haaretz.com/weekend/week-s-end/behind-the-scenes-of-un-nuclear-inspection-of-iran-1.320599, 31 December 2012.
[5] Jeffrey T. Richelson, *Spying on the Bomb* (New York: W.W. Norton, 2005), 503–517.
[6] Steven A. Hildreth, *Iran's Ballistic Missile and Space Launch Programs* (Washington, DC: Congressional Research Service, 6 December 2012), 35–38.

Presumptions rather than analysis have characterized American discourse about the consequences if Iran were to acquire a nuclear weapon. It is widely taken for granted, and repeatedly voiced even by those who disagree among themselves on other aspects of Iran, that the advent of an Iranian nuclear weapon would be a very bad development that would exacerbate instability, or even worse, in the Middle East. Few have challenged this consensus.[7] The consensus, however, is grounded in little more than intuition, augmented by stereotyped images of the Iranian leadership.

Some of the belief that an Iranian nuclear weapon would be a calamity rests on the notion that Iranian leaders are religiously driven radicals who do not think like Western leaders and who cannot be deterred even by the prospect of severe retaliation against their country. The problem with this view is that it simply does not accord with the behavior that Iranian leaders have displayed during the more than three decades of the Islamic Republic's existence. The Iranians have repeatedly demonstrated that they respond to foreign challenges and opportunities with the same considerations of costs and benefits, and of the impact on the interests of their regime, as other leaders do. This has been true even on matters involving Iranian behavior that violated international law or was otherwise objectionable to the West. For example, Iran ended an earlier campaign of assassinating Iranian dissident exiles in Europe when it became apparent that the assassinations were beginning to harm significantly Tehran's relations with European governments. Iranian leaders demonstrated the same carefully calculated way of determining policy even during the most trying experience in the Islamic Republic's history: the eight-year war that began when Saddam Hussein's forces invaded Iran in 1980.[8] The Iranians' prosecution of the war at great cost to themselves demonstrated how fervently they, like most other peoples, resist when their homeland is the target of aggression. The war nonetheless ended when the Iranian supreme leader, Ayatollah Ruhollah Khomeini, "drank the cup of poison," as he put it, in agreeing to a cease-fire when the costs of continuing the war appeared to outweigh any benefits. Khomeini's successors have given every indication of being motivated, as are other leaders, by an interest in maintaining their regime and their power—in this life, not some afterlife. They are subject to the same principles of deterrence as anyone else.

---

[7]A conspicuous exception is Kenneth Waltz, "Why Iran Should Get the Bomb," *Foreign Affairs* 91 (July/August 2012): 2–5. For an argument that does not go as far as Waltz in suggesting that an Iranian bomb would be desirable but explains why it would not be a significant threat, see Paul R. Pillar, "We Can Live With a Nuclear Iran," *Washington Monthly* 44 (March/April 2012,): 13–19.

[8]Bruce Riedel, "If Israel Attacks," *The National Interest* 109 (September/October 2010), 6–13, at 11.

Even many commentators who reject the image of irrational Iranian mullahs subscribe to another part of the conventional wisdom about why an Iranian nuclear weapon supposedly would make the political and security situation in the Middle East markedly worse. This part, which sounds more sophisticated than the hypothesis about mad mullahs, holds that even if Iran never detonated a nuclear weapon, the mere possession of one would enable it to intimidate other states and otherwise to throw its weight around in harmful ways. Intuitively this seems to make sense. Nuclear weapons are serious business. Shouldn't owning them have a serious impact on what the owner can do in his neighborhood?

Moving from intuition to analysis, however, this part of the conventional wisdom breaks down, too. Possession of nuclear weapons can make a difference in international relations only insofar as the possibility that they will be used somehow enters into the thinking of decision makers. If no one believes that is a possibility, the weapons are merely a very expensive adornment in an ammunition bunker. For possession of a nuclear weapon to make possible Iranian intimidation that is not taking place today would require something that Iranian leaders would like to do but currently are dissuaded from doing because of the prospect of some foreign actor retaliating. The issue in question also would have to be seen as so important to Tehran that it could credibly threaten to escalate the matter to the level of nuclear war—and thereby neutralize the other actor's threat of retaliation—with all of the costs and risks such escalation would entail for Iran itself. One struggles to think of any conceivable issue where these conditions would arise.

Nuclear weapons, given their awesome effects, are good for deterring what a regime might consider awesome, particularly the regime's own extinction from foreign attack. This deterrent role is almost certainly the major reason for any interest Iranian leaders have in developing nuclear weapons. But the weapons' very awesomeness makes them too blunt an instrument for accomplishing much else. Accordingly, the record of nuclear proliferation that has already occurred around the globe does not support the notion that nuclear weapons are game-changers that facilitate regional bullying or adventurism.[9] We should have known as much from the extensive body of doctrine about nuclear weapons and escalation that was developed during the Cold War.[10] But the alarmist, conformist approach that has characterized discussion of a possible Iranian nuclear

---

[9] Stephen M. Walt, "The mother of all worst-case assumptions about Iran," 30 November 2012, accessed at http://walt.foreignpolicy.com/?page=2, 1 January 2013; and Todd S. Sechser and Matthew Fuhrmann, "Crisis Bargaining and Nuclear Blackmail," *International Organization* 67 (Winter 2013): 173–195.

[10] A classic text is Herman Kahn, *On Escalation: Metaphors and Scenarios* (New York: Praeger, 1965). On the significance of the nuclear weapons threshold, see chapter 6.

weapon has not encouraged people to crack open textbooks from the Cold War era.

Similar considerations apply to oft-repeated arguments that an Iranian nuclear weapon would somehow embolden Hamas or Lebanese Hezbollah to undertake their own forms of adventurism. Such arguments overstate the tightness of relations between Iran and these two actors. Sunni Hamas was never a client of Shia Iran, although with meager support from elsewhere, it has accepted some Iranian help. Hezbollah was very much Iran's client and is still its ally, but the power and position it has achieved in Lebanon have greatly reduced its dependence on Iran, as well as giving it important equities of its own. Whatever deterrence currently applies to Hamas and Hezbollah does not have to do with Iran's strategic situation. It instead concerns the groups' conventional confrontation with Israel and the political costs that any adventurism would have among their own constituencies and larger courts of opinion. In any event, it is not credible that Iran would assume the extremely large risks to itself of nuclear escalation on behalf of some mischief by Hamas or Hezbollah. The leaders of Hamas and Hezbollah are smart enough to realize that.

What attempts there have been to offer analysis supporting the idea of an Iranian nuclear weapon being especially dangerous show the strains of trying to make a case with a preferred conclusion. Such attempts are laden with worst-case speculation about what a nuclear-armed Iran "could" do in the region, without explaining exactly how the nuclear weapons would make a difference or how Iran could make credible a threat to escalate to nuclear war.[11] Analysis suggesting that war with Iran would be less costly and dangerous than the existence of an Iranian nuclear weapon is prone to self-contradiction, particularly by depicting an Iran that supposedly is too unpredictable to be deterred from initiating a war but that, if on the receiving end of an attack, would be a model of calmness and rationality and would be deterred from striking back.[12] Another variety of self-contradiction is to argue that an Iranian nuclear weapon might be more costly than a war because the existence of the weapon would raise fears of war (which, in turn, would adversely affect the oil market).[13]

---

[11]An example is Ash Jain, *Nuclear Weapons and Iran's Global Ambitions: Troubling Scenarios* (Washington, DC: Washington Institute for Near East Policy, August 2011). For a critical commentary on this monograph, see Paul R. Pillar, "Iran's Nuclear Oats," 29 September 2011, accessed at http://nationalinterest.org/blog/paul-pillar/irans-nuclear-oats-5960, 1 January 2013.
[12]See, for example, Matthew Kroenig, "Time to Attack Iran," *Foreign Affairs* 91 (January/February 2012): 76–86.
[13]This is the main argument in the Bipartisan Policy Center report, *The Price of Inaction: Analysis of Energy and Economic Effects of a Nuclear Iran* (Washington, DC: Bipartisan Policy Center, October 2012).

Expressions of concern about an Iranian nuclear weapon often also posit that the introduction of this weapon would trigger a cascade of nuclear proliferation in the Middle East. As with other presumed effects of an Iranian bomb, the image of a proliferation cascade is merely held as an assumption, repeatedly referred to by politicians and others without supporting analysis. The assumption disregards how, ever since President John F. Kennedy spoke about the prospect of 15 or 20 nations having nuclear weapons by the mid-1970s, actual nuclear proliferation has lagged well behind projections about it. The assumption also does not explain why the development of nuclear weapons by Israel—which, according to Avner Cohen, the foremost historian of the Israeli program, and other researchers who have studied the subject, probably *did* have such weapons at least by the mid-1970s[14]—has not triggered a corresponding response by any of the many Middle Eastern states that have considered Israel an adversary. Most important, close examination of both the capabilities and motivations of the most-plausible Middle Eastern proliferators—particularly Egypt, Saudi Arabia, and Turkey—indicates that an Iranian bomb would be unlikely to lead any of them to cross the nuclear threshold that they so far have refrained from crossing.[15] Even if any of the states had the capability to build a nuclear weapon, negative repercussions from doing so, especially including likely damage to their relations with the United States, would be a significant disincentive.

Stepping back from the fixation on Iran's nuclear program, one has to ask—and future historians are sure to ask—how the sole superpower of the early twenty-first century could come to see this state along the Persian Gulf as posing such a supposedly immense threat. Iran, even before the damage inflicted by the most recent rounds of sanctions, has been a mid-level nation with numerous internal problems, a narrowly based economy dependent on oil exports, and almost no ability to project power at a distance. Estimates of Iranian military spending are uncertain but usually put at between one and one-and-a-half percent of U.S. defense spending, as well as being only one-fifth of military spending by the sheikhdoms on the other side of the Persian Gulf.[16]

---

[14]Avren Cohen, *Israel and the Bomb* (New York: Columbia University Press, 1999), 337–338; and Warner D. Farr, *The Third Temple's Holy of Holies: Israel's Nuclear Weapons* (Maxwell Air Force Base: Air War College, 1999) accessed at http://www.au.af.mil/au/awc/awcqate/capc-pubs/farr.htm, 4 March 2013.
[15]Steven A. Cook, "Don't Fear a Nuclear Arms Race in the Middle East," 2 April 2012, accessed at http://www.foreignpolicy.com/articles/2012/04/02/don_t_fear_a_nuclear_arms_race, 3 January 2012.
[16]Stockholm International Peace Research Institute, SIPRI Military Expenditure Database, accessed at http://milexdata.sipri.org, 2 January 2013; and Anthony H. Cordesman, "The Iran Primer: The Conventional Military," accessed at http://iranprimer.usip.org/resource/conventional-military, 2 January 2013.

THE ROOTS OF DEMONIZATION
The origins of the current American attitude toward Iran are thus not primarily to be found in whatever actual threat Iran poses today to U.S. interests. That raises the question of what does account for the enormous attention and alarmism centered on this subject in American political discourse today. The answer to that question begins with the historically based American way of looking at foreign adversaries. It is supplemented by the historical baggage of the past dysfunctional and strife-ridden relationship between the United States and the Islamic Republic. A further significant ingredient is the position of the government of Israel, which, because of the uncommon role that Israel-related issues play in American politics, has done much to shape U.S. policy and discourse on Iran. All of these factors combine to maintain a political environment in which a grave Iranian threat is taken for granted and any questioning of that threat is dismissed as being outside the mainstream. This set of attitudes is further perpetuated by mutual reinforcement with attitudes in Iran that in some respects mirror attitudes in the United States. Each side's worst presumptions about the other side encourage words and actions that make the presumptions look true.

American Thinking about Enemies
Americans' manner of viewing foreign adversaries today is rooted in the history of their country's past relations with the outside world. Their attitudes have been shaped especially by the most costly and all-consuming episodes in that history, in particular the wars—hot and cold—of the twentieth century. Not having the same experience as, say, Europeans have long had of continuous and unavoidable contact with a variety of neighbors having an assortment of conflicting and parallel interests, American attitudes are disproportionately molded by the great conflicts in which the United States has crossed its ocean moats to confront enemies deemed awful enough and threatening enough to warrant such expeditions. Most Americans thought of the conflicts then, and still think of them, as morally clear struggles between good and bad forces, even if, as with the world wars (and worldwide communism during the Cold War), they actually were complicated multilateral affairs with varieties of interests within the warring coalitions. In short, Americans have a profoundly Manichean way of viewing their interaction with the outside world and their confrontation with foreign adversaries.

The Manichean outlook leads to demonization of the most salient of those adversaries. They are viewed not just as having interests that conflict with those of the United States, but as genuinely evil. Some of those adversaries really have been undeniably evil, with Adolf Hitler being at or near the top of almost any such list. The lasting influence on American thinking of the experience with the Nazis stems partly from the sheer scale and disproportionate impact of World War II and from how the dealings with Germany in the 1930s were tailor-made to become the historical analogy most frequently invoked by anyone arguing that it is necessary to confront some other adversary.[17] The evil of Hitler has, in effect, been transferred by analogy to various later foes of the United States.

Once the United States has become locked in conflict with any adversary, especially if warfare is at least a possibility, other incentives accentuate the demonization. Gaining popular backing for an expensive war (or other expensive confrontation, such as the Cold War) is more feasible when the enemy is perceived as evil rather than being merely the other side of a conflict of interests. This aspect of gaining popular support is reinforced by the American self-image as a peace-loving people who go to war only in response to someone else's aggression. Accordingly demonization, including the Hitler analogy, played an especially important role in the selling of a war that clashed with that image: the one against Saddam Hussein's Iraq, which was an offensive war of choice and thus itself an act of aggression.[18]

Americans need a foreign villain. That has been the case since, beginning with World War II, the United States has had large and expensive overseas commitments that can be sustained only if American citizens support them and believe they understand the need for them. The need for a villain is a matter of public psychology and, because of that, also a matter of politics. As for who can play that role, Saddam Hussein is gone, and the unpleasantness of the Iraq War has provided a political incentive to erase quickly the memory of it (and along with that, some of the lessons from it). Osama bin Laden and his al Qaeda have, of course, been prominent foes over the past decade. But a terrorist group can never fill the same role as a state, and now bin Laden is gone, too. Well-suited on several counts to play the current role of villain is that other state on the Persian Gulf with oil resources and radical politics: Iran.

---

[17]On the use of this and similar analogies in discourse about U.S. policy, with particular reference to the Vietnam War, see Yuen Foong Khong, *Analogies at War: Korea, Munich, Dien Bien Phu, and the Vietnam Decisions of 1965* (Princeton, NJ: Princeton University Press, 1992).
[18]Deputy Secretary of Defense Paul Wolfowitz was especially fond of applying the analogy of Hitler to Saddam Hussein. See Wolfowitz's own description of his use of the analogy, quoted in Derrick Z. Jackson, "A fatal distraction," *Boston Globe*, 26 March 2004, accessed at http://www.boston.com/news/globe/editorial_opinion/oped/articles/2004/03/26/a_fatal_distraction/, 22 January 2013.

Current American attitudes toward Iran illustrate several consequences that commonly flow from demonization of a foreign adversary. One is a disinclination to see any reasonable basis for the adversary's actions, or at least a basis that is compatible with one's own needs or interests. Another is a tendency to underestimate how much of what the regime on the other side does may have broader support among its own population. Yet another is a tendency to see the other side's ambitions as more negative and farther-reaching than they really are. Related to this is an underestimation of the other side's willingness to compromise.

Historical Baggage
The history of Iran's relations with the United States has set the stage for the current deeply antagonistic American attitude toward it. The American view of the Islamic Republic was bound to be initially negative because of the pointedly critical view of the United States that Khomeini and his followers voiced and because they overthrew a regime that had been a significant ally of Washington. By the 1970s, the United States had come to rely on the Shah of Iran, a profuse purchaser of U.S.-made arms, as a major protector of stability and U.S. interests in the Persian Gulf. Even this aspect of the history was not enough to foreordain that the relationship would become as intensely antagonistic as it later did. During the Iranian revolution, views of it within the administration of Jimmy Carter varied, with some members of the administration disparaging the Shah as an autocrat and not mourning his departure.[19] The dominant view of the Shah's ouster, however, was as a shocking setback to U.S. interests in the region.

The experience that did more than anything to color for decades American attitudes toward the Islamic Republic of Iran was the seizing of the American embassy in Tehran in November 1979 and the holding hostage of 52 Americans for 444 days, until the day Carter left office. The hostage crisis was one of the few international events to have, largely through the medium of television, a profound and sweeping impact on the perceptions and emotions of the American public. The perpetuation of the drama for more than a year imparted a remarkable degree of public awareness and familiarity with the story, with some of the hostages and their more-outspoken family members back in the United States becoming

---

[19]Zbigniew Brzezinski, *Power and Principle: Memoirs of the National Security Adviser 1977-1981* (New York: Farrar Straus Giroux, 1983), 354–355; and Gary Sick, *All Fall Down: America's Tragic Encounter with Iran* (New York: Random House, 1985), 68–72.

familiar names. The popular ABC television program *Nightline* began as a nightly report on the hostage saga.

As an act of terrorism against Americans, the seizure of the embassy and its staff also identified Iran in the American consciousness as the number one terrorist state in the world. That status was further cemented over the next several years by terrorism at the hands of Lebanese Hezbollah. Americans were again victims, including in the bombing of the Marine barracks in Beirut in 1983, which was the deadliest terrorist attack against American citizens until September 11, 2001. Hostage-taking in Lebanon, with Americans among the most prominent victims, dragged on through the 1980s.

During the early years of the Islamic Republic, Iran was doing even more than this to earn a deserved reputation as the world's number one terrorist state. Operations included numerous assassinations of exiled dissidents in Europe and elsewhere, and subversive activities in the Middle East and Persian Gulf region. Iranian international terrorism later subsided as Tehran strove to improve its relations with the Europeans and came to realize that survival of the Iranian revolution did not depend on the fomenting of similar revolutions in nearby states. State-sponsored terrorism in general, however, also subsided during the same period,[20] and so Iran has remained in most eyes—including official ones—the leading terrorist-sponsoring state.[21] In any event, past history remains more important in shaping American attitudes about Iran than current patterns of sponsoring terrorism.

The label of arch-terrorist state is reason enough for most Americans to have a firmly embedded view of Iran as an implacable enemy. An added dimension, however, that plays directly into the preoccupation with Iran's nuclear program is the merging of terrorism, in popular fears as well as political rhetoric, with the proliferation of unconventional weapons (or weapons of mass destruction, to use the common vocabulary). Fascination with scenarios of terrorism involving such weapons has prevailed at least since the 1990s; the attack with sarin gas by the Japanese cult Aum Shinrikyo on the Tokyo subway in 1995 stimulated public interest in the subject. The George W. Bush administration's aggressive selling of the Iraq war depended on repeatedly connecting terrorism and weapons proliferation, with the President rhetorically obliterating any distinction between the two in his "axis of evil" speech.[22] The later discrediting of this sales

---

[20]Paul R. Pillar, *Terrorism and U.S. Foreign Policy*, 2d ed. (Washington, DC: Brookings Institution Press, 2003), chap. 6.

[21]U.S. Department of State, *Country Reports on Terrorism 2011*, 31 July 2012, chap. 3; accessed at http://www.state.gov/j/ct/rls/crt/2011/195547.htm, 5 May 2013.

[22]President George W. Bush, State of the Union Address, 29 January 2002, text accessed at http://georgewbush-whitehouse.archives.gov/news/releases/2002/01/20020129-11.html, 22 January 2013.

campaign as it applied to Iraq did not seem to dispel the specter of a nuclear-armed state giving its weapons, or technology to make them, to a terrorist client. The specter gets invoked today in agitation about Iran's nuclear program.[23] It probably contributes to American public perceptions and sentiments about that program, even though there is no known instance during the entire history of the nuclear age of a nuclear-armed state—even one with terrorist clients—doing anything like that. That record is unsurprising, given the absence of any advantage in surrendering control over such weapons or materials, and the very dim prospect of the state achieving any deniability. Iran would be widely and automatically assumed to be behind any appearance of nuclear materials in the hands of a group with which it had an association, such as Hezbollah.

Alongside the history of conflict and confrontation between Washington and Tehran is a meager history of engagement. What engagement there has been has tended to discourage most Americans from more engagement. In this respect, the most significant attitude-forming event also dates from the early years of the Islamic Republic: the Iran-Contra affair of 1985–1986. A U.S. purpose of this secret initiative, which involved the sale of arms to Iran, was to try to secure Iranian help in the release of American hostages in Lebanon. Once revealed, the affair was quickly regarded as a scandal, not only because of the sour taste left by trading arms for hostages but also because of the illegal use of proceeds from the arms sales to fund rebels in Nicaragua, as well as efforts to cover up the entire caper. Some of those involved on the U.S. side were convicted of criminal offenses, and the affair is now seen as perhaps the blackest mark on Ronald Reagan's presidency. The episode poisoned the American political waters for anyone else thinking about initiatives to engage Iran. It also discredited the concept of "moderates" in the regime in Tehran, who were the ostensible Iranian interlocutors.

The next serious U.S. effort to reach out to Tehran, this time publicly, was by the administration of Bill Clinton in its last year in office. In a major speech in March 2000, Secretary of State Madeleine Albright expressed regret for the episodes in U.S.–Iranian history (mentioned below) that have most angered Iranians and took what the administration hoped would be the first step toward a better relationship by removing restrictions on the import of Iranian carpets, caviar, and pistachios.[24] This minor reduction in U.S. economic sanctions against Iran, however significant U.S. officials

---

[23]See, for example, Elliott Abrams, "The Grounds for an Israeli Attack," *World Affairs* 175 (May/June 2012), 25–30, at 26.

[24]Remarks by Secretary of State Madeleine K. Albright before the American–Iranian Council, 17 March 2000, text accessed at http://www.fas.org/news/iran/2000/000317.htm, 22 January 2013.

considered it to be, evidently was less conspicuous to leaders in Tehran than wording in the same speech that referred negatively to "unelected hands" as still being in control of Iranian policy. Iranian leaders took this as one more indication that Washington was less interested in dealing with the regime as it existed than in trying to replace it.[25] The initiative went nowhere, and it entered an American lore according to which the Iranians reject opportunities for a normal or cordial relationship and are the ones to be blamed for the antagonistic nature of the relationship that exists today. Clinton's administration made no further significant effort to reach out to Tehran before giving way to the neoconservative-dominated administration of George W. Bush, which had no interest in talking with the Iranian regime.

Iranian Suspicions and Grievances
The negative impact of the history of U.S.–Iranian relations on American attitudes about Iran has been amplified by the resonance it finds in some similar Iranian attitudes about the United States. The similarity starts with the psychological and political need for a foreign villain, which is at least as strong for the revolutionary regime in Tehran as it is for the United States. More specifically, this is a political need for the hard-liners who have come to dominate the regime, have drawn support from the image they have nurtured as guardians against foreign threats, and use popular perceptions of such threats as a distraction from economic and other domestic difficulties. Regardless of how open the hard-liners may be to improved foreign relations and how much they realize that the incumbent regime would benefit from improvement, in the meantime, a perception of Iran being besieged from abroad serves a domestic political purpose.

The history of U.S.–Iranian relations makes the United States the archenemy from the Iranian viewpoint. That viewpoint highlights different episodes in this history than the American viewpoint does. Some of the relevant history even predates the advent of the Islamic Republic. A particularly salient episode for Iranians is the coup that in 1953 overthrew the populist (and democratically elected) Prime Minister, Mohammad Mosaddegh, and was partly engineered by the United States in cooperation with Britain. Although Mosaddegh was not quite as popular as the recounting of this story sometimes makes him out to be—and although the role of Iranians was greater and the role of Britain and the United States less than in most telling of the tale—Iranians came to see the coup as an indicator of U.S. hostility toward Iran and a U.S. proclivity to trample on

---

[25] Ray Takeyh, *Hidden Iran: Paradox and Power in the Islamic Republic* (New York: Times Books, 2006), 114–115.

the rights and prerogatives of Iranians. For many Iranians, it is as much of an attitude-shaping historical landmark as the hostage crisis is for Americans.

The subsequent close U.S. relationship with Shah Mohammad Reza Pahlavi, whose power was reaffirmed with the ouster of Mosaddegh, is another part of the history that has put the United States in an unfavorable light in Iranian eyes. As the most-important foreign backer of the Shah's regime, the United States shared opprobrium generated by the regime's excesses. This is clearly the case with members of the current regime who worked to overthrow the Shah. The sentiments extend as well to many other Iranians who have unfavorable memories of repression under the Shah.

One of the most-traumatic events for a generation of Iranians is the Iran–Iraq War of 1980–1988, which began with an Iraqi invasion of Iran and in which several hundred thousand Iranians died. This, too, shaped Iranian perceptions of the United States because of a U.S. tilt in favor of Iraq, which was not undone in Iranian eyes by the later U.S. invasion of Iraq and overthrow of Saddam Hussein. U.S. support to Iraq during the war against Iran included arms, training, diplomatic support, and, during the war's final phase, the reflagging of oil tankers of Iraq's Arab allies and direct combat between U.S. and Iranian naval forces. Also during the war's closing months, a U.S. warship shot down a civilian Iranian airliner, killing all 290 persons aboard. The shooting was a mistake by a naval crew thinking it was under attack, but to this day, the Iranian government states that the downing of the airliner was intentional. Many other Iranians also probably believe it was.

Notwithstanding the historical basis for Iranians to perceive hostility from the United States and to feel hostility in return, the Iranian leadership evidently saw an opportunity for improving the relationship following the September 11 terrorist attacks, which the Iranian supreme leader, Ayatollah Ali Khomeini, strongly and publicly condemned.[26] Even though Khomeini also warned against launching a war in Afghanistan, once the United States did intervene in Afghanistan and oust the Taliban regime, Iranian and U.S. officials worked effectively together in midwifing a new Afghan political order under President Hamid Karzai. James Dobbins, the chief U.S. representative at the international conference in Bonn, Germany that reached agreement on creating the new Afghan government, observes that the Iranians were "particularly helpful" in that endeavor.[27] For a few

---

[26] Jim Muir, "Iran condemns attacks on US," BBC News, 17 September 2001, accessed at http://news.bbc.co.uk/2/hi/middle_east/1549573.stm, 16 January 2013.
[27] James Dobbins, "How to Talk to Iran," *The Washington Post*, 22 July 2007, accessed at http://www.washingtonpost.com/wp-dyn/content/article/2007/07/20/AR2007072002056.html, 16 January 2013.

weeks in late 2001 and early 2002, it looked as though Washington and Tehran were moving their relationship to a less-acrimonious path.

Then President George W. Bush declared the "axis of evil" and identified Iran as one of the points of the axis. To the Iranians, this was a shocking response to their post-September 11 cooperation. Being put in the same category as their old enemy Saddam Hussein only made the shock worse. The Iranian leadership still did not give up on the idea of an improved relationship with Washington. One indication of this was an Iranian proposal for negotiating a grand bargain of outstanding differences, with a written proposal to that effect transmitted to the U.S. government in 2003 by Switzerland, which serves as the diplomatic protecting power for the United States in Iran. Some observers have questioned the seriousness of this initiative, but the documentary evidence indicates that it was genuine.[28] The Bush administration, riding high at that moment—with Saddam Hussein having been toppled but the difficulties of the occupation of Iraq not yet having become apparent—made no reply to the overture and even reprimanded the Swiss ambassador for forwarding it. U.S.-Iranian relations were left in a bitter freeze, with no contacts at all for the next several years.

By the time Barack Obama entered the presidency, the United States and Iran were thus locked in a vicious circle of mutually reinforcing perceptions of hostility, which continues to prevail today. An action by one side that can be interpreted as an indication of hostile intentions leads to reactions by the other side, in words or deeds, that in turn are interpreted as hostile. A perception that the other side does not want a better relationship elicits negative or suspicious reactions that the other side perceives in the same way. It is difficult, though not impossible, to get out of such a circle of mistrust and misperception. Such difficulty, far more than any conflict of national interests, inhibits improvement of the relationship today.

Influence of Israel
A major added political factor on the U.S. end of this relationship is the posture of the government of Israel. That government's insistent pushing of the theme that Iran, and specifically a nuclear-armed Iran, poses a grave threat clearly has significantly shaped the handling of the issue in American political discourse and is a leading reason the issue has the prominence that it does. The pushing does not reflect strategic analysis of

---

[28]A recapitulation of this episode and links to the relevant documents are in Nicholas D. Kristof, "Iran's Proposal for a 'Grand Bargain,'" *The New York Times*, 28 April 2007, accessed at http://kristof.blogs.nytimes.com/2007/04/28/irans-proposal-for-a-grand-bargain/, 16 January 2013.

the actual threat that an Iranian nuclear weapon would pose to Israel. Assessments by think tanks and scholars of the size of Israel's nuclear arsenal vary somewhat, but a typical estimate postulates a stockpile of 75–200 weapons accompanied by an assortment of modern delivery systems—a capability far superior to anything Iran could ever hope to achieve in the foreseeable future.[29] The head of the Israeli intelligence service Mossad, like many retired senior Israeli security officials who can speak on the subject even more freely, has denied the frequently heard assertion that an Iranian nuclear weapon would pose an existential threat to Israel.[30] Many ordinary Israelis understandably fear an Iranian nuclear weapon, however, based on the history of the Jewish people and vituperative anti-Israeli rhetoric from Iran, and with the fear stoked by their own government.

The government of Prime Minister Benjamin Netanyahu also has other motives for continuing its agitation on the issue. It naturally would like to maintain Israel's regional nuclear weapons monopoly. It may prefer not even to think twice the next time it uses Israel's conventional military superiority, as it has several times, in conducting operations in neighboring states or territories. The issue of Iran also serves as a distraction from the unsettled conflict between Israelis and Palestinians. The Israeli government and its supporters habitually respond to any raising of the Palestinian issue or the building of Israeli settlements in occupied territory by stating that Iran is the greatest threat to peace and stability in the region and where the international community ought to direct its attention instead.[31] Finally, any rapprochement between Iran and the United States would threaten to weaken Israel's claim to being Washington's sole reliable partner in the Middle East.

Whatever the exact mix of motives, the Israeli agitation about Iran has a big impact on American handling of the issue because of the extraordinary role that preferences of the Israeli government play in American politics.[32] In the United States, the Iran issue has become in large part an Israel issue and a way for American politicians to demonstrate support for Israel. This dimension of the issue underlies the posture that candidate Romney took

---

[29] Robert S. Norris, William M. Arkin, Hans N. Kristensen, and Joshua Handler, "Israeli Nuclear Forces, 2002," *Bulletin of the Atomic Scientists* 58 (September/October 2002): 73–75.
[30] Barak Ravid, "Mossad chief: Nuclear Iran not necessarily existential threat to Israel," *Haaretz*, 29 December 2011, accessed at http://www.haaretz.com/print-edition/news/mossad-chief-nuclear-iran-not-necessarily-existential-threat-to-israel-1.404227, 17 January 2013.
[31] See, for example, a speech by Netanyahu reported in "PM: Iran is greatest world danger, not settlements," *Jerusalem Post*, 8 January 2013, accessed at http://www.jpost.com/DiplomacyAndPolitics/Article.aspx?id=298796, 16 January 2013.
[32] John J. Mearsheimer and Stephen M. Walt, *The Israel Lobby and U.S. Foreign Policy* (New York: Farrar, Straus and Giroux, 2007).

on Iran. It also has shaped the public posture on Iran of Barack Obama's administration. One of the President's strongest and most-prominent declarations that an Iranian nuclear weapon would be unacceptable was in a speech he gave during his re-election campaign to the American Israel Public Affairs Committee.[33]

The Iranian regime has no country comparable to Israel influencing its policies, but Israel itself has figured prominently in destructive Iranian rhetoric. This has especially been true of Mahmoud Ahmadinejad, Iran's President from 2005 to 2013, who found Israel-bashing to be a fruitful theme in domestic politics. Ahmadinejad's rhetoric has been taken in the United States as confirming the worst assumptions about Iranian intentions, even though the Iranian President is not the most important decision maker in the regime on foreign policy or nuclear matters. One piece of bravado seized upon more than any other was in a speech Ahmadinejad gave in 2005, in which he predicted that Israel would eventually go the way of the Shah's regime. Disputes over translation of this speech have continued ever since, but it became the basis for an oft-repeated observation that the President of Iran threatened "to wipe Israel off the map."[34] Some American politicians have gone a step further and asserted falsely that Iran has stated an intention to use a nuclear weapon to accomplish this goal—notwithstanding Iran's public posture that it does not even want a nuclear weapon.[35]

STULTIFICATION OF POLICY

The net effect of all the influences—including history, Israel, and Iranian bombast—on American thinking about Iran is a deeply held and widely shared belief that Iran, and especially its nuclear program, poses a grave danger. In the most-recent biennial survey by the Chicago Council on Global Affairs of American attitudes on foreign policy, 67 percent of respondents said that Iran's nuclear program was a "critical threat to vital U.S. interests." This was the second-most-frequently mentioned threat, only slightly behind international terrorism.[36] Such a climate of

---

[33]Remarks by the President at AIPAC Policy Conference, 4 March 2012, accessed at http://www.whitehouse.gov/the-press-office/2012/03/04/remarks-president-aipac-policy-conference-0, 17 January 2013.

[34]On the translation issue, see Uri Friedman, "Debating Every Last World of Ahmadinejad's 'Wipe Israel Off the Map'," 5 October 2011, accessed at http://www.theatlanticwire.com/global/2011/10/debating-every-last-word-ahmadinejads-wipe-israel-map/43372/, 18 January 2013.

[35]Rep. Michele Bachmann asserted this during her campaign for the Republican presidential nomination. John Bresnahan, "Bachmann: Iran would use nuke against United States, Israel," *Politico*, 18 December 2011, accessed at http://www.politico.com/blogs/politico-live/2011/12/bachmann-iran-would-use-nuke-against-united-states-107923.html, 18 January 2013.

[36]*Foreign Policy in the New Millennium* (Chicago, IL: Chicago Council on Global Affairs, 2012), 14.

public opinion stultifies any political action to improve relations with Iran. Political incentives push in the direction of words and policies that continue the vicious circle of hostility. Actions required to get out of that circle are politically hazardous because they are seen—and political opponents can criticize them—as being soft on Iran.

One of the specific consequences of this environment is the diffidence involved in what little diplomacy there is between Washington and Tehran, which have not had normal diplomatic relations since the hostage crisis more than three decades ago. The transition from George W. Bush to Barack Obama took the possibility of revived diplomacy out of the deep freeze, but the tentativeness each side has displayed in doing business with its bête noire is still apparent. The Obama administration made essentially a single attempt, during its first year in office, at a negotiated agreement with Iran before throwing its energy instead into gaining international support for anti-Iran sanctions. It even rejected an agreement that Brazil and Turkey extracted from Iran in 2010 that included the same Iranian concessions the United States was demanding in 2009. Diplomacy went back in the freezer, emerging only with the start of the current series of talks beginning in 2012.[37]

Another consequence is the unhelpful manner in which the sanctions have been handled, especially by the U.S. Congress. Ostensibly, the purpose of most of the sanctions is to induce Iran to make concessions regarding its nuclear program. In practice, they have instead played a different political role: as a means for American politicians to demonstrate their toughness on Iran (and their support for Israel). Repeatedly voting in favor of additional sanctions against Iran is an easy way to do this. An additional influence on American behavior regarding this subject is the hope of eventually doing away with the Iranian regime. Although regime change is not explicitly stated by most of those voting in favor of added sanctions, that hope almost certainly underlies much of the support for ever-increasing sanctions. Political conditions in Iran do not suggest that it is in a pre-revolutionary situation, but the upheaval in several Arab countries over the past two years has rekindled the hope.

Use of sanctions as leverage for obtaining concessions at the negotiating table requires that they be used flexibly. It is just as important for the other side to believe that relief from sanctions will result from concessions as that a lack of concessions will mean no relief. Use of sanctions as a device for political posturing or as a hoped-for way to hasten regime change,

---

[37]The most-thorough account of the Obama administration's diplomacy on the subject is Trita Parsi, *A Single Roll of the Dice: Obama's Diplomacy with Iran* (New Haven, CT: Yale University Press, 2012).

however, instead implies that the pressure from sanctions should be inflexible and unrelenting. The latter approach has prevailed. In public and congressional discussion, the sweeping and unrelenting nature of sanctions against Iran has come to be treated as an end in itself, with almost no attention to exactly how the sanctions relate to Iranian concessions beyond a simple notion that the Iranians ought to give up and cry "uncle." Meanwhile, the United States and its negotiating partners in the P5 + 1 (the permanent members of the United Nations Security Council plus Germany) have made no proposals that include any relief from sanctions other than those involving spare parts for commercial aircraft and trade in precious metals and petrochemicals.[38] The Iranians have been given no reason to believe that they would receive significant sanctions relief in return for concessions, and thus they have lacked an incentive to concede. Making promises credible is generally harder than making threats credible, and the history of mutual mistrust between the United States and Iran has made it even harder.[39] Inflexibility in the negotiating position of the P5 + 1 has made it harder still.

A similarly unhelpful pattern has characterized threats to use military force. A possible military attack on Iran was discussed originally as an alternative to a negotiated settlement as a way to prevent an Iranian nuclear weapon. The military option was discussed despite the likely counterproductive effect of stimulating an Iranian decision to build the very weapon the attack was intended to prevent. Once negotiations with Iran began but did not yield quick progress, a different purpose of a threatened military attack came to dominate discussions of the issue: the idea of such a threat as an inducement to Iran to make concessions to the P5 + 1 about its nuclear program. This idea gave greater respectability to the concept of launching an offensive war, because threatening such a war could be defended in the name of aiding negotiations. The threats and saber-rattling moves to go with them have been promoted not as a seeking of war but as supposedly a necessary aid to obtaining an agreement.[40]

The threat of armed force, however, probably has impeded rather than aided the reaching of a negotiated agreement. The threats

---

[38] Arms Control Association, "History of Official Proposals on the Iranian Nuclear Issue," August 2012, accessed at http://www.armscontrol.org/factsheets/Iran_Nuclear_Proposals, 30 December 2012; and Arshad Mohammed, "Big powers to offer easing gold sanctions at Iran nuclear talks," Reuters, 15 February 2013, accessed at http://www.reuters.com/article/2013/02/15/us-iran-nuclear-gold-idUS-BRE91E0TP20130215, 16 February 2013.

[39] Robert Jervis, "Getting to Yes With Iran: The Challenges of Coercive Diplomacy," *Foreign Affairs* 92 (January/February 2013): 105–115, at 111.

[40] Among the many who make this argument are James K. Sebenius and Michael K. Singh in "Is a Nuclear Deal with Iran Possible?" *International Security* 37 (Winter 2012/13): 76–77, 89–90.

contribute to the atmosphere of hostility that for years has added to distrust and worst-case assumptions between Tehran and Washington and thereby have made rapprochement more difficult. That the reaching of an agreement would be seen as a backing down in the face of a threat of armed force adds to the political and psychological costs to Iranian leaders of making concessions. Such threats also stimulate rather than diminish Iranian interest in nuclear weapons because of their presumed value as a deterrent against major foreign attack. The more that the brandishing of the threat of military attack makes an attack seem likely, the greater will be the Iranian interest in developing nuclear weapons and the less inclined they will be to make concessions that would preclude that possibility.

The Iranians have good reason to be suspicious of ultimate U.S. and Western motivations, and threats of military force are unhelpful in that respect too. The Iranians do not have to look far to see ample evidence, including in American political rhetoric, in favor of the proposition that the primary U.S. goal regarding Iran is regime change. And they do not have to look far into the past to see a recent U.S. use of military force—participation in the intervention in Libya—that overthrew a Middle Eastern regime after it had reached an agreement with the United States to give up all its nuclear and other unconventional weapons programs. Iranian leaders would have little reason to make concessions about their own program if they believed the same thing was likely to happen to them. This is already a problem; rattling the saber only makes it worse.

Despite all these considerations, the threats continue, not only in general American discourse but in the official position of the Obama administration, which talks about all options being on the table. They continue partly because the notion of threatening an adversary into submission has a simple appeal and primitive believability. They continue also because support for military threats, like support for sanctions, serves the political function of demonstrating firmness on Iran and backing for Israel—and for some, trying to appease the Israeli government enough to dissuade it from launching its own attack.

DIPLOMATIC POSSIBILITIES

The outlines of an achievable agreement between Iran and the P5 + 1 have been apparent for some time. They would include restricting Iran's enrichment of uranium to the lowest levels of enrichment, and even then in quantities corresponding to legitimate peaceful uses. Iranian production of medium-enriched (20 percent) uranium would cease, with existing stocks transferred out of the country. In return, most sanctions would be removed and Iran would be guaranteed a supply of enough 20-percent-enriched uranium to power the research reactor that uses it as fuel. Such a formula would be consistent with Iran's insistence that its nuclear program is entirely for peaceful purposes. The formula is thus attainable in a way that simply pressuring the Iranians into crying "uncle" is not.

Iran reportedly made in the summer of 2012 a proposal to the Europeans that included these basic elements.[41] The Iranian proposal as presented was unacceptable to the P5 + 1 because under it, Iran would have taken its promised steps on uranium enrichment only after the West had removed sanctions. In this respect, the Iranian proposal mirrored that of the P5 + 1, which has called on Iran to take all of its required steps before the P5 + 1 would even consider significant relief from sanctions. The resulting disagreement is common in international negotiations; each side naturally would prefer not to implement its own end of a deal until the other side makes good on its end. Also common is the resolution of such differences by negotiating a schedule of phased implementation in which each side both gives something and gets something in each phase. It is the negotiation of such an implementation sequence, as well as other details such as the exact disposition of the 20 percent-enriched uranium, that remains to be accomplished.

Political impediments to such an agreement persist on both sides but are not insurmountable. Some elements in the Iranian regime that milk foreign hostility for political benefit are unlikely to believe that an improved relationship with the United States and the West works to their advantage, but for the top leadership, this would be outweighed by being able to claim credit for the resulting advantages in economics and prestige. On the U.S. side, a likely challenge is getting congressional cooperation in lifting sanctions, some of which are designated by law as responses to human rights questions or other matters besides the nuclear issue. There also is the potential for the government of Israel, which has disdained the very idea of negotiations with Iran, to be a spoiler.

If such an accord is nevertheless achieved, it would secure for each of the parties its most important stated objectives. For the United States and its P5 + 1 partners, restrictions on Iran's program would preclude it from building a nuclear weapon without major difficulty and conspicuous violations of the agreement that would give ample warning well before actual construction of such a weapon. For Iran, the agreement would bestow respect and acceptance of its nuclear program and would finally gain relief from the economically debilitating sanctions.

---

[41]David E. Sanger, "Iranians Offer Plan to End Nuclear Crisis," *The New York Times*, 5 October 2012.

A nuclear agreement would open the door to a better overall relationship that could bring other benefits to the United States ultimately more important than the nuclear issue itself. A reduction of tension with Tehran would permit a more relaxed and less costly U.S. military posture in the Persian Gulf, which currently is aimed overwhelmingly at Iran. There also would be a potential for positive cooperation with Iran, which, although a weakling in projecting power at a distance, has influence to be reckoned with closer to its own borders. One place with such potential is Afghanistan, where the parallel U.S. and Iranian interests that underlay the cooperation over a decade ago are still present. Another place is Iraq, where Iran is now the dominant foreign influence and where endless violence and instability serve neither U.S. nor Iranian interests.

None of this will turn Iran and the United States into close friends and allies, as they were in the time of the Shah. Differences, some of them sharp, will persist—including on matters related to Israel as long as the Palestinian issue remains unresolved. But the differences can be handled in a more normal way than in the context of the pathological non-relationship that has persisted for over three decades.

The U.S. posture toward Iran is a prominent example of how traumatic history, domestic politics, and emotions that flow from both can overpower more-sober evaluation of the U.S. interests at stake in a foreign relationship. Popular, politically charged sentiment about confronting foreign villains can have benefits; it fueled, for example, the enormous sacrifices by Americans that were necessary to win World War II. The case of Iran shows that it also can have major disadvantages.*

---

*This article was originally published in *Political Science Quarterly* 128 (Summer 2013): 211–231.

Pakistani Opposition to American Drone Strikes

C. CHRISTINE FAIR
KARL KALTENTHALER
WILLIAM J. MILLER

AMERICA'S EMPLOYMENT OF WEAPONIZED unmanned aerial vehicles (UAVs), popularly known as "drones," to kill alleged terrorists in Pakistan's federally administered tribal areas (FATA) fuels sustained controversy in Pakistan. Pakistani outrage has steadily deepened since 2008, when the United States increased the frequency of the strikes.[1] The increasing use of "signature strikes" has been particularly controversial in (and beyond) Pakistan, because such strikes are targeted at "men believed to be militants associated with terrorist groups, but whose identities aren't always known."[2] Whereas personality strikes require the operator to

---

[1] See New America Foundation, "The Year of the Drone: An Analysis of U.S. Drone Strikes in Pakistan, 2004–2012," 2013, accessed at http://counterterrorism.newamerica.net/drones, 9 May 2013.
[2] Adam Entous, Siobhan Gorman, and Julian E. Barnes, "U.S. Tightens Drone Rules," *The Wall Street Journal*, 4 November 2011, accessed at online.wsj.com/article/SB10001424052970204621904577013982672973836.html?mod=WSJ_hp_LEFTTopStories, 9 May 2013.

C. CHRISTINE FAIR is an assistant professor at the Security Studies Program within the Edmund A. Walsh School of Foreign Service at Georgetown University. She has published widely on South Asian security issues and is the author of *Fighting to the End: The Pakistan Army's Way of War*. **KARL KALTENTHALER** is professor of political science at the University of Akron and adjunct professor of political science at Case Western Reserve University. He has published several books and articles on public opinion, counter-terrorism, and political economy. **WILLIAM J. MILLER** is executive director of institutional analytics, effectiveness, and planning at Flagler College. He has published on political attitudes toward various public policies in the United States, Europe, and the Middle East in leading journals.

develop a high level of certainty about the target's identity and location, based on multiple sources such as "imagery, cell phone intercepts and informants on the ground,"[3] operators may "initiate a signature strike after observing certain patterns of behavior."[4] When conducting signature strikes, the United States assesses that the individuals in question exhibit behaviors that match a pre-identified "signature" (for example, pattern of observable activities and/or personal networks) that suggests that they are associated with al Qaeda and/or the Pakistani or Afghan Taliban organizations.[5] Because the identity of the target is unknown, even during the strike, it is possible that these persons are innocent civilians, a possibility that both current and former U.S. government officials concede.[6] While the George W. Bush administration employed both personality strikes from 2004 and signature strikes from 2008 in Pakistan, the administration of Barack Obama has redoubled the use of both types.[7] This has ignited public protests against the drones in Pakistan, particularly in Pakistan's urban areas—far removed from the tribal areas where drones are employed. It has also galvanized a vigorous debate within Pakistan's National Assembly, which tried, but ultimately failed, to curtail the strikes.

While the use of armed drones clearly antagonizes segments of Pakistan's polity, it is only one of several issues causing conflict between Pakistan and the United States. Others include the infamous Raymond Davis affair of early 2011, in which Davis—a CIA contractor—shot and

---

[3] Greg Miller, "CIA Seeks New Authority To Expand Yemen Drone Campaign," *The Washington Post*, 18 April 2012, accessed at http://articles.washingtonpost.com/2012-04-18/world/35453346_1_signature-strikes-drone-strike-drone-program, 9 May 2013.

[4] Columbia Law School Human Rights Clinic and Center for Civilians in Conflict, "The Civilian Impact of Drones: Unexamined Costs, Unanswered Questions," 2012, 32–33, accessed at http://civiliansinconflict.org/uploads/files/publications/The_Civilian_Impact_of_Drones_w_cover.pdf, 9 May 2013.

[5] Micah Zenko, *Reforming U.S. Drone Strike Policies*, January 2013, accessed at http://www.cfr.org/wars-and-warfare/reforming-us-drone-strike-policies/p29736?co=C009601, 9 May 2013; "The Civilian Impact of Drones." Behaviors that the CIA may interpret as probative of involvement with hostile forces include traveling in convoys of vehicles that behave similarly to fleeing al Qaeda or Taliban; presence in areas that seem to be terrorist training camps; and participating in what the CIA judges to be militant gatherings, perhaps because they are armed, and so forth. See Cora Currier, "How Does the U.S. Mark Unidentified Men in Pakistan and Yemen as Drone Targets?" *ProPublica*, 1 March 2013, accessed at http://www.propublica.org/article/how-does-the-u.s.-mark-unidentified-men-in-pakistan-and-yemen-as-drone-targ, 9 May 2013. On the CIA targeting Pakistani Taliban members as well as al Qaeda and the Afghan Taliban, see Jonathan Landay, "Obama's drone war kills 'others,' not just al Qaida leaders," *McClatchy.com*, 9 April 2013, accessed at http://www.mcclatchydc.com/2013/04/09/188062/obamas-drone-war-kills-others.html#storylink=cpy, 9 May 2013.

[6] "The Civilian Impact of Drones," 33.

[7] Entous, Gorman, and Barnes, "U.S. Tightens Drone Rules;" Cora Currier, "Everything We Know So Far About Drone Strikes," *Propublica.com*, 5 February 2013, accessed at http://www.propublica.org/article/everything-we-know-so-far-about-drone-strikes, 9 May 2013.

killed two men whom he claimed were menacing him in Lahore. (Pakistan-based journalists suspect that the two men were in the employ of Pakistan's intelligence agency, the ISI.) The ensuing row over Davis's fate—the United States claimed that he had diplomatic immunity, while Pakistan insisted that he face trial for murder in Pakistan—spawned protests in Lahore and beyond and deepened Pakistanis' belief that the United States is indifferent to the loss of Pakistani life.[8] Just as Washington and Islamabad were getting beyond the Davis-related turbulence, the May 2011 raid on Osama bin Laden's hideout in the Pakistani cantonment town of Abbottabad again rocked the relationship. As both countries struggled to overcome the resulting frost in relations, the November 2011 U.S.–NATO attack on a Pakistani military outpost at Salala, which led to the deaths of 24 Pakistani soldiers, and the U.S. refusal to apologize once more brought the relationship to the breaking point. Pakistan's civilian and military leaders face mounting pressure to cease active cooperation with United States, including on the drone program.[9]

Yet despite the many sources of strain in U.S.–Pakistan relations, drones are often depicted as the single most significant irritant. This view is buttressed by the belief—which has become a truism in Western and even Pakistani media—that not only do most Pakistanis know about the program, they overwhelmingly oppose it. Foes of the drone program also suggest that the strikes help to create more terrorists than they eliminate.[10] But the conventional wisdom about Pakistanis' universal opposition to the drones is not empirically buttressed. Polling data from Pew[11] demonstrate that nearly two thirds of Pakistanis have never even heard of the drone program, despite the media coverage it has

---

[8]Omar Waraich, "U.S. Diplomat Could Bring Down Pakistan Gov't," *Time.com*, 9 February 2011, accessed at http://www.time.com/time/world/article/0,8599,2047149,00.html, 9 May 2013; C. Christine Fair, "Spy for a spy: the CIA-ISI showdown over Raymond Davis," *ForeignPolicy.com*, 10 March 2011, accessed at http://afpak.foreignpolicy.com/posts/2011/03/10/spy_for_a_spy_the_cia_isi_showdown_over_raymond_davis, 9 May 2013.

[9]For a succinct but insightful overview of this, see Teresita C. Schaffer and Howard B. Schaffer, *How Pakistan Negotiates with the United States: Riding the Roller Coaster* (Washington, DC: United States Institute of Peace, 2011).

[10]International Human Rights and Conflict Resolution Clinic At Stanford Law School and Global Justice Clinic at NYU School Of Law, "Living Under Drones: Death, Injury, and Trauma to Civilians From US Drone Practices in Pakistan," 2012, accessed at http://livingunderdrones.org/wp-content/uploads/2012/10/Stanford-NYU-LIVING-UNDER-DRONES.pdf, 9 May 2013; Chris Woods, "Drone War Exposed—the Complete Picture of CIA Strikes in Pakistan," *Bureau of Investigative Journalism*, 10 August 2011, accessed at http://www.thebureauinvestigates.com/2011/08/10/most-complete-picture-yet-of-cia-drone-strikes, 9 May 2013.

[11]Pew Research Global Attitudes Project, Spring 2010 Survey Data, accessed at http://www.pewglobal.org/2010/05/08/spring-2010-survey-data/, 9 May 2013.

received in Pakistan and beyond. Among the minority of respondents (35 percent) who had heard of the program, nearly one third said that drone strikes are necessary to defend Pakistan from extremist groups. A slight majority (56 percent) of the one third who were familiar with drones said that drone strikes are not necessary to protect Pakistan, and nearly one in two (49 percent) Pakistanis who were familiar with the program believe that the strikes are being conducted without their government's approval. Yet this figure is not that much greater than the 33 percent who believe that their government has given its approval for these strikes.[12] Clearly, Pakistani public opinion is less informed, and much less unanimous, than is often presumed.

In this paper, we seek to explain why some Pakistanis oppose the drone program while others support it. Because the vast majority of the sample indicated that they had not heard of the drone program, we must also determine the predictors of those who are unaware of this program, despite the enormous publicity it receives. To achieve the first goal, we rely upon elite discourse analysis of Pakistani writings on this sensitive subject. We examine arguments advanced by both Pakistani opponents and proponents of the use of drones to put forth several testable hypotheses that may explain support for and opposition to the U.S. drone program in Pakistan. To test these hypotheses, we leverage recent Pakistani survey data collected by Pew's Global Attitudes Project. This dataset provides us with a dependent variable (support for the drone program), as well as several potential explanatory variables that can instrument for our proposed hypotheses. Selection effects restrict the size and composition of persons answering the question that comprises our dependent variable. To contend with these selection effects, we employ the Heckman selection model, which allows us to control for the characteristics of those who are not familiar with the program as well as for other explanatory variables that may predict attitudes about the program among those who were familiar with it and expressed an opinion about it.

We find that more highly educated males with higher levels of Internet use are more likely than other groups to know about the program and thus to be included in our dataset. Among the minority of survey participants who both had heard of the program and expressed an opinion about it, opposition could be traced principally to the elite media discourse on the drone strikes. Media coverage of the strikes focuses on their human costs

---

[12]Pew Global Attitudes Project, "Little Knowledge of Drone Strikes in Pakistan," 12 August 2010, accessed at http://pewresearch.org/databank/dailynumber/?NumberID=1069, 9 May 2013.

and commonly expresses distrust of the United States. We show that less-educated Pakistanis, women, and persons who view the United States as an enemy are more likely to oppose the drone program, all else being equal. We do not find other potential explanations, such as support for political Islam, to be relevant.

The remainder of this article is organized as follows. In the next section, we present a brief overview of the drone program in Pakistan and the controversy surrounding it. We focus on the debate in Pakistan, which is most germane to Pakistani opinion formation. Second, we draw several hypotheses from these debates that we will test through our probit models. Third, we present the data that we will use in this analysis and detail the methodology employed for data handling and modeling. Fourth, we present the main findings of this effort. This article concludes with a consideration of the implications of our findings.

U.S. DRONE STRIKES: INDISCRIMINANT DEATH FROM ABOVE OR THE LEAST-WORST OPTION

The American use of UAVs against militants in Pakistan probably began in 2004, with a strike in South Waziristan which targeted a militant commander named Nek Mohammad. Drone use remained sporadic for several years: between 2004 and 2007, there were only nine attacks. Yet the Bush administration became increasingly convinced that drone attacks were an effective way to defeat the militants in FATA, and in 2008, it launched 33 strikes, a major increase over previous years. When Barack Obama became President, he substantially increased the use of drone strikes, consistent with his strategic objective of defeating al Qaeda. In 2009, there were 53 drone strikes; in 2010, the "year of the drone," there were 118 drone attacks; and in 2011, there were 70 drone attacks.[13]

Curiously, despite the attention on the drone program in international media, the program, which is conducted under the auspices of the U.S. Central Intelligence Agency (CIA), is still technically covert. Accurate information about the program is thus very difficult to obtain, and even accounts in peer-reviewed journals contain many errors.[14] U.S. government officials are generally prohibited from even acknowledging any particular

---

[13] Peter Bergen and Katherine Tiedemann, *The Year of the Drone: An Analysis of US Drone Strikes in Pakistan, 2004–2010* (Washington, DC: New America Foundation, 2010); New America Foundation, "The Year of the Drone."

[14] See, for example, Brian Glyn Williams, "The CIA's Covert Predator Drone War in Pakistan, 2004–2010: The History of an Assassination Campaign," *Studies in Conflict & Terrorism* 33: 871-892. Williams's account of the origins of the program is simply wrong in many places and is generally discordant with the history recounted to one of the authors by Richard Clarke and others.

drone strike in Pakistan, despite the fact that drones are heavily reported in Pakistani and international media.[15] Author interviews with numerous U.S. and Pakistani officials since 2009, however, suggest that the program took shape during the tenures of Pakistani President Pervez Musharraf and President Bush. As a U.S. official explained to one of the authors in 2009, President Musharraf originally authorized the drone strikes, although he restricted their use to FATA. In order to keep his authorization secret, however, Pakistan would "protest" such an ostensibly flagrant violation of Pakistan's sovereignty.[16] It remains contested to what degree Pakistan's previous government—or elements thereof—continued to cooperate with the United States prior to its term ending in March 2013. While American officials interviewed by the authors maintain that the Pakistanis cooperate on selecting some targets, Pakistani civilian and military officials insist that there is no cooperation and that the attacks violate Pakistani sovereignty.[17] It remains to be seen how the newly elected Pakistani government, under Prime Minister Nawaz Sharif and his Pakistan Muslim League-Nawaz (PML-N), will contend with the drone program.

The Pakistani drone program may not long remain under the auspices of the CIA. Increasing judicial and congressional frustration with the official secrecy surrounding the otherwise extremely visible program, as well as nagging questions about the degree to which drone strikes are covered by the 2001 Authorization for Use of Military Force, have prompted Obama officials to consider shifting the program from the CIA to the Department of Defense.[18] The CIA-conducted drone strikes are a covert action falling under Title 50. Should the Department of Defense assume control, the

---

[15] Acting U.S. Ambassador to Pakistan met with anti-drone Code Pink activists in November 2011. Even discussing the existence of the program and the possible outcomes of the strikes caused Hoagland to remark that "I probably just, you know, got into big trouble with what I just said." "Acting US ambassador to Pakistan met with Code Pink, discussed 'classified' drone casualty counts," *The Daily Caller*, 5 November 2011, accessed at http://dailycaller.com/2012/11/05/acting-us-ambassador-to-pakistan-met-with-code-pink-discussed-classified-drone-casualty-counts/#ixzz2EJ4GxBjr, 9 May 2013. However, in April 2013 the Obama administration offered its first detailed justification of a program it had previously refused to discuss. See Charlie Savage, "Top U.S. Security Official Says 'Rigorous Standards' Are Used for Drone Strikes," *The New York Times*, 30 April 2013, accessed at http://www.nytimes.com/2012/05/01/world/obamas-counterterrorism-aide-defends-drone-strikes.html?_r=0, 12 May 2013.
[16] Jonathan Landay, "U.S. secret: CIA collaborated with Pakistan spy agency in drone war," *McClatchy.com*, 4 April 2013, accessed at http://www.mcclatchydc.com/2013/04/09/188063/us-secret-cia-collaborated-with.html#storylink=cpy, 9 May 2013.
[17] Landay, "U.S. secret;" Mark Mazzetti, "A Secret Deal on Drones, Sealed in Blood," *The New York Times*, 6 April 2013, accessed at http://www.nytimes.com/2013/04/07/world/asia/origins-of-cias-not-so-secret-drone-war-in-pakistan.html?ref=markmazzetti&_r=0&pagewanted=all, 9 May 2013.
[18] Greg Miller and Karen DeYoung, "Administration debates stretching 9/11 law to go after new al-Qaeda offshoots," *The Washington Post*, 6 March 2013, accessed at http://articles.washingtonpost.com/2013-03-06/world/37500569_1_qaeda-drone-strikes-obama-administration, 9 May 2013.

program would come under Title 10 and would be carried out as a clandestine activity. Although the two are often conflated, the distinction between clandestine and covert action is important. A covert action is one in which the involvement of the sponsoring government is meant to remain secret. A clandestine activity, on the other hand, is intended to remain a secret, but should it be revealed, it can be publicly acknowledged.[19] Thus, if the drone program came under Title 10, U.S. officials *could*, in principle, discuss it. But while there may be more transparency under Title 10, such activities actually receive less oversight than those carried out under Title 50, which are under the purview of the intelligence committees of both the House and the Senate. Thus, it remains unclear whether transferring the drone program to the Department of Defense will have a significant effect on the transparency of the program.[20]

The restriction of drone strikes within Pakistan to FATA, which comprises seven tribal agencies and six frontier regions, is important for several often-underappreciated reasons. First, and foremost, Pakistan's constitution does not apply to FATA. Instead, FATA is governed by a colonial governance instrument called the Frontier Crimes Regulation, or FCR. As a consequence, foreign journalists are prohibited from travelling to FATA without the approval of the ministry of interior and/or an escort from the military and intelligence services. Even ordinary Pakistanis cannot legally visit the area unless they themselves have family ties there. Thus, it is extremely difficult to obtain accurate information from what has long been something of an informational black hole. These restrictions serve the Pakistani state's interests because it has long used FATA to host a dizzying array of Islamist militant groups operating in Afghanistan, India, and even Pakistan itself.[21] Thus, some of Pakistan's most-hardened Islamist militants have found sanctuary in FATA.

Second, each agency is governed by a government representative known as a "political agent." The political agent works with tribal elders, called maliks, who collaborate, in part because of their desire to retain their privileged status and in part because of payments received from the

---

[19]Andru E. Wall, "Demystifying the Title 10-Title 50 Debate: Distinguishing Military Operations, Intelligence Activities & Covert Action," *Harvard Law School National Security Journal* 3 (December 2011): 85–142.
[20]Spencer Ackerman, "Little Will Change if the Military Takes Over CIA's Drone Strikes," *Wired.com*, 20 March 2013, accessed at http://www.wired.com/dangerroom/2013/03/military-drones, 9 May 2013.
[21]Hussain Haqqani, *Pakistan: Between Mosque and Military* (Washington, DC: Carnegie Endowment for International Peace, 2005); Barnett R. Rubin, *The Fragmentation of Afghanistan* (New Haven, CT: Yale University Press, 2002); Rizwan Hussain, *Pakistan and the Emergence of Islamic Militancy in Afghanistan* (Burlington, VT: Ashgate, 2005); Praveen Swami, *India, Pakistan and the Secret Jihad: The Covert War in Kashmir, 1947-2004* (London: Routledge, 2007).

government via the agent. The political agent is responsible for administrative duties and ordinary law and order. At his discretion, he can refer a civil dispute to a council of maliks (*jirga*), which decides how the dispute should be resolved. The jirga's decree is final and binding and no appeal is available. Perhaps the most-controversial aspect of the FCR is the wide-scale coercive powers it affords the state for "controlling, blockading, and taming a 'hostile and unfriendly tribe.'"[22] These coercive powers include "collective punishment," under which the state is authorized to seize "wherever they may be found, all or any of the members of such tribe, and all and any property belonging to them or any of them" for any offense committed by one or more members of a tribe. The state can even banish or exile an individual or group of individuals from an agency altogether.[23] In effect, entire communities can be ousted from their homes, fined, and have their revenues and properties seized or even forfeited altogether, "simply because a murder or culpable homicide was committed or attempted in their area."[24] Because "the application of collective punishment...disregards individual culpability and identifies the innocent with the guilty" and violates numerous provisions of Pakistan's own constitution, the applicable provisions have been struck down by Pakistan's high courts, with no effect.[25] The FCR is also inconsistent with several international conventions to which Pakistan is a signatory, including the Universal Declaration of Human Rights, which affords everyone the right to an effective remedy by competent national tribunals and protection from arbitrary arrest, detention, and exile.[26]

Despite the fact that Pakistan's own high courts have demanded that the FCR be repealed, no government has ever done so. In fact, the state has long made use of the coercive powers it provides. In 2004, the Pakistani Army, under the leadership of Army Chief and President Pervez Musharraf, used collective punishment to roust foreign Islamist militants in Waziristan. They used and threatened to use home demolition, the seizure of businesses, and the forfeiture of other properties and assets to persuade locals to

---

[22]Osama Siddique, "The Other Pakistan: Special Laws, Diminished Citizenship and the Gathering Storm," 5 December 2012, accessed at http://dx.doi.org/10.2139/ssrn.2185535, 9 May 2013.
[23]Gulman S. Afridi, "FCR's Collective Responsibility," *The Dawn*, 2 January 2012, accessed at http://dawn.com/2012/01/02/fcrs-collective-responsibility, 9 May 2013.
[24]Siddique, "The Other Pakistan," 11.
[25]Afridi, "FCR's Collective Responsibility."
[26]Aamenah Yusafzai, "Bringing Justice to FATA," *Dawn.com*, 23 November 2010, accessed at http://blog.dawn.com/2010/11/23/bringing-justice-to-fata, 9 May 2013. Technically, aspects of the FCR have been amended via a presidential order in August 2011. However, none of these have been implemented. G.M. Chaudhry, The Frontier Crimes Regulation, 1901–as amended on 27 August 2011: summary of 2011 amendments (Islamabad: National Democratic Institute, 2013).

surrender foreigners living amongst them. During Pakistan's military operations in FATA, which began in 2002 and continue today, the army has denied individuals and specific tribes access to major roads that prevented them from escaping the conflict and reaching humanitarian aid.[27]

These aspects of FCR, which render Pakistanis who live in FATA "lesser citizens," have enormous and nearly universally unacknowledged implications for the U.S. use of armed drones in FATA. As noted above, under the FCR, an entire family or clan can be punished just because one member has granted terrorists sanctuary in his home. This clause has been used to justify the Pakistani air strikes and draconian army operations that have caused enormous civilian casualties and forced displacement. As of March 2013, the United Nations reported that there were still some 758,000 persons who had been internally displaced due to ongoing security operations in FATA as well as parts of Khyber-Pakhtunkhwa.[28] Part of the unrecognized legitimizing discourse surrounding the use of armed drones in FATA is the unfortunate fact that residents of FATA are second-class citizens, and the legal regime under which they are governed permits the state to ignore individual innocence and guilt. The United States exploits this predicament, but Pakistan perpetuates it by sustaining a legal regime that discriminates between the citizens of the so-called "settled areas," where the constitution applies, and those lesser citizens under the rule of the FCR.

There is a third, equally unappreciated aspect of the tribal areas: because FATA is governed under the FCR, it has no police forces; instead, paramilitary, military, and tribal militia forces keep order. Thus, the arrest of militants, collection of evidence, and subsequent prosecution in Pakistan's courts is not a viable option in FATA. (In contrast, high-value targets captured in the rest of Pakistan are tried under Pakistani law or, in some cases, remanded to the United States.) Thus, while law-and-order approaches may be infinitely preferable to the use of armed drones, successive Pakistani governments have closed this route by choosing to defer bringing the area and its people fully under Pakistan's constitution.[29] Thus, the only

---

[27] Yusafzai, "Bringing Justice to FATA"; Azmat Hayat Khan, "FATA," in Pervaiz Iqbal Cheema and Maqsudul Hasan Nuri, eds., *Tribal Areas of Pakistan: Challenges and Responses* (Islamabad: Islamabad Policy Institute, 2005). Surprisingly the FCR was critically discussed in U.S. Department of State, Bureau of Democracy, Human Rights and Labor, "2004 Country Reports on Human Rights Practices–Pakistan," 28 February 2005, accessed at http://www.state.gov/g/drl/rls/hrrpt/2004/41743.htm, 9 May 2013.

[28] United Nations Office for the Coordination of Humanitarian Affairs, "Humanitarian Dashboard-Pakistan," March 2013, accessed at http://www.unocha.org/pakistan/reports-media/ocha-reports, 9 May 2013.

[29] Joshua T. White, "The Shape of Frontier Rule: Governance and Transition, from the Raj to the Modern Pakistani Frontier," *Asian Security* 4 (2008): 219–243.

alternatives to doing nothing to combat the militants in FATA, who operate against international forces in Afghanistan and who are responsible for killing some 43,000 Pakistanis since September 11, are devastating and indiscriminate Pakistani military operations or Special Forces raids into Pakistani territory by Afghanistan-based troops.[30]

American and Pakistani officials understood that the FCR would frustrate the ability of foreign and even Pakistani journalists to learn about the drone program, allowing both states to cultivate confusion about its origins. Indeed, in the early years, the Pakistan military actually took credit for the attacks, which they said were conducted with conventional attack aircraft (for example, F-16s and attack helicopters).[31] Daniel Markey, a member of the Secretary of State's Policy Planning Staff from 2003 to 2007, has said that

> Musharraf's consent represented both that of the Pakistani military and its civilian government. Not only did he grant his consent, but initially, the Pakistani military tried to take credit for these kinds of attacks—claiming that they weren't the work of drones, but Pakistani air strikes. This wasn't a very credible claim on Pakistan's part, but it worked for a while because the strikes were initially much less frequent than they are now. And the misdirection helped the Pakistani government weather the domestic backlash.[32]

---

[30]Like many databases, the Pak Institute for Peace Studies is not always clear about what sorts of attacks it tallies and what criteria it uses to code different kinds of violence. These numbers are taken from their annual reports from 2008 and 2011. They reported that 7,107 Pakistanis had been killed in 2011; 10,003 in 2010; 12,632 in 2009; 7,997 in 2008; 3,448 in 2007; 907 in 2006; and 216 in 2005, for a total of 42,310. Pak Institute for Peace Studies, *Pakistan Security Report 2008* (Islamabad: PIPS, 2008); Pak Institute for Peace Studies, *PIPS Security Report 2009*, accessed at http://san-pips.com/index.php?action=books&id=main; Pak Institute for Peace Studies, *Pakistan Security Report 2011* (Islamabad: PIPS, 2011); Pak Institute for Peace Studies, "Civilian Casualties in Armed Conflicts in Pakistan: Timeline 2012," 2012, accessed at http://san-pips.com/index.php?action=reports&id=tml2, 9 May 2013.

[31]In March 2013, *The New York Times* reported that the United States had taken the unusual step of disavowing two drone strikes. Such a disavowal is odd, since the drone program is a covert action and thus U.S. officials cannot acknowledge its existence. Given that Pakistan has no armed drone capability, there are a few possible explanations for the event. First, it is possible that the attack was a conventional strike, carried out by Pakistan, which the Pakistanis wanted to blame on the United States. Second, the strike may have been carried out by an American drone after all, and the officials cited in the story were simply wrong or seeking to engage in information management. Third, it may be that there was no drone strike to begin with. Because no Pakistani or U.S. official will discuss this incident with the authors, we are unable to evaluate the merits of the story. Declan Walsh, "U.S. Disavows 2 Drone Strikes Over Pakistan," *The New York Times*, 4 March 2013, accessed at http://www.nytimes.com/2013/03/05/world/asia/us-disavows-2-drone-strikes-over-pakistan.html?pagewanted=all, 9 May 2013.

[32]Daniel Markey comments transcribed in Ritika Singh, "Lawfare Podcast Episode #20: Daniel Markey on U.S.–Pakistan Terrorism Cooperation and Pakistan's Extremist Groups," 27 September 2012, accessed at http://www.lawfareblog.com/2012/09/daniel-markey-on-u-s-pakistan-terrorism-cooperation-and-pakistans-extremist-groups, 9 May 2013.

Musharraf did not follow through on any of his public complaints, confirming the mutual understanding that such protests were political drama for domestic consumption. Markey explains that "one can only assume ... that the private messages from the Pakistani government were different from their public messages."[33]

As Markey makes clear, however, Pakistan was unable to sustain the pretense that its military was conducting the operations. Local residents found missile fragments with American markings, and Pakistani media eventually caught on to the story. Furthermore, the increasing U.S. use of drone attacks made the cover story increasingly untenable. Throughout much of the Bush presidency, American drones were rarely employed in Pakistan, and thus, Pakistan's claims of responsibility were not robustly challenged. This changed as drone strikes became increasingly common under the first Obama administration and as Pakistan transitioned from a military government led by President Musharraf to one that is nominally democratic.

From Washington's point of view, it may be enough that the United States conduct drone operations in Pakistan with the continued support of Pakistan's intelligence agency, the Interservices Intelligence Directorate (ISI), and the army, which oversees the ISI.[34] But the drone program raises many questions for Pakistan's citizens. For one thing, Pakistanis routinely hear their politicians decrying the drones, yet the strikes continue. As the Pew data indicate, many Pakistanis suspect that their government is colluding with the United States, but so far, few Pakistanis have demanded that their government make clear the extent to which it tolerates or even actively facilitates U.S. drone operations. Politicians remain silent, even as media reports continue to reveal the degree to which the Pakistani civilian government and military have been complicit in the program.[35]

In the wake of the November 2011 U.S.–NATO attack on the Pakistani military outpost at Salala, Pakistan civilian and military stakeholders came

---

[33]Singh, "Lawfare Podcast Episode #20."
[34]For a graphic of all suspected U.S. drone bases in Pakistan, see The Bureau of Investigative Journalism, "CIA drones quit one Pakistan site – but US keeps access to other airbases," 15 December 2011, accessed at http://www.thebureauinvestigates.com/2011/12/15/cia-drones-quit-pakistan-site-but-us-keeps-access-to-other-airbases, 9 May 2013.
[35]"Wikileaks: Kayani wanted more drone strikes in Pakistan," *Pakistan Express Tribune*, 20 May 2011, accessed at http://tribune.com.pk/story/172531/wikileaks-kayani-wanted-more-drone-strikes/, 9 May 2013; Rob Crilly, "Wikileaks: Pakistan privately approved drone strikes," *The Telegraph*, 1 December 2010, accessed at http://www.telegraph.co.uk/news/worldnews/wikileaks/8172922/Wikileaks-Pakistan-privately-approved-drone-strikes.html, 9 May 2013; Jim Sciutto and Lee Ferran, "WikiLeaks: Pakistan Asked for More, Not Fewer Drones," *ABC News The Blotter*, 20 May 2011, accessed at http://abcnews.go.com/Blotter/wikileaks-cable-pakistan-asked-fewer-drones/story?id=13647893#.ULQtE-NewV8E, 9 May 2013; Landay, "U.S. secret"; Mark Mazzetti, "A Secret Deal on Drones."

under increasing pressure from a restive population to decrease cooperation with United States, including their facilitation of the drone program. Pakistanis, like Americans, are generally not privy to details about the degree to which the Pakistani security establishment collaborates with the United States on drone operations and, like American opponents of the program, often object to it as a violation of Pakistani sovereignty.[36] In an effort to publicly punish the United States and appease increasing public outcry over the Salala episode, while making few actual changes to the status quo, Pakistan's Parliament forced the United States to cease operations at the Shamsi airbase. Shamsi, however, was only one of the bases that the United States used to stage drone strikes in Pakistan.

The ruckus over Shamsi exposed significant fissures in Pakistan's civil-military relations. First, the declaration was political theatre in the first degree: no U.S. personnel were stationed at Shamsi at the time. Second, the United States continues to use other bases in Pakistan for drone flights. Third, U.S. government officials have told the authors that Pakistan's intelligence agency continues to collaborate with the CIA on these strikes. (Pakistani officials deny that they are doing so.) Moreover, while political actors publicly question the army's right to sell Pakistan's sovereignty to the United States,[37] U.S. State Department cables released, without authorization to WikiLeaks, show that Pakistan's current political elites are at most indifferent to drone strikes, and that many, in fact, support the program.[38]

Thus, ordinary Pakistanis are left to question why drones are used against citizens and foreigners alike in FATA and which (if any) Pakistani authority authorizes the strikes. The program also raises troubling

---

[36]See Chris Rogers, "Legality of U.S. Drone Strikes in Pakistan," Center for Research and Security Studies, Islamabad. N.d., accessed at http://crss.pk/downloads/Reports/Special-Posts/Legality-of-US-Drone-Strikes-in-Pakistan.pdf, 9 May 2013; Joshua Foust and Ashley S. Boyle, "The Strategic Context of Lethal Drones: A framework for discussion," American Security Project, 16 August 2012, accessed at http://americansecurityproject.org/featured-items/2012/the-strategic-context-of-lethal-drones-a-framework-for-discussion/, 9 May 2013.

[37]Inter alia, John Reed, "Pakistan Boots U.S. From Drone Base," *Defensetech.com*, 30 June 2011, accessed at http://defensetech.org/2011/06/30/pakistan-boots-u-s-from-drone-base/, 9 May 2013; "US-Pak intelligence cooperation continues," *The Dawn*, 23 January 2012, accessed at http://dawn.com/2012/01/23/us-pak-intelligence-cooperation-continues/, 9 May 2013; Chris Woods, "CIA drones quit one Pakistan site — but US keeps access to other airbases," *The Bureau of Investigative Journalism*, 15 December 2011, accessed at http://www.thebureauinvestigates.com/2011/12/15/cia-drones-quit-pakistan-site-but-us-keeps-access-to-other-airbases/, 9 May 2013; "Pakistan Helps U.S. Drones Campaign: Reuters," *HuffingtonPost.com*, 22 January 2012, accessed at http://www.huffingtonpost.com/2012/01/22/pakistan-us-drones-campaign_n_1221774.html, 9 May 2013.

[38]"US embassy cables: Pakistan backs US drone attacks on tribal areas," *The Guardian*, 30 November 2010; Jim Sciutto and Lee Ferran, "WikiLeaks: Pakistan Asked fore More, Not Fewer Drones," *ABCNews.com*, 20 May, 2011, accessed at "US embassy cables: Pakistan backs US drone attacks on tribal areas," *The Guardian*, 30 November 2010.

questions about civil-military relations in Pakistan: what—if any—powers do civilian leaders wield over the program, not to mention the Pakistani military, which is supposed to be subordinate to civilian control? Equally, Pakistanis—and Americans—lack knowledge about basic aspects of the program: who is targeted and why, with what actual outcome, and with what eventual effect upon Pakistani or American security?

THE ARGUMENT

Pakistan's Urdu-language media (private television, radio, and print) is almost universally anti-drone, while Pakistan's English-language publications, aimed at an elite readership, take a slightly more sympathetic attitude. Given unequal access to these debates across Pakistan (a function of access to media, as well as of literacy in Urdu and English), we seek to understand how those Pakistanis who are aware of the drone program form an opinion about it. Since the average citizen of any country does not know much about security policy issues, how does she form her views? Public opinion researchers have argued that societal and political elites play a very large role in shaping what the public thinks about policy issues, particularly policy issues they do not understand very well. John Zaller,[39] in a seminal book on the origins of public attitudes, argues that elites play a large role in framing issues and shaping their presentation in the mass media and public discourse. The role of elites in shaping opinion is even greater in developing countries with relatively low literacy rates, where the governing elite have a high control over information. Members of the mass public most often assume that elites have better information on issues than they themselves do, and take their cues on complex issues from those whom they consider knowledgeable.[40] As Arthur Lupia argues,[41] the more expert the elite is assumed to be on an issue, the more likely it is that citizens will follow elite cues on that issue.

Not only is the perceived expertise of the opinion maker important to shaping views on security issues, but so is the ability of the individual to discern a strong argument from a weak one. People who are better educated will probably have access to a greater base of knowledge and to more channels of information than those with a very basic level of education or no education at all. Thus, the more-educated have the tools to be more

---

[39]John Zaller, *The Nature and Origins of Mass Opinion* (Cambridge: Cambridge University Press, 1992).
[40]Arthur Lupia, *The Democratic Dilemma: Can Citizens Learn What They Need to Know?* (Cambridge: Cambridge University Press, 1998).
[41]Ibid.

discriminating about the information that media outlets provide on security issues.

How does the argument about elite discourse pertain to Pakistan and the drone debate? The Pew data show that most Pakistanis are not aware of the drone campaign; only about one third of the public is aware that drones are being used to kill militants on Pakistan's soil. Our Heckman selection model analysis shows that those who do offer an opinion on the drones are those who are more educated, male, and have access to the Internet. Thus, the data suggest that the Pakistani debate over drones is waged among elites, who nonetheless differ in key ways, such as level of education, literacy in English, access to non-Urdu media, and the like.

We contend that the information available to Pakistanis is central to forming their attitudes on the drone program. The less educated a Pakistani is, the more likely it is that she will have access to limited sources of information about the drone program, and that those sources of information will be in the vernacular and take a more-nationalistic tone. Literate but moderately-educated Pakistanis will have access to Urdu newspapers and (for the minority who can afford it) Urdu television; the Urdu media is overwhelmingly against the strikes. Highly educated Pakistanis, on the other hand, have access to the more-positive accounts of the drone program available through English-language television (including foreign channels) and newspapers, and the Internet. Thus, less-educated Pakistanis are less likely to be positive about the drone program than are the highly educated.

The highly educated population, most of which speaks English, has access to a broader and more-diverse media selection, such as newspapers like *The Dawn*, *The Express Tribune*, and the *Daily Times*, among others. While most of the coverage of drones in Pakistani English-language media is negative, the English-language media gives space to pro-drone views that are completely absent from the Urdu language media. Thus, higher levels of education provide elite Pakistanis with a broader range of views on the desirability of the drone strikes. Most importantly, higher levels of education, and the ability to read and understand English, give a citizen access to pro-drone arguments, which in Pakistan are only available in English-language sources. We argue that those Pakistanis who have positive attitudes toward the drone strikes are the elite *within* the elite in Pakistani society.

The nature of the media coverage in Pakistan means that those who are exposed solely to Urdu-language media are unlikely to hear any pro-drone arguments. The less educated an individual is, the more likely it is that he or she does not speak English and seeks only Urdu media, which is overwhelmingly anti-drone. Thus, the less-educated have narrower exposure to views on the subject and are likely to be more opposed to the drones. This argument produces the following hypothesis:

> *H1: The lower the respondent's level of education, the more likely the respondent is to oppose drone strikes in Pakistan.*

There is an important gender component to this argument. Pakistani men tend to be far better educated and better informed about political matters than Pakistani women, and as a result, they have much greater access to different channels of information. The differences in education between the genders in Pakistan are quite stark: among males above the age of 10, 69 percent are considered "literate," and 69 percent have had some kind of formal education. In contrast, among females above 10 years of age, only 45 percent are literate and 44 percent have had some kind of formal education.[42] Thus, we surmise that women are more likely than men to oppose drone strikes because of their lower levels of education and access to information. This yields our second hypothesis:

> *H2: Women are more likely to oppose drone strikes than men.*

To understand how elite discourse may shape opinion, it is necessary to first describe the lineaments of the drone debate in Pakistan. Whereas most discussions of the drone program primarily concentrate on the arguments of those who oppose it, we must also identify the reasoning put forth by those who support drone use. These arguments—for and against—are laid out in the next section.

ANTI-DRONE ARGUMENTS IN PAKISTAN

Pakistanis who oppose drone strikes offer numerous criticisms of the program. First and foremost is the issue of sovereignty. Pakistan's Foreign Minister, Hina Rabbani Khar, among numerous other Pakistani leaders, denounced the strikes as "unlawful, against international law, and [a] violation of sovereignty."[43] It may be that the many Pakistanis who hear such cries of protest from their government officials become convinced that the drone strikes violate domestic and international legal norms and are not representative of the wishes of their democratically elected

---

[42]Pakistan Bureau of Statistics, "Percentage Distribution of Population by Age, Sex Litracy [sic] and Level of Education-2008-09," n.d., accessed at http://www.pbs.gov.pk/sites/default/files/Labour%20Force/publications/lfs2008_09/t03.pdf, 9 May 2013.

[43]"Drones violate sovereignty, Pakistan tells UN," *PakTribune*, 31 October 2012, accessed at http://paktribune.com/news/Drones-violate-sovereignty-Pakistan-tells-UN-254545.html, 9 May 2013.

government. Thus, some Pakistanis may conclude that the drone strikes are carried out in defiance of the wishes of Pakistan's democratic government. This gives rise to an important testable hypothesis:

> *H3: Those who value democracy more in Pakistan will be more likely to oppose drone strikes.*

A second important issue is the lack of information about who was targeted in the drone strikes, with what cause, and with what outcomes. Various international and Pakistani organizations have attempted to investigate civilian casualties resulting from the strikes. Prominent organizations involved in this effort include the International Human Rights and Conflict Resolution Clinic at Stanford Law School and the Global Justice Clinic at the NYU School of Law;[44] the Bureau of Investigative Journalism (BIJ);[45] and the New America Foundation (NAF).[46]

According to the BIJ, there have been 352 drone strikes in Pakistan, of which 300 have taken place under the Obama administration. Together, these drone strikes have killed between 2,590 and 3,383 persons, of whom anywhere between 472 and 885 have been civilians, including 176 children. In addition, the BIJ assesses that between 1,255 and 1,408 persons have been injured by drones.[47] NAF reaches somewhat similar figures (to be expected, as it uses essentially the same news reports): "337 CIA drone strikes" since 2004, which have killed between 1,932 to 3,176 people. Of those killed, between 1,487 and 2,595 were reported to be militants, and between 257 and 310 civilians.[48] Despite the uncertainty about the actual status of the victims of the strikes, the attacks receive regular coverage in the Pakistani print media (such as the newspapers *The Dawn* in English and *Jang* in Urdu), as well as television and radio. The coverage focuses upon the alleged collateral damage from drone strikes, including scenes of destroyed vehicles and houses, and the bodies of people supposedly killed in the strikes.

A third interesting element of the Pakistani debate over drones is the involvement of Islamist militant leaders. One of the most important anti-drone spokesmen from this group is Hafez Saeed, the leader of the

---

[44]International Human Rights and Conflict Resolution Clinic At Stanford Law School and Global Justice Clinic at NYU School Of Law, "Living Under Drones."
[45]Bureau of Investigative Journalism, "The Covert Drone War," accessed at http://www.thebureauinvestigates.com/category/projects/drones, 9 May 2013.
[46]New America Foundation, "Year of the Drone."
[47]Bureau of Investigative Journalism, "Covert War on Terror—The Data," accessed at http://www.thebureauinvestigates.com/category/projects/drone-data, 9 May 2013.
[48]New America Foundation, "Year of the Drone."

international terrorist organization Lashkar-e-Taiba (LeT, now operating under the name Jamaat-ud-Dawa, JuD). (The United States Department of State has declared both LeT and its alias, JuD, to be foreign terrorist organizations.) Saeed has petitioned the Punjab High Court to declare the strikes illegal,[49] and his organization has led many protests against the drone program and other forms of cooperation with the United States. JuD also took the lead in organizing an alliance of Islamist political leaders and militant activists called the Difah-e-Pakistan Council (Defense of Pakistan Council.)[50] Given that the drone strikes target al Qaeda and the Pakistani and Afghan Taliban, the allies of JuD and other jihadi groups, we may surmise that those who do not fear the influence of such groups may be more likely to oppose drone strikes. This gives rise to a fourth hypothesis:

> *H4: Those who do not believe that al Qaeda poses a serious threat to Pakistan will be more likely to oppose drone strikes.*

That said, mainstream Islamist political parties (often called Ulema parties because of their involvement with the ulema, or religious scholars), and right-of-center politicians, such as Imran Khan and Nawaz Sharif, also oppose drones.[51] Opposition to drones overlaps significantly with support of an increased role for Islam in governance: Nawaz Sharif made a highly publicized effort to impose Islamic law in Pakistan and even tried to declare himself the "Amir-ul-Momineen" (leader of the faithful) before he was deposed by General Musharraf in 1999.[52] Imran Khan, a former cricketer and international lothario, has in recent years re-invented himself as a pious Pakistani and nationalist politician who has voiced vocal support for Sharia.[53] In some cases, furthermore, Islamist political actors are

---

[49]"JuD drone petition: LHC postpones hearing of case," *Pakistan Express Tribune*, 2 November 2012, accessed at http://tribune.com.pk/story/459621/jud-drone-petition-lhc-postpones-hearing-of-case, 9 May 2013.

[50]See "Drone, NATO attacks, MFN decision blasted," *The Nation*, 23 January 2012, accessed at http://www.nation.com.pk/pakistan-news-newspaper-daily-english-online/national/23-Jan-2012/drone-nato-attacks-mfn-decision-blasted, 9 May 2013.

[51]"Imran Khan's Pakistan anti-drone drive halts for night," *BBC News.com*, 6 October 2012, accessed at http://www.bbc.co.uk/news/world-asia-19854297, 9 May 2013; "Nawaz demands end to drones," *The Nation*, 30 August 2012, accessed at http://www.nation.com.pk/pakistan-news-newspaper-daily-english-online/lahore/30-Aug-2012/nawaz-demands-end-to-drones, 9 May 2013; "Jamaat e Islami calls to shoot down drones," *Lahore Times*, 6 June 2012, accessed at http://www.lhrtimes.com/2012/06/06/jamaat-e-islami-calls-to-shoot-down-drones/#ixzz2E0tqNWDM, 9 May 2013.

[52]"PML(N)-A Family Affair," *Pakistan Today*, 6 March 2012, accessed at http://www.pakistantoday.com.pk/2012/03/06/comment/editors-mail/pmln-a-family-affair, 9 May 2013.

[53]See "Imran Khan demands the imposition of shariat in Pakistan," *Daily Express*, 21 January 2009, accessed at http://letusbuildpakistan.blogspot.com/2009/01/imran-khan-demands-imposition-of.html, 9 May 2013.

identical with, or have strong ties to, overtly militant leaders.[54] This gives rise to another testable hypothesis:

> *H5: Those who want to see Islam play a greater role in the state should be more likely to oppose drone strikes.*

Finally, at the core of the drone debate is a deep suspicion about the United States and its intentions vis-à-vis Pakistan. Survey data now show that Pakistanis view India, their traditional rival, more favorably than they do the United States. Many Pakistanis believe that the Americans are at war not with terrorists, but with Islam and Muslims.[55] The Pakistani public has a long and deeply held antipathy toward the United States. Table 1 shows the pattern of anti-American views among Pakistanis dating back to 2002, when Pew started asking about favorability toward the United States in Pakistan.

As can be seen in the table, 69 percent of Pakistani respondents had an unfavorable view of the United States in 2002, and only 10 percent had a favorable view of the country. In 2010, 68 percent of Pakistanis had an unfavorable view of the United States, and only 17 percent had a favorable view of the country. Given that the drone strikes did not really start in a

TABLE 1
Opinion Toward the United States

	Favorable	Unfavorable	DK/Refused
Pakistan			
Spring 2010	17	68	16
Spring 2009	16	68	16
Spring 2008	19	63	17
Spring 2007	15	68	16
Spring 2006	27	56	17
Spring 2005	23	60	17
Spring 2004	21	60	18
May 2003	13	81	6
Summer 2002	10	69	20

Source: Pew Research Center's Global Attitudes Project

[54] C. Christine Fair, "The Militant Challenge in Pakistan," *Asia Policy* 11 (January 2011): 105–137.
[55] Pew Research Center, "Pakistani Public Opinion Ever More Critical of U.S: 74% Call America an Enemy," 27 June 2012, accessed at http://www.pewglobal.org/2012/06/27/pakistani-public-opinion-ever-more-critical-of-u-s/, 9 May 2013; World Public Opinion.org; "Public Opinion in the Islamic World on Terrorism, al Qaeda, and US Policies," 25 February 2009, accessed at http://www.worldpublicopinion.org/pipa/pdf/feb09/STARTII_Feb09_rpt.pdf, 9 May 2013; World Public Opinion.org, "Muslims Believe US Seeks to Undermine Islam," 24 April 2007, accessed at http://www.worldpublicopinion.org/pipa/articles/brmiddleeastnafricara/346.php, 9 May 2013.

significant way in Pakistan until 2008, we cannot logically surmise that the high degree of disfavor toward the United States, has been principally driven by the drone strikes. Most Pakistanis were anti-American before the drones became a subject of public discourse. The drone strikes definitely did not help America's image with most Pakistanis, but they are not the primary cause of anti-Americanism in the country.

Anti-Americanism has deep roots in Pakistan. This legacy of negative opinions of the United States comes from a sense that the United States has often wronged Pakistan over the decades. Many Pakistanis felt that the United States abandoned Pakistan after the Soviets withdrew from Afghanistan in 1988, leaving Pakistan to deal with the resulting chaos. The United States also imposed harsh sanctions on Pakistan after it tested nuclear weapons. Finally, the United States has historically been willing to support military dictators in Pakistan as long as those individuals were viewed as pro-American. The United States appears as an impediment to the growth of a stable, functioning democracy in Pakistan, and the majority of Pakistanis view it with distrust. This gives rise to another testable hypothesis:

> *H6: Those who believe the United States is an enemy of Pakistan are more likely to oppose drone strikes than those who do not see the United States as an enemy.*

ARGUMENTS OF PAKISTANI DRONE PROPONENTS

While the voices of Pakistan's drone supporters are rarely heard, the Pew data demonstrate that a sizeable number of Pakistanis who know about the drones support their use. We can discern the bases of their support by reviewing the pro-drone op-eds written by Pakistanis in Pakistani and foreign newspapers. These writers argue that something must be done to eliminate the Islamist militants in the tribal areas and the threat they pose to Pakistanis. Pakistan's military operations have not always been successful and they have often come at a high price: the Pakistani army's spring 2009 operation against the Pakistani Taliban in Swat displaced over 3 million persons, over and above the 800,000 (or more) who had been displaced that year from the tribal areas due to military operations.[56] In late summer 2009, a fact-finding mission sent to Swat by Pakistan's Human Rights Commission documented extrajudicial killings by the

---

[56]Internal Displacement Monitoring Centre, "Millions of IDPs and Returnees Face Continuing Crisis," 2 December 2009, accessed at http://www.internal-displacement.org/8025708F004BE3B1/(httpInfoFiles)/9F1885E236952592C12576800057602F/$file/Pakistan_Overview_Dec09.pdf, 9 May 2013.

security forces and even mass graves.[57] U.S. State Department cables released through WikiLeaks reveal that U.S. officials knew about the killings but kept them secret.[58] The United States did not act until October 2010, after a video surfaced that appeared to show Pakistani troops shooting bound and blindfolded young men. The United States invoked Leahy Amendment sanctions, precluding U.S. military assistance to the units involved in the abuses.[59] Pakistanis are also very familiar with the devastation associated with Pakistan's use of combat aircraft in Swat, South Waziristan, and elsewhere. In October 2009, Pakistan deployed fighter-bomber aircraft in the tribal areas, causing residents to flee when theirs homes were destroyed.[60]

Given that the various displaced persons fled to major cities throughout the country, and also the vigorous media coverage of these unpopular military operations, Pakistanis are fully aware that the alternative to the drones may be much more unpleasant. Thus, those who support the drones do so because they believe that the strikes are the least-bad option, and also that doing nothing is not acceptable.[61] As with the foregoing section, we review these arguments in support of the drone program to generate testable hypotheses.

Perhaps the most important reason some Pakistanis support the use of drones is that they believe that the drones are killing terrorists, which Pakistan either cannot or will not tackle on its own. Moreover, drone proponents will often note that the drones kill foreign and Pakistani militants whose very presence in Pakistan vitiates Pakistan's claims of sovereignty and endangers the state. As one editorial in *The Pakistan Express Tribune* recently opined, "The real threat to our nation comes

---

[57]Human Rights Commission of Pakistan, "Serious concerns over mass graves, extrajudicial killings, IDPs' plight in Swat: HRCP," 12 August 2009, accessed at http://hrcpblog.wordpress.com/2009/08/22/serious-concerns-over-mass-graves-extrajudicial-killings-idps%E2%80%99-plight-in-swat-hrcp, 9 May 2013.

[58]Declan Walsh, "US 'kept Pakistani army Swat murders secret,'" *The Guardian*, 30 November 2010, accessed at http://www.guardian.co.uk/world/2010/nov/30/us-pakistani-army-swat-murders-secret, 9 May 2013.

[59]"'Abusive' Pakistani units lose aid," *Al Jazeera*, 22 October 2010, accessed at http://www.aljazeera.com/news/americas/2010/10/2010102271611937887.html, 9 May 2013. Unfortunately, this punitive measure was undermined by the nearly simultaneous announcement of 2 billion dollars in military aid to Pakistan. Eric Schmitt and David E. Sanger, "U.S. Offers Pakistan Army $2 Billion Aid Package," *The New York Times*, 22 October 2010, accessed at http://www.nytimes.com/2010/10/23/world/asia/23policy.html?pagewanted=all&_r=0, 9 May 2013.

[60]One of the authors visited South and North Waziristan with the Pakistan army in August 2010 and observed first-hand the massive devastation resulting from these strikes. See also, "Displaced tell of fear after 100,000 flee army assault,"*The Dawn*, 19 October 2009, accessed at http://archives.dawn.com/archives/145043, 9 May 2013.

[61]C. Christine Fair, "Pakistan's Own War on Terror: What the Pakistani Public Thinks," *Journal of International Affairs* 63 (Fall/Winter 2009): 39–55.

from the heavily armed outfits marching across our northern areas, rather than the strikes made by unmanned planes."[62]

Drone supporters may also weigh the potential loss of innocent life due to drones against the much larger problem of terrorism in Pakistan. Mohammad Taqi's critique of the Stanford–NYU Law School report on drones for the English-language *Daily Times* argues that the report is methodologically flawed,[63] but also points out that it is completely silent about

> the psychological effects of terrorist attacks on the general population all over Pakistan.... For example, compared to a total of roughly 350 drone attacks since 2004, there were well over 600 terrorist bombings and more than 1,000 fatalities across Pakistan. In addition, over 35 targeted attacks on the Shia and other minorities took place in 2011, causing over 500 deaths. But apparently the idea of the study was to highlight only the alleged atrocities by the US, while glossing over the reign of terror unleashed over Pakistanis at large by those holed up in FATA and their handlers in and cohorts in "mainland" Pakistan.[64]

Thus, for Taqi, the costs of drones are worth paying if the strikes degrade the ability of terrorist groups' to attack Pakistanis. Taqi is essentially

---

[62]"A question of Sovereignty," *The Pakistan Express Tribune*, 13 December 2012, accessed at http://tribune.com.pk/story/478880/a-question-of-sovereignty/?fb_action_ids=10151199413465003&fb_action_types=og.likes&fb_source=aggregation&fb_aggregation_id=288381481237582, 9 May 2013.

[63]This report did, in fact, have numerous methodological flaws. First and foremost, it relied upon interviews conducted among a convenience sample of 130 persons. These interviews were conducted well outside of the tribal areas and were "arranged through local contacts in Pakistan....The majority of the [69] experiential victims were arranged with the assistance of the Foundation for Fundamental Rights" (International Human Rights and Conflict Resolution Clinic At Stanford Law School and Global Justice Clinic at NYU School Of Law, "Living Under Drones," 2–3). The Foundation for Fundamental Rights is the leading opponent of drones in Pakistan and thus is a party to the debate rather than an impartial organization dedicated to an objective understanding of the issue. Much of the report's evidence is thus derived from interviews fielded among a small sample that is deeply tainted by selection bias. The authors make no attempt to identify Pakistanis who evince some support for drones, much less incorporate their views into the report. Equally dismaying, the authors of the report take all interview-derived information as authoritative and make no effort to independently confirm oral statements by invoking forensic or munitions experts or other scientific means of validating witness statements. The authors do not disambiguate the various causes of similar outcomes. For example, they note that Pakistani interlocutors described these "experiential victims" as exhibiting clinical signs of post-traumatic stress disorder due to their experience (howsoever direct or indirect) of either drone strikes or drone surveillance. Although the strikes are carried out in areas that are also tormented by enormous terrorist violence, restrictive and violent social regimes enforced by the local Taliban, extensive Pakistani military and paramilitary and intelligence presence, the authors simply assume that any such instances of depression can be attributed to drones alone. In short, the authors arrive at sweeping conclusions that are fundamentally unsupported by the report's thin and dubious empirical foundation.

[64]Mohammad Taqi, "Shooting down drones with academic guns?" *The Daily Times*, 4 October 2012, accessed at http://www.dailytimes.com.pk/default.asp?page=2012\10\04\story_4-10-2012_pg3_2, 9 May 2013.

arguing that the drones serve Pakistan's interests while also advancing those of the United States.

Mohammad Zubair, a lawyer from Peshawar with family ties to the tribal areas, is a vocal supporter of drones. He recalls the revelations of Air Chief Marshal (Retired) Rao Qamar Suleiman, who admitted in a 2011 *Daily Times* article that Pakistan's Air Force had flown "5,000 strike sorties and dropped 11,600 bombs on 4,600 targets in Pakistan's troubled tribal areas since May 2008."[65] In contrast to what he calls the "media's unverifiable reports" of innocent drone casualties, "the internally displaced persons of South Waziristan and people of North Waziristan [from the bombing campaign of the Pakistan Air Force] tell a different story about such attacks, albeit in whispers, due to fear. The IDPs claim that drones did not disrupt their social life or cause infrastructural damage or kill innocent civilians because of the precise and targeted nature of their attacks."[66] Thus, Zubair's arguments in support of drones derive from a reasoned comparison of the other more-damaging options to eliminate a threat that he believes is real and a menace to the state.

Zubair is not alone in voicing the view that the drones largely kill actual terrorists and are much preferable to the massive damage caused by the air force's bombing campaign, which displaced millions of Pakistanis and destroyed whole villages. Nor is he alone in condemning the Pakistani state for failing to exert itself over these areas to protect these vulnerable citizens.[67] Farhat Taj, an outspoken Norway-based researcher from the Tribal Areas, has questioned many of the reports of high civilian casualties, based on their failure to provide "verifiable evidence of civilian 'casualties'… i.e. names of the people killed, names of their villages, dates and locations of the strikes," as well as an "inadequate" collection methodology.[68]

Ali Arqam, writing in English on the Internet, presents a similar set of arguments for drone attacks. He argues that whatever harm drones do, it is less than that done by Pakistan's military actions and the "indiscriminate suicide bombings and other terrorist attacks by the nexus of Jihadist groups that have taken over" parts of the tribal areas.[69] Arqam, like Taqi, criticizes the recent Stanford–NYU Law School report for ignoring the

---

[65]Muhammad Zubair, "Drone attacks: myth and reality," *The Daily Times*, 4 June 2012, accessed at http://www.dailytimes.com.pk/default.asp?page=2012\06\04\story_4-6-2012_pg3_4, 9 May 2013.
[66]Zubair, "Drone attacks: myth and reality."
[67]Ibid.
[68]Farhat Taj, "Drone attacks: challenging some fabrications," *The Daily Times*, 2 January 2010, accessed at http://www.dailytimes.com.pk/default.asp?page=2010\01\02\story_2-1-2010_pg3_5, 9 May 2013.
[69]Ali Arqam, "Questioning the veracity of FFR-assisted Stanford report on drone attacks," *Let Us Build Pakistan*, 5 October 2012, accessed at http://criticalppp.com/archives/229457, 9 May 2013.

effect that terrorism has had on many Pakistanis. He observes that no one asked the "46,000 and counting victims of Jihadist terrorism in Pakistan about the psychological effects of seeing their near and dear ones obliterated in market places"; the authors did not ask Pakistan's religious minorities, who are the targets of sectarian terrorist groups, "about the psychological effects of seeing gruesome beheadings and executions of pilgrims and laborers on the basis of their religious identity"; nor did the report address the concerns of "Pashtun families as well as PPP, ANP, JUIF and other political activists, leaders and even those Deobandi clerics who were massacred for opposing the Taliban and their methods?"[70] For Arqam, doing nothing will ultimately result in a greater loss of life, well beyond the tribal areas; drones are preferable to the alternative (military action) because they target terrorists more accurately and thus cause less loss of innocent life.[71]

These authors provide some insights into the factors that lead Pakistanis to support drones. Pakistani drone supporters recognize that the drones do kill innocent civilians. But they still support the strikes because they believe that FATA-based terrorists do more harm than the drones, and that targeted killings are the least-bad option for dealing with Pakistan's terrorism problem. This reasoning is thrown into sharp relief by the fact that many of these drone supporters (including Taj, Taqi, Shah, and Zubair) have family ties to FATA. Thus, we suspect, along the lines of H4, that those who believe al Qaeda and other militant groups pose a serious threat to Pakistan are more likely to support drones and less likely to oppose them. It is also worth noting that authors from FATA understand the implications of the FCR: families offering shelter or other assistance to "terrorists" put their household and extended families at risk. Thus, for those in FATA, "innocence" has a different legal and social connotation than it does in the rest of Pakistan. Unfortunately, Pew did not survey FATA residents. Finally, conspicuously absent in these pro-drone pieces is any expression of the belief that the United States is at war with Pakistan. For these interlocutors, it is not that the Americans are trampling Pakistan's sovereignty; rather, Pakistan has not bothered to exert it own

---

[70] Ibid.
[71] There are numerous pro-drone articles in the Pakistani media, most making the same arguments as the pieces discussed above. See, for example, Saroop Ijaz, "Game of Drones," *Pakistan Express Tribune*, 6 October 2012, accessed at http://tribune.com.pk/story/447920/game-of-drones/, 9 May 2013; Pir Zubair Shah, "My Drone War," *Foreign Policy*, 27 February 2012, accessed at http://www.foreignpolicy.com/articles/2012/02/27/my_drone_war; Farhat Taj, "A Survey of Drone Attacks in Pakistan: What Do the People of FATA Think?" 5 March 2009, accessed at http://www.airra.org/newsandanalysis/droneattack-survey.php, 9 May 2013.

sovereignty over FATA. Thus, we anticipate that, consistent with H6, those who do not believe that the United States is an enemy of Pakistan are less likely to oppose U.S. drones in Pakistan.

DATA AND METHODS

The data used in this analysis came from the 2010 Pew Global Attitudes Survey, which included questions about drone strikes in Pakistan.[72] The survey was conducted in Pakistan's four provinces: Punjab, Sind, Northwest Frontier Province (now known as Khyber Paktunkhwa), and Balochistan. For security reasons, the survey was not fielded in FATA. To get an idea of how much Pakistanis know about the drone strikes, respondents were asked: *How much, if anything, have you heard about drone attacks that target leaders of extremist groups: a lot, little, or nothing at all?* Of the responses, the largest category was nothing at all, with 43 percent. Don't know/refused was the second largest response category with 22 percent. Of those who responded that they knew something about the drones, 21 percent said they knew a little and 14 percent said they knew a lot. Thus, in 2010, only 35 percent of the sample claimed that they knew something about the drone program, whereas 43 percent stated they knew nothing about it. It is clear from these responses that a minority of Pakistanis are familiar with the drone strikes.

In order to gauge opposition to the drone strikes, the respondents were asked: *Please tell me whether you support or oppose the United States conducting drone attacks in conjunction with the Pakistani government against the leaders of extremist groups.* The breakdown of response to this question was that 23 percent support the drone strikes, 32 percent oppose the drone strikes, and 45 percent do not know or refuse to answer the question. Thus, a plurality of Pakistanis either do not know about the drone strikes or refuse to answer the question. Table 2 shows a breakdown

TABLE 2
Please Tell Me Whether You Support or Oppose the United States Conducting Drone Attacks in Conjunction with the Pakistani Government Against Leaders of Extremist Groups

	Pakistan (n = 1,040)	Punjab (n = 568)	Sind (n = 273)	Balochistan (n = 66)	Northwest Frontier Province(NWFP) (n = 133)
Support	40.2 percent	42.8 percent	35.9 percent	39.4 percent	38.3 percent
Oppose	59.8 percent	57.2 percent	64.1 percent	60.6 percent	61.7 percent

[72]We employ 2010 data from the Pew Global Attitudes Project because that is the most-recent survey to include a battery of questions about the drone program in Pakistan and for which full access to the dataset is available. The 2012 dataset was still embargoed at the time of writing.

of Pakistani attitudes toward drone strikes among those respondents who answered the question.

As the table shows, the majority of respondents who knew about the drone strikes or offered an opinion were opposed to them, with nearly 60 percent opposed to 40 percent in favor. A minority, albeit a significant minority, views the drone strikes as positive.

The 2010 Pew survey allows us to examine some of the attitudes that surround the topic of drone strikes. The survey instrument includes a series of questions dealing with the necessity of the strikes, their toll on innocent civilians, and the degree to which the Pakistani government is assenting to the American drone strikes. Table 3 shows the results of answers to these questions, first across Pakistan and then by province.

The first question to examine is: *How much, if anything, have you heard about the drone attacks that target leaders of extremist groups—a lot, a little, or nothing at all?* This is the gateway question to the questions about the merits and drawbacks of the drone strikes. If a respondent answers *nothing at all*, they are not asked the immediate subsequent questions about the drone strikes. If they answer, *a lot* or *a little*, they are asked what they think about the drone strikes. The responses to this question are discussed above.

The first follow-up question is: *For each of the following statements about the drone attacks, please tell me whether you agree or disagree: They*

TABLE 3
For Each of the Following Statements about the Drone Attacks, Please Tell Me Whether You Agree or Disagree

	They are necessary to defend Pakistan from extremist groups				
	Pakistan (n = 629)	Punjab (n = 320)	Sind (n = 201)	Balochistan (n = 8)	NFWP (n = 100)
Agree	37.2 percent	33.4 percent	37.3 percent	50.0 percent	48.0 percent
Disagree	62.8 percent	66.6 percent	62.7 percent	50.0 percent	52.0 percent

	They kill too many innocent people				
	Pakistan (n = 689)	Punjab (n = 339)	Sind (n = 213)	Balochistan (n = 23)	NFWP (n = 114)
Agree	94.8 percent	95.6 percent	92.0 percent	100.0 percent	96.5 percent
Disagree	5.2 percent	4.4 percent	8.0 percent	0.0 percent	3.5 percent

	They are being done without the approval of the Pakistani government				
	Pakistan (n = 586)	Punjab (n = 312)	Sind (n = 175)	Balochistan (n = 14)	NFWP (n = 85)
Agree	55.6 percent	64.1 percent	46.3 percent	42.9 percent	45.9 percent
Disagree	44.4 percent	35.9 percent	53.7 percent	57.1 percent	54.1 percent

are necessary to defend Pakistan from extremist groups. Thirty-seven percent of Pakistanis agreed with this statement and 63 percent disagreed. Thus, a pattern emerges that is very similar to the question about support for and opposition to drone strikes.

The next question in the series concerned collateral damage. It asks: *For each of the following statements about the drone attacks, please tell me whether you agree or disagree: They kill too many innocent people.* This question elicited very strong responses. Ninety-five percent of those surveyed agreed that the strikes killed too many innocents, while only 5 percent believed that they did not.

The final question in the series asked: *For each of the following statements about the drone attacks, please tell me whether you agree or disagree: They are being done without the approval of the Pakistani government.* The responses to this question show that Pakistanis are much less united on this point than on the question of civilian casualties. Fifty-six percent agreed that the drone strikes are carried out without the approval of the Pakistan government, and 44 percent disagree.

In summary, these questions show that more Pakistanis oppose the drone strikes than favor them, that they think the strikes kill too many innocent people, and that they are slightly more likely to believe that the United States carries out the strikes without the consent of the Pakistani government.

While the targets of the drone strikes are religiously motivated militants, religious beliefs are not at the root of opposition to drone strikes. This study argues that the principal determinant of opposition to the drone strikes in Pakistan is the degree to which a Pakistani has access to a range of different opinions on the drone attacks. In other words, the less educated a citizen is, and the less access she has to information and commentary about the drone strikes, the more likely she is to oppose the attacks.

MODELING OPPOSITION TO U.S. DRONE STRIKES IN PAKISTAN

This study uses a Heckman probit model to explain opposition to U.S. drone strikes in Pakistan. The model tests hypotheses related to respondents' attitudes toward the United States, various Pakistani authorities, and militant groups, their religious beliefs, and their exposure to various types of media. Because of the larger number of missing cases resulting from some questions, we would be left with a significantly smaller sample if we opted to not employ an appropriate Heckman selection model. Why are there so many missing cases?

The literature on public opinion gives two general reasons why respondents choose not to answer survey questions. The first has to do with actual and perceived knowledge. Krosnick and Milburn argue that some individuals simply do not know enough about the subject of a question and choose not to answer for fear of appearing foolish.[73] Others perceive themselves as insufficiently knowledgeable and also do not answer. Thus, one reason for non-response is a lack of objective knowledge of the subject matter, and another reason is a lack of confidence that one is able to answer such questions. Krosnick and Milburn find that both the less-knowledgeable and women (no matter their level of knowledge) tend to have higher non-response rates than males and the more-knowledgeable.

Adam Berinsky argues that another reason individuals may choose not to answer some survey questions is social desirability effects.[74] If a question comes up and the respondent does not want to give her sincere answer, which may be one that she believes to be socially undesirable, she may choose to simply not answer the question and avoid the discomfort of either lying or stating her true beliefs.

Both types of reasons may be at play in the data utilized here. Pakistan is a highly unequal society when it comes to education. The illiteracy rate, particularly among women, is very high by international standards. Drone strikes and terrorism are both highly controversial issues, and asking about them can easily cause discomfort among respondents. Table 4 shows the correlations of the don't know/no response with the independent variables used in the study's analysis.

TABLE 4
Pearson Correlation Coefficients for Independent Variables and Don't Know/No Response Respondents

Variable	Correlation
Education	−.272**
Gender	−.254**
Internet usage	−.167**
Pro-democracy	−.149**
United States is enemy	−.136**
Islamic influence	.059*
Income	.049*
Al Qaeda is a threat	.003

**Correlation significant at the .01 level (2-tailed)

[73] Jon Krosnick and Michael Milburn, "Psychological Determinants of Political Opinionation," *Social Cognition* 8 (1990): 49–68.
[74] Adam Berinsky, "The Two Faces of Public Opinion," *American Journal of Political Science* 43 (1999): 1209–1230.

As we can see from the correlations, the Pakistanis most likely to refuse to answer the drone question or to say they don't know are the less-educated, women, and less-informed. These results make sense in light of the political knowledge and social desirability effects discussed above. The less-educated and women are likely to be less aware of the drones issue and are also less confident about their responses being based on correct information; therefore they chose not to respond.

We thus chose to utilize a Heckman selection model, which includes a selection function and a response function. In this case, the selection function will be similar to a regular binary logistic model, analyzing the factors that contribute to disapproval of drones. In this case, the dependent variable in the second model is also dichotomous. Thus, we use the Heckman probit model (as opposed to the standard Heckman selection model in which the response function uses ordinary least squares). Specific problems related to model specification are discussed below.

The dependent variable that we use in this analysis is a question that asks: *Now I'm going to ask you a list of things that the United States might do to combat extremist groups in Pakistan. For each one, please tell me whether you would support or oppose it*. The respondent is then offered: *Conducting drone attacks in conjunction with the Pakistani government against leaders of extremist groups*. The respondent is then offered the choice of: support, oppose, don't know, or refuse to answer.[75]

The independent variables are operationalized in the following manner. Education is operationalized with a question that asks the respondent the highest level of education she has completed. The more educated one is, the more likely one is to oppose drone strikes. We also use gender as a proxy for level of information, as we know that men tend to be more informed about political issues in Pakistan than women.

The anti-Americanism argument is operationalized using a straightforward question about favorability toward the United States: *Overall, do you think of the United States as more of a partner of Pakistan, more of an enemy of Pakistan, or neither?* We predict that respondents who say that they view the United States as more of an enemy of Pakistan will be more likely to oppose the drone strikes.

The argument about support for democratic norms is operationalized using the question: *Democracy is preferable to any other kind of*

---

[75]Given that many of the independent variables ask respondents questions that could pull on the same underlying values, it is important to ensure that multicollinearity is not an issue for our model. To do so, we obtained Variance Inflation Factor Scores. The mean VIF was 1.26, with the highest 1.64. All are well below the typical threshold of 10 for excessive collinearity.

government. The respondent was given the option of agreeing or disagreeing with that statement. We hypothesize that those who agree with the statement will be less supportive of drones.

One of the major arguments made in favor of drone strikes in Pakistan is that they kill foreign terrorists such as al Qaeda. Thus, we hypothesized that those who fear al Qaeda would be more in favor of drone strikes. We used the following question to operationalize this: *How serious a threat is al Qaeda to our country? Is it a very serious threat, a somewhat serious threat, a minor threat, or not a threat at all?* We predict that those who do not think al Qaeda is a threat to Pakistan will be more opposed to the drone program.

The variable relating to a respondent's view on the role Islam should play in Pakistan is operationalized by the question: *How much of a role do you think Islam plays in the political life of our country—a very large role, a fairly large role, a fairly small role, or a very small role?* If the respondent answered the question, they were then asked: *In your opinion, is this good or bad for the country?* If the respondent answered that Islam played a fairly small or very small role in the political life of the country and that this was bad, signifying Islamist tendencies, we expect that he or she would be more likely to oppose drone strikes. Likewise, if the respondent said that Islam played a fairly or very large role in the political life of the country and that this was good, we would expect him or her to be more likely to oppose drone strikes.

We do not use the survey questions about the necessity of drone strikes, whether too many innocents are killed, or whether they are done with or without the approval of the Pakistani government, because these questions had too many missing cases and would not allow for analysis of the variation in responses toward the dependent variable.

We add a control for income. This variable is added because it could have effects on the dependent variable, although we do not have theoretical priors about its causal relationship to the dependent variable.

ANALYSIS

The data came from the 2010 Pew Global Attitudes Survey, which collected the views of 2000 Pakistanis on a range of issues. Because of missing cases resulting from some questions, we used a sample of 1,681 respondents.

Before proceeding, a brief discussion of the Heckman model is necessary. Although the purpose and nature of the methodology is clear, there is some disagreement about model specification and execution. Derek Briggs suggests that "it does not matter whether the covariates in the selection function differ from those in the response schedule."[76] He goes on to note that it is often suggested that the selection function contain at least one variable not included in the outcome model or that the response model contain none of the variables included in the selection function. In a test of the Heckman model, Briggs found that selection functions containing slightly different model specifications can produce vastly different results. Furthermore, flawed model specification can produce inflated standard error results due to multicollinearity.

The first model in Table 5 presents an analysis of which Pakistanis opt to respond to questions related to drones. While our previous analysis of the correlation between "don't know" responses and our dependent variable demonstrates which citizens are more or less likely to respond, the response model allows us to use the Heckman model to do so. We suggest that males are more likely to respond, along with individuals who are more highly educated and better informed. Since we must include a variable in the response model that is not in the selection model, we choose to include a

TABLE 5
Heckman Logistic Regression Results

Dependent Variable-Oppose Drones

Independent Variables	Selection Model Coeff.	Standard Error	Response Model Coeff.	Standard Error	Marginal Effects
Pro-democracy (high = agree)			−.081	.070	
Al Qaeda is a threat (high = very serious threat)			.007	.030	
Islamic influence (high = large and good)			.020	.013	
Education (high = post-graduate)	.273***	.030	.131***	.041	.038
Gender (high = male)	.713***	.065	.538***	.085	.157
United States is enemy (high = more of an enemy)			−.143**	.053	.042
Income (high = more income)			−.043	.032	
Internet usage (high = more usage)	.419***	.135			
Constant	−1.130	.083	−1.296	.248	
N	888		793		
Wald X^2	90.84				
Prob > X^2	.000				
Log likelihood	−1,539.18				
LR test of independent equations	4.22				
Prob > X^2	.040				

Note: Figures are unstandardized coefficients shown alongside standard errors.
*$p < .1$; **$p < .05$; ***$p < .01$.

---

[76]Derek C. Briggs, "Causal Inference and the Heckman Model," *Journal of Educational and Behavioral Statistics* 29 (2004): 397–420, at 404.

variable that asks respondents how often they use the Internet. We believe those who use the Internet more regularly will be more aware of and knowledgeable about the drone program, and consequently more likely to respond. The same logic applies to Pakistanis who are more educated. Ultimately, we find evidence that being male, highly educated, and a regular Internet user makes respondents significantly more likely to respond to the question about drones that we use as our dependent variable in the response model.

The second model in Table 4 shows support for different hypotheses raised in this study. We will discuss each of our hypothesized categories of explanations presented in the response model. Beginning with the democratic norms category, we find no statistically significant relationship between attitudes toward democracy and attitudes toward drone strikes.

Looking at the support-for-militancy category, we do not find a significant relationship between Pakistani attitudes toward al Qaeda and support for drone attacks. Likewise, support for Islamism is not found to be a significant predictor: the variable utilized in our analysis (which combines questions about the amount of influence Islam has in Pakistan along with whether that influence is good or bad) does not have a clear relationship with citizen opinions of drones. Attitude toward the United States—as measured through a question asking if the United States is an enemy of Pakistan—is found to be a significant predictor of opinion about drones at the .01 level. Individuals who believe the United States is an enemy are more likely to oppose drone strikes.

Turning to our hypothesis regarding access to information, both predictors are statistically significant at the .01 level. Individuals with more education and males are both more likely to support the use of drones in Pakistan than other categories of respondents. Our sole control variable—income—does not emerge as a significant predictor in our response model.

Because we use the Heckman probit, the coefficients we present in Table 4 do not portray the marginal effects of the independent variables on the dependent variable. To help present a fuller picture, we report the marginal effects of our significant variables in Table 4 as well. The marginal effects measure the probability of a respondent opposing drones when all independent variables are held at their mean except for the variable of interest, which is moved from its minimum to its maximum value. Thus, we are able to assess the substantive effect of each independent variable to explain variation in the dependent variable. When we examine our model, the most substantively significant variable appears to be gender, with a first difference of .157. This means that solely by moving the variable from female to male, while holding all other variables at their mean or median, we see a 15.7 percent increase in the likelihood that a respondent will oppose drone strikes. Perceptions of the United States as an enemy (4.2 percent) and education (3.8 percent), all have smaller substantive effects.

CONCLUSIONS

This analysis sought to understand the landscape of Pakistani public opinion about American drone strikes in FATA. We used a Pew Global Attitudes Project survey from 2010 that has one of the best available question sets on Pakistani attitudes toward drone strikes. Our overview of Pakistani attitudes toward drone strikes shows that most Pakistanis (at least 43 percent) are unaware of the drone strikes in FATA. Those who are aware of the strikes and have an opinion oppose them by a margin of 20 percent.

The next goal of the study was to explain the variation we see in Pakistani public opinion toward the drone strikes: why do some Pakistanis oppose the drone strikes while others do not? We hypothesized that the primary driver of opposition to the drone strikes was the anti-drone discourse in the popular media. Since most Pakistanis' only source of information on the drone program is the Urdu-language media, they are exposed to a steady stream of negative stories about the drone strikes. We expected that the most-educated Pakistanis would be more likely to support the drone strikes because they tend to have access to more-varied sources of information (some of them in English) and thus are exposed to the pro-drone arguments presented in more-sophisticated Pakistani media sources, as well as in foreign media.

The results of the analysis bear out our argument. Pakistanis who have little education are most likely to be opposed to the drone strikes. Pakistani women, who are generally poorly educated and excluded from political discussions, tend to be more negative about the drones than men, as we expected.

We also found, as we expected, that views on the United States predict respondent views on drone strikes. The more negative the respondent was about the United States in general, the more likely he or she was to oppose drone strikes.

Interestingly, our prediction that a respondents' views on political Islam would influence her attitude toward the drone strikes was not borne out by the data. Respondents with Islamist tendencies did not seem more likely either to oppose or favor the strikes. This result illustrates the breadth and diversity of the Islamist spectrum in Pakistan; most Islamists do not support the militants who are the targets of the strikes.

Fear of or support for al Qaeda also does not seem to have much effect on Pakistanis' thinking about drones. This may be because Pakistanis think of the Pakistani Taliban as the main target of drone strikes. The Pakistani Taliban poses a much greater threat to Pakistan than al Qaeda does.

What do these results tell us about where public opinion in Pakistan is headed? We know that Pakistani public opinion matters when it comes to this issue. The media reacts to it, as does the government and even the military. Public opinion does not drive policy on this issue, but it constrains the range of options available to U.S. and Pakistani authorities. The United States is trying to reduce the negative consequences of drone strikes, in FATA in particular, in order to minimize the chances of enflaming public sentiment. This effort includes the use of new, more-accurate weapons, but also a reduction in strikes. The United States is even giving Pakistan unarmed surveillance drones so that the drone war will no longer be solely an American effort. The drone war is not just a war against militants; it is also a fight to win over the Pakistani public.

This analysis makes a case that the U.S. government should be more assertive and transparent about its use of armed drones in Pakistan, and also that it should try to reach the large percentage of the population that does not know about the program in order to shape opinion in favor of the drone strikes. This outreach may involve radio, non-cable TV (such as *Pakistan TV*), or even local media, such as SMS texting in Urdu. The fact that so few Pakistanis have fixed attitudes about the program shows that there is, in fact, room for a genuine struggle over Pakistani public opinion. But the U.S. government, which has refused to discuss the program in Pakistan or even the United States, has not even entered the fray.*

---

*This article was originally published in *Political Science Quarterly* 129 (Spring 2014): 1–33.

The Rationality of Radical Islam

QUINTAN WIKTOROWICZ
KARL KALTENTHALER

WHY DO ISLAMIST RADICALS ENGAGE in high-cost/risk activism that exposes them to arrest, repression, and even death? At a group level, it appears perfectly rational: zealous contention places enormous pressures on adversaries and increases the likelihood that the group will achieve its objective. Robert Pape's study of suicide terrorism provides some empirical evidence that extreme forms of activism do indeed produce concessions from opponents.[1] Yet, although extreme tactics may be deployed as part of a logical, coherent, and rational strategy to maximize group goals, is it "rational" for the *individual* perpetrators? Why not free-ride off the efforts of others rather than jeopardize personal self-interest?

We argue that radical Islamic groups offer spiritual selective incentives to individuals who are concerned with the hereafter. Although some radical Islamists are compelled by economic incentives or personal psychological needs that may have nothing to do with religious conviction (the need for revenge against perceived oppressors, a need for a sense of empowerment, or a desire for prestige), religion matters for many. In cases where individuals take spirituality seriously, movement ideologies offer

---

[1] Robert Pape, "The Strategic Logic of Suicide Terrorism," *American Political Science Review* 97 (August 2003): 343–362.

QUINTAN WIKTOROWICZ has served in two senior positions at the White House and is the author of *Radical Islam Rising: Muslim Extremism in the West*. **KARL KALTENTHALER** is professor of political science at the University of Akron and adjunct professor of political science at Case Western Reserve University. He has published several books and articles on public opinion, counter-terrorism, and political economy.

strategies for fulfilling divine duties and maximizing the prospects of salvation on judgment day. In essence, these ideologies serve as heuristic devices or templates that outline the path to salvation. Where individuals believe that the spiritual payoffs outweigh the negative consequences of strategies in the here and now, high-cost/risk activism is intelligible as a rational choice.

This article uses al-Muhajiroun as a case study to demonstrate the rationality of radical Islam. Based in the UK, with branches throughout the Muslim world, this movement supported al Qaeda; *jihad* against the United States in Afghanistan, Iraq, and Saudi Arabia; terrorism against Israel; attacks against the United Nations; military coups against governments throughout the Muslim world; and the establishment of an Islamic state in Britain. After September 11, it garnered extraordinary media attention in the UK and raised serious concerns among governments combating Islamic terrorism. Although it was less radical than groups such as al Qaeda, al-Muhajiroun openly promoted an assortment of extremist causes and is a good example of high-cost/risk activism. The movement was formally disbanded in October 2004, but its activists continue to operate through two successor organizations: al-Ghurabaa' (the Strangers) and the Saviour Sect. Al-Muhajiroun's leader and founder, Omar Bakri Mohammed, left the UK for Lebanon in August 2005 and was barred from returning as a result of the British government's crackdown on Islamic extremism after the terrorist attacks on the Tube system earlier in July.[2]

The focus of this article is on how spiritual incentives inspire Islamic radicalism. As a result, it does not directly address why individuals initially chose al-Muhajiroun over more moderate Islamic organizations that require less sacrifice. Nor does it focus on the process of preference reordering. These are important issues and are addressed extensively by the first author in a separate publication, which points to the importance of social networks, low levels of prior religious knowledge, identity crises, negative experiences with moderate Islamic figures and organizations, the public outreach activities of al-Muhajiroun, and perceptions about the credibility of the movement's leader as compared with moderate alternatives and radical rivals.[3] All of these drew individuals into study circles, where they were socialized into the movement ideology.

---

[2] For details on the dissolution, see Quintan Wiktorowicz, *Radical Islam Rising: Muslim Extremism in the West* (Lanham, MD: Rowman & Littlefield, 2005), 213–217.
[3] Wiktorowicz, *Radical Islam Rising*.

For those who eventually accepted the ideology as "true Islam" (and this was heavily influenced by perceptions about the credibility of the movement leader as an interpreter of Islam rather than the superiority of al-Muhajiroun's spiritual incentives relative to other groups),[4] why did they engage in high-cost/risk activism? Why not simply continue taking lessons without graduating to riskier behaviors? In other words, why not free-ride off the sacrifice of others?

We argue that the choice to move to high-cost/risk activism can be understood as a rational decision if we take the content of the movement's ideology seriously. Al-Muhajiroun's ideology outlines an *exclusive* strategy to salvation, which entails a number of costly and risky behaviors. Any deviations from this strategy mean that an individual will not enter Paradise, thus eroding tendencies toward free-riding. For those who accepted the movement ideology and sought salvation, a refusal to engage in high-cost/risk activism was tantamount to violating self-interest, because it meant that they would go to Hell.

Before proceeding, it is important to note limitations in conducting fieldwork on radical Islamic groups. The primary obstacle is access. Although surveys and large samples are preferable, they are rarely possible, given the secretive nature of these movements. As a result, one is left with small samples of respondents and ethnographic methods, if access is granted. In this study, the first author conducted thirty interviews (many tape-recorded) with movement leaders and activists and interacted with about one hundred other activists and movement "supporters." In addition, he attended movement-only lessons, public study circles, demonstrations, and community events, and collected movement documents and audio/written materials, including leaflets, protest announcements, training books, taped lessons/talks, and press releases. Although this hardly represents a probability sample of individuals, publications, and activities, the fieldwork results offer rare empirical evidence that addresses individual rationality.

RATIONAL RADICALISM?
Most studies of the causes of Islamism offer a grievance-based explanation implicitly rooted in functionalist social psychology accounts of mass behavior, which view collective action as derived from exogenous structural strains, system disequilibrium, and concomitant pathologies (alienation, anomie, atomization, normative ambiguity, etc.) that create individual

---

[4]See Wiktorowicz, *Radical Islam Rising*.

frustration and motivation for "deviant" social behavior.[5] The model posits a linear causal relationship in which structural strains, such as modernization, industrialization, or an economic crisis, cause psychological discomfort, which, in turn, produces collective action. The implication is that participation is the result of "irrationality."

The preponderance of research argues that the underlying impetus for Islamic activism derives from the crises produced by failed secular modernization projects in the Middle East.[6] Rapid socioeconomic transformations and manipulated economic policies concentrated wealth among the Westernized elites, state bourgeoisie, and corrupt government officials. Large swathes of the population, in contrast, faced housing shortages, insufficient municipal services and infrastructure, rising prices, declining real wages, and unemployment. The professional classes and lumpen intelligentsia, in particular, faced blocked social mobility and relative deprivation as a result of economic malaise and widespread employment preferences that emphasized *wasta* (connections) above merit.[7] The crises were compounded by the bitter Arab defeat in the 1967 war with Israel, the legacy of colonialism and cultural imperialism, and political repression.[8] According to this perspective, individuals responded by seeking to re-anchor themselves through a religious idiom.

Rather than viewing Islamists as grievance-stricken reactionaries, recent research has reconceptualized Islamic activists as strategic thinkers engaged in cost-benefit calculations. Lisa Anderson, for example, observes that "the closer the movements were to the prospects of sharing power, the

---

[5]See, for example, Ralph H. Turner and Lewis Killian, *Collective Behavior* (Englewood Cliffs, NJ: Prentice-Hall, 1957); William Kornhauser, *The Politics of Mass Society* (Glencoe, IL: The Free Press, 1959); Neil J. Smelser, *Theory of Collective Behavior* (New York: Free Press, 1962).

[6]Susan Waltz, "Islamist Appeal in Tunisia," *Middle East Journal* 40 (Autumn 1986): 651–670; R. Hrair Dekmejian, *Islam in Revolution: Fundamentalism in the Arab World*, 2nd ed. rev. (Syracuse, NY: Syracuse University Press, 1995); Valerie J. Hoffman, "Muslim Fundamentalists: Psychosocial Profiles" in Martin E. Marty and R. Scott Appleby, eds., *Fundamentalisms Comprehended* (Chicago, IL: University of Chicago Press, 1995); Mahmud A. Faksh, *The Future of Islam in the Middle East* (Westport, CT: Praeger, 1997).

[7]Saad Eddin Ibrahim, "Anatomy of Egypt's Militant Islamic Groups: Methodological Notes and Preliminary Findings," *International Journal of Middle East Studies* 12 (December 1980): 423–453; Hamied N. Ansari, "The Islamic Militants in Egyptian Politics," *International Journal of Middle East Studies* 16 (March 1984): 123–144; Henry Munson, Jr., "The Social Base of Islamic Militancy in Morocco," *Middle East Journal* 40 (Spring 1986): 267–284; Waltz, "Islamist Appeal in Tunisia," 651–670; Hoffman, "Muslim Fundamentalists"; Carrie Rosefsky Wickham, *Mobilizing Islam: Religion, Activism, and Political Change in Egypt* (New York: Columbia University Press, 2002), chapter three.

[8]Yvonne Y. Haddad, "Islamists and the 'Problem of Israel': The 1967 Awakening," *Middle East Journal* 46 (Spring 1992): 266–285; Franois Burgat and William Dowell, *The Islamic Movement in North Africa* (Austin: Center for Middle Eastern Studies at The University of Texas at Austin, 1993); Nikki R. Keddie, "The Revolt of Islam, 1700 to 1993: Comparative Considerations and Relations to Imperialism," *Comparative Studies in Society and History* 36 (July 1994): 463–487; John L. Esposito, *Islam and Politics*, 4th ed. (Syracuse, NY: Syracuse University Press, 1998).

more pragmatic they appeared to be."[9] Empirical studies of the Muslim Brotherhood in Jordan illustrate this point: the Brotherhood has demonstrated its willingness to sacrifice ideological ideals for political gains.[10] And movement activists make strategic decisions about organizational resources and relationships,[11] participation in political alliances,[12] responses to economic liberalization,[13] and intra-movement competition.[14]

Even radical movements previously described as unflappable, ideological zealots trapped by rigid adherence to dogma are now analyzed as strategic thinkers. Shaul Mishal and Avraham Sela, for example, argue that Hamas strategically responds to changes in the political context.[15] Prior to the al-Aqsa intifada in 2000, the growing popularity of the Palestinian-Israeli peace process challenged the viability of Hamas. Strict intransigence toward peace was likely to erode support from a population that sought an end to the economic and social hardships of occupation, thereby threatening the organizational survival of Hamas. In response, Hamas tactically adjusted its doctrine to accommodate the possibility of peace by framing it as a temporary pause in the *jihad*. Mohammed M. Hafez uses an implicit rational-actor model to explain Muslim rebellions in Algeria and Egypt during the 1990s. He contends that violence erupted as a response to "an ill-fated combination of institutional exclusion, on the one hand, and on the other, reactive and indiscriminate repression that threaten[ed] the organizational resources and personal lives of

---

[9]Lisa Anderson, "Fulfilling Prophecies: State Policy and lslamist Radicalism" in John L. Esposito, ed., *Political Islam: Revolution, Radicalism, or Reform?* (Boulder, CO: Lynne Rienner, 1997), 26.

[10]Sabah El-Said, *Between Pragmatism and Ideology: The Muslim Brotherhood in Jordan*, policy paper no. 3 (Washington DC: The Washington Institute for Near East Policy, 1995); Glenn Robinson, "Can Islamists Be Democrats? The Case of Jordan," *Middle East Journal* 51 (Summer 1997): 373–388; Malik Mufti, "Elite Bargains and the Onset of Political Liberalization in Jordan," *Comparative Political Studies* 32 (February 1999): 100–129; Quintan Wiktorowicz, *The Management of Islamic Activism: Salafis, the Muslim Brotherhood and State Power in Jordan* (Albany: The State University of New York Press, 2001).

[11]Christopher Alexander, "Opportunities, Organizations, and Ideas: Islamists and Workers in Tunisia and Algeria," *International Journal of Middle East Studies* 32 (November 2000): 465–490; Wiktorowicz, *The Management of Islamic Activism;* Ziad Munson, "Islamic Mobilization: Social Movement Theory and the Egyptian Muslim Brotherhood," *The Sociological Quarterly* 42 (Fall 2001): 487–510; Diane Singerman, "The Networked World of Islamist Social Movements" in Quintan Wiktorowicz, ed., *Islamic Activism: A Social Movement Theory Approach* (Bloomington: Indiana University Press, 2004), 143–163.

[12]Benjamin Smith, "Collective Action with and without Islam: Mobilizing the Bazaar in Iran" in Wiktorowicz, ed., *Islamic Activism*, 185–204; Jillian Schwedler, "The Islah Party in Yemen: Political Opportunities and Coalition Building in a Transitional Polity" in Wiktorowicz, ed., *Islamic Activism*, 205–228.

[13]M. Hakan Yavuz, "Opportunity Spaces, Identity, and Islamic Meaning in Turkey" in Wiktorowicz, ed., *Islamic Activism*, 270–288.

[14]Janine Astrid Clark and Jillian Schwedler, "Who Opened the Window? Women's Activism in Islamist Parties," *Comparative Politics* 35 (April 2003): 293–312.

[15]Shaul Mishal and Avraham Sela, *The Palestinian Hamas: Vision, Violence, and Coexistence* (New York: Columbia University Press, 2000).

Islamists."[16] To defend themselves against regime repression, the Islamists went underground and formed exclusive organizations, leading to a process of encapsulation and radicalization. Stathis N. Kalyvas views the Islamist-led massacres that plagued Algeria in the 1990s as strategic assaults intended to deter civilian defections "in the context of a particular strategic conjuncture characterized by (a) fragmented and unstable rule over the civilian population, (b) mass civilian defections toward incumbents and (c) escalation of violence."[17] Several scholars have argued that the tactic of suicide bombing is rational in that it helps Islamic (and other) terrorist groups achieve their group goals.[18] And Michael Doran conceptualizes al Qaeda as a rational actor, arguing that "when it comes to matters related to politics and war, al Qaeda maneuvers around its dogmas with alacrity."[19] In this understanding, "al Qaeda's long-term goals are set by its fervent devotion to a radical religious ideology, but in its short-term behavior, it is a rational political actor operating according to the dictates of realpolitik."[20]

Although these studies represent a clear departure from caricatures of zealots narrowly driven by grievances, they tend to focus on the group as the unit of analysis. In other words, tactics and activism are viewed as rational in the sense that they are effective means for promoting group goals. But what about the individuals who actually engage in activism on behalf of the group? Why do individuals within these groups voluntarily agree to engage in personally risky actions? In research on Islamic extremism, there has been surprisingly little research at the *individual* level of analysis from a rational-actor perspective.

In addressing this lacuna, our starting point is the rational-choice emphasis on individual strategies designed to produce personal payoffs. The strategy (or action) is the *best means* for the actor to achieve her most desired outcome or preference, given available information. Rational-choice theory does not provide an explanation of preference formation, but rather offers a framework for explaining strategy choices under a given

---

[16] Mohammed M. Hafez, *Why Muslims Rebel: Repression and Resistance in the Islamic World* (Boulder, CO: Lynne Rienner, 2003), 21–22.
[17] Stathis N. Kalyvas, "Wanton and Senseless? The Logic of Massacres in Algeria," *Rationality and Society* 11 (August 1999): 245.
[18] Ehud Sprinzak, "Rational Fanatics," *Foreign Policy* 120 (September/October): 66–73; Assaf Moghadam, "Palestinian Suicide Terrorism in the Second Intifada: Motivations and Organizational Aspects," *Studies in Conflict and Terrorism* 26 (March/April 2003): 65–92; Pape, "The Strategic Logic of Suicide Terrorism," 343–362.
[19] Michael Doran, "The Pragmatic Fanaticism of al Qaeda: An Anatomy of Extremism in Middle Eastern Politics," *Political Science Quarterly* 117 (Summer 2002): 178.
[20] Ibid., 182.

set of stable, ordered preferences. Rationality is evaluated in terms of whether the strategy is intended to obtain an individual's primary preference, not according to whether the preference itself seems reasonable to the outside observer. In other words, we cannot judge an action as irrational simply because we do not agree with the studied actor's preference ordering. As long as the actor committing the action believes that she is seeking to optimize her top preference, the individual is acting in a rational manner.[21]

So how does a rational-choice perspective help us understand the high-cost/risk activism of the activists in al-Muhajiroun and other radical Islamic groups? On the face of it, participation seems to defy the logic of collective action. Islamic radicals are, in essence, offering to produce collective goods that will benefit all Muslims: establishment of the Islamic state, expulsion of the United States from Muslim lands, divine justice, etc. This presents a classic collective action problem: why would individuals choose to contribute to the production of the collective good when they can free-ride off the efforts of others? This question is especially pertinent given the risks and costs associated with radical Islamic activism.

Rational-choice theory points to the use of selective incentives or side payments as means of inducing participation and overcoming the free-rider dilemma. These are benefits that individuals only accrue if they contribute to the collective good.[22] Although early models of rational choice assumed that individuals were primarily interested in maximizing some wealth function,[23] scholars have since expanded their view of human preferences. For example, rational-choice studies of voting behavior have focused on nontangible incentives to explain why an individual chooses to vote regardless of whether her vote is really likely to maximize the probability of producing a particular public policy outcome vis-à-vis the election. Voting is seen as providing nontangible psychological gratification for those who feel as though they are fulfilling their civic duty.[24]

Most radical Islamic groups offer a nontangible *spiritual* incentive to attract participants: participation produces salvation on judgment day and

---

[21]Jon Bister, "Introduction," in Jon Bister, ed., *Rational Choice* (New York: New York University Press, 1986), 4.
[22]Mancur Olson, *The Logic of Collective Action* (Cambridge, MA: Harvard University Press, 1965), 133–134.
[23]Gary Becker, "The Economic Approach to Human Behavior" in Jon Elster, ed., *Rational Choice*, 109.
[24]Brian Barry, *Sociologists, Economists, and Democracy* (New York: Macmillan, 1978); William Riker and Peter Ordeshook, "A Theory of the Calculus of Voting," *American Political Science Review* 62 (March 1968): 25–42; William Riker and Peter Ordeshook, *Introduction to Positive Political Theory* (Englewood Cliffs, NJ: Prentice Hall, 1973).

entrance to Paradise in the hereafter. The difference among Islamic groups is over *how the spiritual payoff should be pursued* (that is, strategy). Each proffers its ideology as an "efficient" (and often exclusive) path to salvation, which serves as a heuristic device for indoctrinated activists to weigh the costs and benefits of certain actions and behaviors. A cornerstone of these ideological templates is that individuals must face high risks and costs because God demands this as a condition for the spiritual payoff. In other words, radical Islamists choose to face great personal risks and costs because otherwise they are not pursuing their self-interest. Just as importantly, because individuals are judged as *individuals* on judgment day according to whether they personally followed the commands of God, free-riding jeopardizes salvation.

In this sense, even seemingly altruistic behavior can be understood as rational self-interest. A study of Mother Teresa, for example, argues that:

> While empathetic and self-sacrificial, Mother Teresa's charity ... was not altruistic, that is, motivated strictly by the desire to benefit the recipient without expectation of external reward. "Works of love," she laid down, "are always a means of becoming closer to God" (Mother Teresa 1985: 25).... Closeness to God, not the alleviation of human pain itself, was the preferred religious product. Indeed in Mother Teresa's assessment, poverty, suffering, and death were positive occasions of divine contact and imitation.[25]

This is not to argue that tangible selective incentives are irrelevant. Islamic groups in Egypt, for example, provide material incentives to attract supporters, including jobs, health services, education, day care, and financial support.[26] In Jordan, the Muslim Brotherhood's charity network provides patronage employment and selective access to goods and services.[27] Both Hamas and Hizballah provide social services and basic goods and services to communities and supporters. And there is evidence that at least some (although most likely a small minority) of those who joined the Armed Islamic Group in Algeria did so to obtain the economic benefits of insurgency, such as smuggling.[28] The point is not to dismiss these material payoffs, but rather to highlight the importance of nontangible incentives as

---

[25] Susan Kwilecki and Loretta S. Wilson, "Was Mother Teresa Maximizing Her Utility? An Idiographic Application of Rational Choice Theory," *Journal for the Scientific Study of Religion* 37 (June 1998): 211.
[26] Denis J. Sullivan, *Private Voluntary Organizations in Egypt: Islamic Development, Private Initiative, and State Control* (Gainesville: University of Florida Press, 1994); Wickham, *Mobilizing Islam*.
[27] Wiktorowicz, *The Management of Islamic Activism*, 83–110.
[28] Luis Martinez, *The Algerian Civil War* (New York: Columbia University Press, 2000).

well. This is particularly important when considering radical Islamic groups that offer few tangible rewards but demand risky activities.

We argue that in the case of al-Muhajiroun, the perceived spiritual payoffs outweighed the risks and costs associated with activism for those who chose to participate. Indoctrinated individuals viewed activism and even risk itself as means to achieve salvation and entrance into Paradise. Guided by the movement ideology, participants viewed suffering and effort as a testament to the certitude of belief (assurance that they would achieve the spiritual payoffs). From this perspective, the strategy of high cost/risk is strategically rational.

A CASE STUDY: AL-MUHAJIROUN

Omar Bakri Mohammed (known as OBM) launched al-Muhajiroun (AM) in the UK in 1996 after leaving Hizb uh-Tahrir.[29] It subsequently became the most visible radical Islamic movement in the country and spread throughout the UK in a number of different cities and neighborhoods. AM also established branches in a variety of other countries, including Lebanon, Ireland, the United States, and Pakistan (this branch eventually claimed independence from the overall al-Muhajiroun movement), which were connected through cyberspace meetings, lectures, lessons, and public events.

After September 11, AM became a central focus in debates about political expression and national security in the UK because of its support for the use of violence. A core tenet of the movement was the use of military coups to establish Islamic states wherever there are Muslims, including Britain. It also condoned the use of violence against Western militaries operating in Muslim countries. AM activists encouraged Britons to fight for the Taliban against American-led forces in Afghanistan,[30] and AM issued a statement supporting *jihad* against coalition forces in Iraq in 2003.[31] OBM and leaders in AM issued other controversial statements as well, including *fatwas* (jurisprudential opinions) condoning attacks against John Major and Tony Blair if they set foot in a Muslim country and a statement supporting the 1998 U.S. embassy bombings in Africa.[32]

---

[29] AM was originally formed in Saudi Arabia as a "cover" for Hizb uh-Tahrir activities during the 1980s, but OBM was forced to flee the country and settled in the UK.
[30] *The Observer*, 28 October 2001; *The Associated Press*, 7 January 2002; *Agence France Presse*, 4 December 2002.
[31] Al-Muhajiroun, "Fight the Invaders vs. Stop the War," 20 March 2003.
[32] These statements were widely covered in the press and confirmed in the first author's interviews with Omar Bakri in 2002.

Perhaps the most contentious action came a year after September 11 when AM sponsored a conference titled "A Towering Day in History" at the Finsbury Park Mosque, reflecting upon the consequences of the attacks and the aftermath for Muslims. The advertising for the conference was framed in such a way that it implied a "celebratory tone," and the press billed it as an event commemorating the triumph of September 11, which did not sit well with the public.[33] Eight months later, reports indicated a possible connection between al-Muhajiroun and the British suicide bombers who killed three Israelis during an attack on Mike's Place, a bar in Tel Aviv.[34] This was followed by advertise ment for a second September 11 event titled "The Magnificent 19" (referring to the nineteen hijackers), which was prevented from being held.

In the UK, there were 160 "formal members" known as *hizbis* (partisans). The small number reflects a selective induction process: individuals only became members after the leadership was convinced that they had fully internalized the movement ideology. As OBM explained, a member of the movement "is an identical copy of the way I think, and he has my adopted culture [ideology], and he teaches it to the people."[35] These activists were qualified to develop and teach others: they were authorized to give lessons and to speak to the public on behalf of the movement. As "life cells," formal members were often sent to other countries to establish branches, indicating OBM's confidence in their ideological internalization.

There were also 700 "students," who took weekly lessons taught by OBM and the formal members. Although these students were not formal members, the vast majority participated in the array of movement activities and took on risk and cost on behalf of the cause. Some even held leadership positions. In the U.S. branch of the movement in the 1990s, for example, the al-Muhajiroun's spokesperson was not actually a formal member. He did not attend the formation meeting that established the branch in 1996, and lived in Springfield, Missouri, far away from the New York City branch headquarters and the movement leadership.[36] To confuse matters further, many of the students referred to themselves as "members," something the

---

[33] See, for example, "Radical Muslim Clerics to Meet on Sept. 11 to Celebrate Anniversary of Attacks," *The Associated Press*, 7 September 2002; "London Rally to 'Celebrate' Terror Attacks," *Sunday Times*, 8 September 2002; "Fanatics to Meet to 'Celebrate' Twin Towers Terror Attacks," *Sunday Mirror*, 8 September 2002.

[34] "British Urged to Curb Anti-Semitic Incitement," *The Times*, 14 May 2003. Al-Muhajiroun responded to the reports by denying the connection ("Blatant Lies from the Sunday Times," al-Muhajiroun Press Release, 4 May 2003).

[35] First author's interview with Omar Bakri Mohammed, London, December 2002.

[36] First author's interview with this activist by phone, April 2003.

formal members encouraged to make students feel important.[37] To make some distinctions, in this article we use the term "activist" to refer to both formal members as well as committed students who participated in risky activism. "Member" refers only to those committed activists who actually went through the formal membership process (the *hizbis*).

At the periphery of the movement, there were thousands of "contacts," potential participants who attended a handful of lessons and events.[38] These contacts were, in effect, sampling al-Muhajiroun's activities to see whether they wanted to become more deeply involved. Although newspapers erroneously reported an estimated 7,000 al-Muhajiroun "members," this number probably accurately represented the number of contacts. Alone, however, the number tells us very little, inasmuch as it is impossible to determine the level of commitment within this aggregate. Some contacts may have come to a single public event. Others may have indulged in deeper religious sampling and may have progressed toward becoming actual students.

Participation in the high-profile and contentious activism of the movement carried a number of costs and risks for activists, particularly in the post-September 11 period. There were enormous commitments of time and energy, including religious training, outreach projects, and public demonstrations. Activists sacrificed relationships with former friends, family, and the mainstream Muslim community. And they were subject to an assortment of laws related to terrorism, treason, public order, and inciting religious and racial hatred. Arrests were common, and activists were conscious that their participation risked legal consequences. At first glance, it appears that they were engaged in irrational behavior that threatened self-interest.

COSTS FOR THE COMMITED ACTIVIST

Gregory L. Wiltfong and Doug McAdam argue that in deciding whether to participate in activism, individuals are influenced by a subjective assessment of costs and risks.[39] *Risks* are threats to an individual's well-being, such as threats to employment or physical safety. *Costs* are factors associated with the demands of participation that require the sacrifice of other commitments or interests. According to rational-actor models, we expect that individuals are unlikely to participate in high-risk, high-cost activism

---

[37]First author's interviews with various activists, UK, March, June, and December 2002.
[38]First author's interview with Omar Bakri Mohammed, December 2002.
[39]Gregory L. Wiltfang and Doug McAdam, "The Costs and Risks of Social Activism: A Study of Sanctuary Movement Activism," *Social Forces* 69 (June 1991): 987–1010.

unless there is an offsetting payoff. From this perspective, the behavior of AM activists appears irrational at first glance, given the dangers and sacrifices derived from belonging to the movement.

Perhaps one of the most important indicators of high *cost* is the time commitment, as demonstrated by the dizzying array of weekly activities. Although these activities were only required for formal members, committed students participated in them as well, thus incurring the general time costs. So although the activities detailed below are outlined in terms of formal-member requirements, they were attended by activists in general.

Members were required to attend a two-hour study session held by the local *halaqah* (circle) every week, unless they were excused because of traveling needs, sickness of a family member, an emergency, or permission of the leader.[40] These circles were intensive, member-only religious lessons that revolved around the movement ideology, and students had to spend time preparing. Given the intensity of these sessions, a lack of preparation incurred the ire of OBM and social pressure from other participants, thereby discouraging consistent indolence.[41] The overall tone at these lessons was captured in the movement bylaws: "Each member must understand that the Halaqah is a serious discussion and not a chat."[42] Although the *halaqah* sessions were only scheduled for two hours, many ran much longer. The first author attended a Thursday session at the movement's headquarters that lasted from 9:00 p.m. until 1:30 a.m. Interviews with participants indicated that this particular lesson typically ran until 5:00 a.m.

Members were required to host at least one public study circle, which was advertised at the local mosque and in the movement newsletter; and there were numerous AM-sponsored public talks, *tafsirs* (explanations of Qur'anic verses), and community events, which were intended to draw interest from potential recruits.[43] Although some of these activities were not "required," all those interviewed stated that they tried to go to as many as possible, in some instances traveling with OBM throughout the country (usually during the evenings). The first author's own participation at public talks and community events in London, Slough, and Luton indicated that this was indeed the case.

Every Saturday, members were required to set up a *da'wa* (propagation) stall in their local community from 12:00 p.m. until 5:00 p.m. In reality, these tended to start a bit later (usually a half hour or an hour late) but

---

[40] Al-Muhajiroun, *The Administration of al-Muhajiroun*, no date.
[41] This pressure was observed by the first author at a movement-only lesson in June 2002.
[42] Al-Muhajiroun, *Administration*.
[43] Ibid.

generally lasted at least four hours. They were held outside local Tube stops, public libraries, municipal buildings, and other public locales. The stalls reflected an activist *da'wa*, which centered on raising public awareness about the plight of Muslims and responsibilities in defending the global *umma* (Muslim community). Activists put up posters, chanted slogans, shouted through loudspeakers, and interacted with observers and passing pedestrians. In effect, these were small protest rallies, usually attended by about ten to twenty local activists.

Members also participated in weekly demonstrations that lasted approximately two hours. The particular topic of the protests varied from week to week, depending upon the "pressing issue" of the day, and they could be volatile events. At a rally outside the Pakistani embassy, protesters screamed "Musharaf, we are coming to kill you!" and chanted slogans, such as "Musharaf watch your back, Bin Laden coming back."[44] Other examples include demonstrations against the governments of Egypt, India, and Qatar. There were also a number of other required functions, including a monthly meeting of all members and special events (such as during Ramadan). In addition, the movement encouraged members to commit themselves to independent activities and community outreach (for example, following politics and news, studying the ideas of other movements, and promoting the movement ideology through interactions at work, school, and the mosque). This was based on movement principles about the necessity of action and outreach;[45] and interviews indicated that movement members were dedicated to more than the bare minimum and voluntarily promoted the movement ideology in every aspect of their lives. One must also take into account routine Muslim rituals (prayer, fasting during Ramadan, etc.) and social interactions with other members, which often involved religious discussion, movement planning, and solidarity building. Considering that most members had jobs or were in school, this was an enormous sacrifice of time.

There was a set of disciplinary measures that provided sanctions for members who did not attend the required activities.[46] For example, if on three separate occasions within a single year a member failed to attend the *halaqah* or monthly gatherings or refused to distribute movement materials or attend movement activities (without a good excuse), the disciplinary proceedings called for the "complete expulsion from all Halaqah and closed monthlies and exclusion from all Administrative procedures of

---

[44]This event was tape-recorded by the first author.
[45]Al-Muhajiroun, *Administration*.
[46]Ibid.; first author's interviews with leaders and other members, 2002.

Al-Muhajiroun (including informing him/her about Al-Muhajiroun activities) for a period specified by the Mu'tamad [the leader responsible for the country branch of the move ment]."[47] In some cases, an individual might have legitimately believed he or she had a valid excuse. If the leadership did not agree, however, the individual was temporarily excluded from all *halaqahs* and closed monthlies for a minimum period of one month. In this case, the leader could also levy a modest fine before readmitting the offender.[48]

These sanctions were for *formal* members alone; and although this implies the importance of sanctions in motivating action, as Mancur Olson argues for small group dynamics, the fact that activists who were *not* formal members participated in many of the risky and costly activities indicates that there must have been some other incentive.

To maintain the flexibility necessary for the frenetic schedule of movement activities, some activists chose less-lucrative employment opportunities (part-time jobs, for example), thus incurring a material cost. Members were also required to pay dues and donate a portion of their salary to the movement, because AM was self-funded.[49] The donation was according to the individual's ability to pay (it generally seemed to follow the calculations used for Islamic charity).

Time commitments and the ideological views of the movement frequently produced social costs, the most important of which was related to family pressures. Almost uniformly, respondents in this study noted their parents' opposition to activism. Parents did not object to religious education per se, but they believed in a personal, apolitical Islam and set different goals, such as getting *halal* (religiously permitted) food in schools.[50] Some concerned parents contacted Zaki Badawi, founder of the Muslim Council of Britain, and asked him to intervene after discovering their children's involvement.[51] This kind of family opposition created social pres sure not to participate.

Nonetheless, activists defied their parents and participated. As one respondent put it, "They warn you and say don't go with these people, but then they see you are firm and what can they

---

[47] Al-Muhajiroun, *Administration*.
[48] Ibid.
[49] In an effort to maintain its independence, AM relies solely on its membership for funding and has, at least according to one member, turned down some sizable donations, including one from the Iranian government.
[50] For the typical concerns of Muslims in the UK, see Tariq Modood, "The Place of Muslims in British Secular Multiculturalism" in Nezar Al Sayyad and Manuel Castells, eds., *Muslim Europe or Euro-Islam: Politics, Culture, and Citizenship in the Age of Globalization* (Lanham, MD: Lexington Books, 2002).
[51] First author's conversation with Zaki Badawi, London, June 2002.

do?"[52] A Somali member reiterated this sentiment: "If the boys are convinced, the parents can't do much. They can tell them not to go, but they can't stop it."[53]

One rather common way that activists attempted to avoid familial friction was by hiding their involvement.[54] This, however, did not necessarily eliminate the social cost, because the ideology required propagation, leading to heated debates with family members. There is little evidence that traumatic altercations shattered families or created irreconcilable differences, but they certainly produced tensions. One joiner recalled that because his father "stands with Union Jack," they used to have rather heated discussions.[55] Another recounted a story in which he shocked his extended family as they discussed the stand-off between Pakistan and India in 2002 by boldly declaring his support for nuclear war. This, he argued, was a religious obligation and for the sake of Islam. His father was a staunch supporter of Britain, and this created a great deal of consternation.[56] These types of interactions indicate that although parental ignorance about participation may have softened family pressure, it was unlikely to eliminate the cost altogether.

RISKY ACTIVISM

All public displays of activism entail some risk, whether it is the possibility (even if remote) that a rally will degenerate into chaos or (in more extreme cases) result in death. One common measure of risk in studies of protest is the perceived possibility of arrest.[57] By this measure, the personal risk for those involved in AM was high. Large numbers of movement activists were arrested, and each public event was seen as a risky venture in which police intervention and arrest (or at least threats of arrest) were possible. The risks became accentuated in the post-September 11 period because al-Muhajiroun was often accused of supporting terrorism.

Arrests (or threats of arrest) frequently occurred at the *da'wa* stalls. It was not the act of protesting itself that raised risk but rather the

---

[52] First author's interview with Hassan, London, June 2002. Note: for rank-and-file members, pseudonyms or other anonymous indicators are used to protect the privacy of respondents.
[53] First author's interview with Somali member, London, June 2002.
[54] First author's interviews with Somali member, Kamal, and Mohammed (movement leader), London, June 2002.
[55] First author's interview with Rajib, Slough, June 2002.
[56] First author's interview with Khalid, London, June 2002.
[57] See, for example, Wilftang and McAdam, "The Costs and Risks of Social Activism," 987–1010.

presentation of grievances. Activists used "moral shock"[58] to evoke emotional responses and elicit sympathy for the cause, whether it was the plight of Iraqis, the Israeli occupation of Palestinian territories, or Indian repression in Kashmir. Pictures are more effective in generating visceral responses from observers, so AM activists used shocking pictures of mutilated and decapitated bodies. Pictures of malnourished or mutilated children were common because they evoked the most consistent emotional response, regardless of whether observers were Muslim. These pictures, more than anything else, drew the ire of police, who were frequently in attendance at the stall or were called in by local business owners and concerned citizens. Altercations with police over whether the pictures were "free speech" often led to arrests.

This was confirmed by observations at a *da'wa* stall outside a public library in London. About ten activists gathered around a display table and an easel adorned with grotesque pictures of the "oppressed": mutilated bodies from the alleged Israeli "Jenin massacres" (the UN did not find any evidence to support the accusations).[59] The pictures, to say the least, were shocking images—an old man with half his face missing, children with massive injuries, and bodies with organs exposed through the skin. The graphic nature of the pictures prompted a flood of calls to the police,[60] and six officers responded and arrived at the stall about an hour after it opened. The protesters were told that they could continue their message verbally and use pictures of bombed buildings, but that they had to remove the pictures of the mutilations. A heated argument ensued. The demonstrators argued that they were merely showing "the truth" (facts that the Western media refused to publish) so that people would understand what was happening to Muslims world wide. The police retorted that the pictures were offensive and that because they were being displayed in a public place, bystanders (including children) had no choice about exposure. The argument was impassioned, and the police threatened arrest. In this particular case, the pictures were taken down. AM activists cited the confrontation as another example of Western repression against Muslims. Interviews with various members of AM, a police officer at the scene, and eight participants at the stall

---

[58] James M. Jasper and Jane Poulsen, "Recruiting Strangers and Friends: Moral Shocks and Social Networks in Animal Rights and Anti-Nuclear Protests," *Social Problems* 42 (November 1995): 493–512; James M. Jasper, *The Art of Moral Protest: Culture, Biography, and Creativity in Social Movements* (Chicago, IL: University of Chicago Press, 1997).
[59] For more on the Israeli incursion into Jenin, see Human Rights Watch Report, "Jenin: IDF Military Operations," May 2002, accessed at http://www.hrw.org/reports/2002/israel3/, 18 April 2006.
[60] First author's interview with the lead police officer at the scene, London, June 2002.

indicated that this kind of altercation was common. Demonstrators were most frequently arrested under the Public Order Act, which provided wide latitude for police officers at the scene to determine whether it represented a public disturbance warranting arrest.[61]

There are other instances in which activists faced risk because of the content of the message. In one example, two members were arrested under the Public Order Act at a protest against homosexuals, because of a leaflet entitled "Gay Today, Pedophile Tomorrow?" They were both convicted and fined £160.[62] Another activist was arrested during a verbal tirade against Israel.[63] In a famous case, Iftikhar Ali, a movement leader, was arrested after distributing leaflets quoting passages from the Qur'an in a context that authorities interpreted as a threat against the Jewish community. He was found guilty of inciting racial hatred (Jews are considered an ethnic group under UK law) and sentenced to a £3,000 fine, a £1,500 reimbursement cost, and 200 hours of community service.[64] Several members lost employment as a result of their activism (religious discrimination is not currently covered by British law). And there was the ever-present risk of arrest under the new terrorism laws.

Anjem Choudary, the leader of the UK branch of AM, aptly summarized the risks and costs of participation:

> Being part of al-Muhajiroun is not really the most prestigious thing. People don't become a part and say "mashallah" [what God has willed, indicating a good omen] and go around saying I am a member of al-Muhajiroun because obviously we get attacked by the government and our members are arrested regularly at demonstrations and at stalls because they speak out openly and publicly about what they believe. They might get arrested because they talk about homosexuality or they might think he is a homophobe or think he is racist and anti-Semitic because he is talking about Palestine. We have had a number of prosecutions. You met Iftikhar Ali. He is the first person in this country to be arrested for incitement to religious hatred for quoting a verse from the text [Qur'an] which was considered to be racist. This has never happened before. It is a landmark decision and he is a member of our organization. If they join and stay that is because they believe in the cause, they believe in the struggle. We ask our members to interact with the culture and to go out regularly on talks and demonstrations, and they will attend weekly and monthly gatherings, and a fair amount of their time will be taken up. And obviously they will be asked

---

[61]Ibid.; first author's interviews with AM members, London, 2002.
[62]First author's interview with one of the arrested activists, London, June 2002.
[63]First author's interview with this activist, London, June 2002.
[64]See http://news.bbc.co.uk/2/hi/uk_news/england/1966839.stm, accessed 18 April 2006.

to contribute financially as well, because we don't receive any finances from the government. We contribute ourselves.[65]

In addition to the costs and risks of activism, there is an important question as to whether there would be a payoff in which the movement achieved its goals. Although AM may have affected the political views of some Muslims, its prospects for success in the UK were minimal, given that a primary stated goal was the establishment of an Islamic state in Britain. Even OBM recognized the futility: "Practically, it is not going to happen except in a Muslim country."[66]

The sense that activism was against individual self-interest is deepened by the availability of other fundamentalist groups whose activities entailed fewer risks (and lower costs, in some cases), including Hizb uh-Tahrir, Jama'a Tabligh, and various reformist Salafi groups, such as those at the Brixton Mosque and Jam'iat Ihyaa' Minhaaj al-Sunnah. In fact, AM offered very few unique selective incentives. For example, solidary incentives derived from group identity, social interactions, and religious activities were offered by other fundamentalist groups, including moderate movements. There were no material incentives, in the sense of magazines or concrete outputs available only to formal members. And other movements and groups offered similar purposive incentives because of their fervent religious missions. According to AM members themselves, all of the fundamentalist movements (moderate and radical, including AM) shared about 95 percent of the same religious precepts. So why take on the costs and risks? Without making a tautological argument (and implying that somehow radicals are deviants and psychologically disturbed because they get a psychological payoff from engaging in risky behavior), the observer is left with the initial impression that this behavior violated the principle of self-interest and thus reflects the irrationality of zealotry.

SPIRITUAL INCENTIVES AND HIGH-COST/RISK ACTIVISM

To make sense of why individuals would still participate in such activism, regardless of high costs/risks and the prospects for free-riding, one must address activist views of incentives and strategic assessments of utility. These were rooted in the movement ideology, which offered guidelines about what activists must do to achieve salvation. Deviations from the ideological proscriptions were interpreted as threats to an individual's utility maximization and desire to be saved on judgment day.

---

[65] First author's interview with Anjem Choudary, by phone, June 2002.
[66] First author's interview with OBM, London, June 2002.

The cornerstone of AM's ideology was its particular understanding of *tawhid*—the oneness of God. *Tawhid* begins with the *shahada*, or testimony of faith that signals a conversion to Islam: "I testify that there is no God except Allah and that Mohammed is His messenger." It defines God as the only true lord and sovereign of the universe worthy of worship. The Qur'an and *hadiths* (recorded traditions of the Prophet) are filled with dire warnings about the consequences for those who violate *tawhid* by ascribing partners to God (*shirk*) (in other words, polytheism):

> Lo! Whoso ascribeth partners unto Him, for him Allah has forbidden Paradise. His abode is in the Fire. For evil-doers there will be no helpers (Qur'an 5:72).
> Lo! Allah forgiveth not that a partner be ascribed Unto Him. He forgiveth (all) save that to who He will. Whoso ascribeth partners to Allah, he hath indeed invented a tremendous sin (Qur'an 4:48).

Although all Muslims accept the general principle of *tawhid*, there are differences over its precise meaning and application. Many Islamic fundamentalists, for example, reject traditional Sufi practices, such as praying at the tombs of saints, as examples of *shirk*. Even within the Islamic fundamentalist community there are differences. Some Islamic activists, for example, accept the possibility of working through democratic institutions, whereas others view adherence to man-made law as egregious *shirk*. What constitutes *shirk* is a matter of contention among Muslims.

For al-Muhajiroun activists, every action, decision, and behavior was seen as an act of worship if it was in accordance with divine law. Any deviation from the straight path of Islam, in contrast, represented a violation of *tawhid*. Those who adhered to *tawhid* gained entrance to Paradise; those who engaged in *shirk* would suffer the hellfires:

> Tawheed prevents man from eternally remaining in the Hellfire. The Prophet Mohammed (SAW) stated in an authentic report: Whoever dies and has so much as a mustard seed of faith in his heart shall enter al-Jannah [the garden of Paradise]. Faith here signifies a correct belief in Allah and His Messenger Mohammed (SAW) and all that they instructed, commanded and prohibited for mankind."[67]

The calculus for individuals is clear: follow the divine rules and receive a spiritual payoff; remain deviant and suffer eternal consequences. But what are the divine rules and how does an individual Muslim identify proper

---

[67] Omar Bakri Mohammed, *Kitab ul-Imaan*, movement training manual, n.d., 17.

adherence? Islamic movements offer religious interpretations represented in ideologies as guidelines to answer this question. These ideologies are, in essence, outlines of strategies for obtaining the spiritual payoff—what individuals must do to ensure salvation.

All Islamic fundamentalist groups base their proffered strategies on the model of the Prophet Mohammed—the Muslim exemplar whose path (*Sunna*) is considered the perfection of Islam in practice. There are divergences, however, over the specifics of the prophetic paradigm and its application in the contemporary context. Each group believes it is following the proper model and interpretation, and these differences matter in terms of the potential for salvation. The Prophet predicted that the Muslim community would fracture into sects after his death and warned his followers to remain focused on his example and the Qur'an for guidance: "I am leaving you two things and you will never go astray as long as you cling to them. They are the Book of Allah and my Sunnah."[68] Many fundamentalist groups believe that there is one correct understanding of the straight path of Islam; ipso facto, all others are deviations and will not receive divine reward. This thinking is based upon authentic *hadiths*, such as "And this Ummah will divide into seventy-three sects all of which except one will go to Hell and they are those who are upon what I and my Companions are upon."[69] Many groups consider themselves to be this "saved sect" (*firqa al-najiyya*) and therefore argue that their adherents will be saved on judgment day.

Al-Muhajiroun's particular interpretation of the model and its relevance for salvation was aptly captured by Omar Bakri Mohammed:

> The [prophetic] methodology is the only way. If I follow it, I remove the sin from my neck. The only way of accepting His command [God] is by following the methodology of the messenger of the Prophet Mohammed. So the Prophet he cultured society; he exposed man made law in society (commanding good and forbidding evil); and he sought support from those sincere [Muslims in the army] who accept Islam from him and give him power from the army. This is the only way we can remove the sin from our neck.[70]

OBM and other AM activists concluded that the only way for individuals to ensure personal salvation was to engage in these activities so as to

---

[68] As quoted in Jam'iat Ihyaa' Minhaaj Al-Sunnah, *A Brief Introduction to the Salafi Da'wah* (Ipswich, UK: Jam'iat Minhaaj Al-Sunnah, 1993), 5.
[69] Ibid., 3.
[70] First author's interview with Omar Bakri Mohammed, December 2002.

"remove the sin" from their necks. Thus, regardless of the risks and costs, individuals had to promote a proper understanding of Islam (a radical interpretation that included support for *jihad* against the United States, Russia, Israel, and others); publicly denounce un-Islamic behavior (including democracy) through overt activism; and work to establish the Caliphate (Islamic state) by means of a military coup (even in the UK).

Al-Muhajiroun argued that because the Prophet accomplished these duties by working with a group, individual Muslims must do likewise to "remove the sin" from their necks and receive a payoff in the hereafter. The AM ideology distinguished between divine duties that can be fulfilled as an individual and those that can only be fulfilled by working with other Muslims. The central argument is that the Prophet and his companions worked as individuals when they addressed *individuals*, but formed collectivities when addressing society. The various divine duties of activism, in particular, were fulfilled by working as groups. For AM, this was reflected in Qur'an 3:104: "Let there rise from among you group(s) calling society to Islam, commanding society to do what Allah orders and to refrain from what He forbids and these (group(s)) are the ones who are successful" (AM translation).

The emergence of a group, however, is not enough to remove sin. Those who fail to participate remain sinful and thus are not part of the saved sect. More importantly for a rational-choice perspective, group membership or belonging alone does not produce the desired spiritual payoff. The group is merely a vehicle for fulfilling individual obligations, so individuals still must engage in the methodology and fulfill duties to remove the sin from their necks. As Omar Bakri explained:

> If any one of them or some of them did a duty or engaged in any duty e.g. political struggle in any part of the world, it does not mean that all of them are rewarded for it, nor does it mean that all the members are fulfilling their duties, rather those who did it alone will be rewarded and will remove the sin from their necks whereas the others remain sinful if they did not fulfill their duties.[71]

This is because, as Omar Bakri argued, "Allah (swt) will account as individuals [on Judgment Day], not as an entity."[72] Where salvation on judgment day is a concern, this ideological precept essentially undermined the potential for free-riding within the group. Each individual had to engage in activism within the group, because he or she would not benefit

---

[71]Omar Bakri Mohammed, Questions and Answers, "Is the group an entity?" n.d.
[72]Ibid.

from the work of others. Only active participants received the payoff. Anjem Choudary, the UK leader of al Muhajiroun, nicely summarized the spiritual incentive for joining the movement: "The only benefit that they [the activists] have, which is a great benefit unto itself, is that they fulfill a duty and ultimately will be rewarded in the hereafter. We don't pretend they are going to get anything apart from that."[73]

A refusal to replicate the model in terms of the method (working with a group) or the specific duties jeopardized an individual's status in the hereafter. In effect, such a refusal was a rejection of *tawhid* and thus evidence of apostasy.[74]

Within the mechanism of the group, individuals had to fulfill three primary divine duties: educate Muslims about proper Islam (i.e., the movement ideology), including exhortations to *jihad*; actively command good and prevent evil through overt (and controversial) activism; and struggle to establish an Islamic state through a military coup. First, individuals had to engage in *tarbiya* (culturing society in proper Islamic belief and behavior) and *da'wa* (propagation). For al-Muhajiroun, this necessitated lessons and activities to teach people about their divine duties and responsibilities as Muslims, according to movement precepts. An important component of this was promoting support for *jihad* against infidels in Muslim lands as an individual Muslim obligation: "Any aggression against any Muslim property or land by any Kuffar [unbelievers] or non-Muslim forces whether American, British or Jews of Israel makes Jihad (i.e. fighting) against them an obligation upon all Muslims."[75] This mandated armed struggles against the Russians in Chechnya; the United States in Afghanistan, Iraq, and Saudi Arabia; India in Kashmir; Israel (both in the occupied territories and the state of Israel, which AM considered Muslim territory); and the United Nations (specifically in Iraq).[76]

Because *tawhid* demands the full application of divine law, al-Muhajiroun argued that all Muslims are obligated to fulfill the responsibility of *jihad* or risk jeopardizing salvation. Omar Bakri was explicit about this utility calculation at a conference titled "Terrorism and Osama Bin Laden" held in East London in 2000: "You all have an obligation to support the

---

[73] First author's interview with Anjem Choudary.
[74] Under many understandings of Islamic law, the ultimate sanction for an individual convicted of apostasy is death, although this is rarely enforced in practice.
[75] Shari'ah Court of the UK (an al-Muhajiroun organization headed by Omar Bakri), "Fatwa against the Illegitimate State of Israel," n.d.
[76] See, for example, Shari'ah Court of the UK, Case No. Russia *I* F4l, Fatwa Concerning the Russian Aggression, n.d.; Shari'ah Court of the UK, Fatwa on Jihad against the Illegitimate State of Israel; al-Muhajiroun Press Release, "The United Nations-A Legitimate Target?" 25 August 2003.

jihad. Or you will be punished on the Day of Judgment! You will get a reward for fighting. You must send your children to jihad."[77] Obviously, calling for such action amounted to support for terrorism and, in certain instances, even implied sedition when the call to *jihad* involved British interests, but the risks were acceptable for those who calculated costs and benefits in terms of the hereafter.

To save themselves and fulfill their duties toward *jihad*, AM activists practiced what they preached by providing not only verbal support but financial and physical assistance as well. AM openly raised money for *jihads* throughout the Muslim world, especially for Chechen rebels, *jihadis* in Kashmir, and *Hamas* in the Palestinian territories. Changes in anti-terrorism laws, however, made this fundraising illegal. Interviews with Omar Bakri indicate that financial support for the struggles might still have occurred through charity front organizations, which raised money for general "charitable" purposes. A number of activists actually went to fight in the *jihads*, not as representatives of al-Muhajiroun as an organization but as individuals fulfilling their personal duty to God "to support their Muslim brothers and sisters."[78]

The second divine duty fulfilled through the group was the command to promote virtue and prevent vice (*al-amr bi'l-ma-ruf wa'l-nahy 'an al-munkar*). Activism to fulfill this obligation was a required duty that must be fulfilled to follow *tawhid* and remain a Muslim. The movement cited the following *hadith*: "There is no prophet that Allah sent before me but he had supporters and companions who did what he said and obeyed his commands. After them there are many successors and they will say what they don't do and do what Allah forbids. Whoever fights them with his hand is a believer, whoever fights them with his tongue is a believer, whoever fights them with his heart is a believer and if you do nothing you can't claim you are a Muslim."[79] The punishment for those who failed to rise is the hellfires. The true believers and activists would receive eternal reward.

The third divine duty was to work for the reestablishment of the Caliphate (Islamic state). Once again, this duty was posited in terms of individual interest in removing sin to ensure personal salvation. Al-Muhajiroun argued that initially, after the collapse of the Caliphate in 1924, its reestablishment was a collective duty (*fard kifaya*), meaning an obligation that can be fulfilled by some on behalf of the *umma*. However,

---

[77] Aaron Klein, "My Weekend with the Enemy," *The Jerusalem Post*, 30 May 2000.
[78] Al-Muhajiroun press release, November 5, 2001.
[79] Omar Bakri Mohammed, *Jihad: The Method for the Khilafah?* (London: MNA Publications, no date), 19.

after a period of time without an Islamic state, "working to establish the Khilafah [Caliphate] [becomes] Fard [a divine duty] upon all Muslims (i.e., Fard Kifayah Muhattam) or a sufficient duty binding immediately without a time limit upon all Muslims and those who engage in it remove the sin and the burden on their necks until they accomplish the task. Whereas those who do not engage in working to establish the Khilafah nowadays are sinful [except for those exempted in sharia]."[80]

For AM, the proper method for establishing the Islamic state was a military coup. As a result, activists contacted members of the military in an attempt to foment a military rebellion that would seize power and establish the Caliphate. Because the religious sources did not specify a particular locale for the Islamic state, Muslims were obligated to work to establish it wherever they lived, including the UK.

In terms of individual calculations, it is irrelevant whether the prospects were likely to succeed. Omar Bakri readily admitted that the establishment of an Islamic state in the UK was highly unlikely. But success did not matter, because individuals are judged on the basis of whether they *worked* to establish the Caliphate. In other words, salvation does not hinge upon whether activists actually succeeded in reaching stated movement goals; they are judged according to whether they worked toward these objectives. The duty is the effort and not the outcome of collective action. The Qur'an emphasizes that divine reward and punishment are meted out according to whether individuals "go forth in the cause of Islam" (that is, exert effort):

> O ye who believe! What is the matter with you, that, when ye are asked to go forth in the cause of Allah, ye cling heavily to the earth? Do ye prefer the life of this world to the Hereafter? But little is the comfort of this life, as compared with the Hereafter. Unless ye go forth, He will punish you with a grievous penalty, and put others in your place; but Him ye would not harm in the least. For Allah hath power over all things (Qur'an 9:38-39).

When asked about whether a demonstration in front of the Indian embassy attracted much attention and support, Anjem Choudary could thus dismiss the importance of a large showing and media coverage as relatively irrelevant, because he "had fulfilled [his] duty to command good and forbid evil."[81]

---

[80] Omar Bakri Mohammed, Questions and Answers, "Are we obligated to work for the Khilafah" n.d.
[81] First author's interview with Anjem Choudary.

Rational-choice studies of rebellion have argued that individuals assess the prospects for success when deciding whether to participate;[82] but in the case of radical Islam, this outcome may be less important. At the individual level, the primary objective is not the establishment of an Islamic state or the success of a demonstration. These are only ways of fulfilling obligations to God, which, in turn, is the only way to achieve salvation. In terms of personal calculations, the very act of participation in itself produces the payoff in the hereafter.

Not only is high-cost/risk activism necessary to produce the desired outcome, but the act of suffering itself is viewed as a divine signal that the activist is on the right path and will achieve salvation as part of the saved sect. The Prophet initially suffered at the hands of the Quraysh (the dominant tribe in Mecca), yet continued to fulfill his obligations to God. AM activists emphasized that regardless of the difficulties, true believers speak out:

> The Prophet [Mohammed] and all the Anbiyya [Prophets], all the Sahabas [Companions], they got tortured, they struggled, they went through pain. For what? Was it because they testified? It was because they implemented in action. The Lord said "Why do you say something that you do not do, you do not act upon?" When we see the Prophet Mohammed, and the Anbiyya, and the Sahabas, they struggled, they did da'wa, they commanded good and forbid evil, they exposed the idolatry of the society, and they introduced the shahada. But no one is doing that today. This is an obligation that is upon every single Muslim when they see *munkar* [evil]. When they see evil and corruption, it becomes an obligation.[83]

This historical precedent was used for *qiyas* (reasoning by analogy), whereby hardships were interpreted as evidence that they were on the right path. In other words, what rational-actor models typically view as risks and costs associated with activism were in fact benefits to the AM participant who viewed them as confirmation of the correctness of belief:

---

[82]Susanne Lohmann "A Signaling Model of Informative and Manipulative Political Action," *American Political Science Review* 88 (June 1993): 319–333; Susanne Lohmann, "Dynamics of Informational Cascades: The Monday Demonstrations in Leipzig, East Germany, 1989-1991," *World Politics* 47 (June 1994): 42–101; Karl-Dieter Opp, *The Rationality of Political Protest: A Comparative Analysis of Rational Choice Theory* (Boulder, CO: Westview Press, 1989); Karl-Dieter Opp, Peter Voss, and Christiane Gem, *Origins of a Spontaneous Revolution: East Germany, 1989* (Ann Arbor: University of Michigan Press, 1993).

[83]First author's interview with Somali member.

> Al-Muhajiroun says, "Look at the Prophet Mohammed, he went to Taif, and he got stones thrown at him." I think why did he get stones thrown at him and we aren't getting stones thrown at us? So when I see the police and they come to us and speak to us, I say *"alhamdulillah* [praise be to God], we are on the right path." If they didn't come to us and said we are very nice people, we are wrong, because Allah said in the Qur'an: the Jews and Christians will never be happy with you until you follow their way of life.[84]

Activists believed that if the authorities treated them well, it was a sign that they were on the wrong path. The Prophet was attacked by the authorities of his day. Obviously, he was on the straight path as the messenger of God, and the authorities were unbelievers. Drawing an analogy to the present, activists believed that if the police or government accommodated a movement, it was a sign of incorrect beliefs. This was reflected in AM's disdain for the Muslim Council of Britain and scholars and movements throughout the Muslim world that cooperate with regimes. The ideology framed overtures and friendly gestures by the authorities as signs of an insidious plot to destroy the truth of Islam, based upon Qur'an 9:8: "Verily if the unbelievers have authority over you, they will not respect you any trust, agreement, or covenant. With their mouths they will have fair words in front of you but their hearts are averse from you and most of them are rebellious, betrayers, and wicked" (AM translation). As one respondent put it:

> I feel good because I feel that [our way] is the only way, because the only way to be a good Muslim is like this—as long as someone is struggling and finds everything against him, then that person is on the right path. The only way to know that someone is really on the right path is, for example, that all the leaders are against him, all the government people are against him. And they don't compromise. So as long as someone is trying and struggling then hopefully he is on the right path. The Prophet he was like that as well. Everyone was against him. He got kicked out of his home land, Mecca, and he had to go to Medina. So that is the way we look at it.[85]

In addition, respondents also maintained that suffering was part of a more general test of certitude and commitment. One activist argued that "it is a test for everyone. And Allah even said that there will be a time when the majority of people will leave Islam or will neglect Islam, and that He will replace people with those who fulfill his command."[86] Others referred to an

---

[84]Ibid.
[85]First author's interview with sixteen-year-old member, London, June 2002.
[86]First author's interview with Islam (local leader), London, June 2002.

oft-quoted *hadith* as evidence of the test of will: "Hold all of you fast to the rope of Allah and do not separate yourselves."

As a result, activists reveled in their tales of confrontation with the police as proof of their own beliefs and eventual salvation.[87] Suffering was affirmation, and movement participants saw themselves as following in the Prophet's shoes, in a way living his experience in modem times. The fact that the activists were condemned by the mainstream Muslim community furthered their conviction and certitude, because the Prophet and his companions were a minority in a sea of *jahiliyya* (disbelief). This produced quite a heady sense of purpose and certitude in a mission that was seen as providing activists with strategies for producing the spiritual payoff.

Comprehending radical Islam necessitates rendering individual decisions about participation and behaviors intelligible. Although recent work has shown that extremism is strategically rational at the group level, there is far less theorizing and data about the individual level of analysis. To address this, we have offered a rational-choice explanation that focuses on spiritual incentives. Radical Islamic movements offer an important spiritual incentive: join the group and engage in risky and costly activism and receive eternal salvation as part of the saved group.

This challenges perspectives that dismiss the possible usefulness of a rational-actor approach to Islamic activism. Roxanne Eueben, for example, argues that "even the most austere version of rational actor theory has very little to say about fundamentalism because, given its basic assumptions, it concludes only that fundamentalists have a revealed preference for fundamen talism."[88] But this kind of argument confuses religious methods with goals or interests. The preference is not for fundamentalism. Fundamentalism is a strategy or method for obtaining the preference of salvation as an end. It is a way of approaching religious interpretation that emphasizes literalism and strict adherence to *tawhid*. Activists follow this interpretive approach because they view it as an exclusive strategy for the pursuit of Paradise. If we recognize that value and instrumental rationalities are frequently related, radical Islamic activism becomes intelligible within a rational-actor framework.

---

[87]This was observed by the first author in several instances, including a large gathering of members prior to a lesson, where they swapped stories about confrontations with police.
[88]Roxanne L. Euben, *Enemy in the Mirror: Islamic Fundamentalism and the Limits of Modern Rationalism* (Princeton, NJ: Princeton University Press, 1999), 33.

We fully recognize that not everyone who participates in radical Islamic groups is driven by spiritual desires. It is folly to assume uniformity. In addition, there are almost certainly important differences between the utility calculations of leaders and those of followers and affiliates. This, of course, is open to empirical investigation. Our point is to initiate a broader understanding of rational action in the study of radical Islam by emphasizing the role of beliefs and relationships among ideology, individual utility calculations, and behavior. If we accept that religion does matter, seemingly irrational behavior becomes understandable as a rational choice.*

---

*This article was originally published in *Political Science Quarterly* 121 (Summer 2006): 295–319.

The Soft Underbelly of American Primacy: Tactical Advantages of Terror

RICHARD K. BETTS

In given conditions, action and reaction can be ridiculously out of proportion.... One can obtain results monstrously in excess of the effort.... Let's consider this auto smash-up.... The driver lost control at high speed while swiping at a wasp which had flown in through a window and was buzzing around his face.... The weight of a wasp is under half an ounce. Compared with a human being, the wasp's size is minute, its strength negligible. Its sole armament is a tiny syringe holding a drop of irritant, formic acid.... Nevertheless, that wasp killed four big men and converted a large, powerful car into a heap of scrap.
—Eric Frank Russell[1]

TO GRASP SOME IMPLICATIONS OF THE NEW FIRST PRIORITY in U.S. foreign policy, it is necessary to understand the connections among three things: the imbalance of power between terrorist groups and counterterrorist governments; the reasons that groups choose terror tactics; and the operational advantage of attack over defense in the

---

[1] William Wolf in Eric Frank Russell, *Wasp* (London: Victor Gollancz, 2000, originally published 1957), 7.

RICHARD K. BETTS is the Director of the Saltzman Institute of War and Peace Studies at Columbia University and has been a member of the National Commission on Terrorism and on advisory panels for the Director of Central Intelligence. His latest books are *American Force* and *Enemies of Intelligence*.

interactions of terrorists and their opponents. On September 11, 2001, Americans were reminded that the overweening power that they had taken for granted over the past dozen years is not the same as omnipotence. What is less obvious but equally important is that the power is itself part of the cause of terrorist enmity and even a source of U.S. vulnerability.

There is no consensus on a definition of "terrorism," mainly because the term is so intensely pejorative.[2] When defined in terms of tactics, consistency falters, because most people can think of some "good" political cause that has used the tactics and whose purposes excuse them or at least warrant the group's designation as freedom fighters rather than terrorists. Israelis who call the Khobar Towers bombers of 1996 terrorists might reject that characterization for the Irgun, which did the same thing to the King David Hotel in 1946, or some Irish Americans would bridle at equating IRA bombings in Britain with Tamil Tiger bombings in Sri Lanka. Anticommunists labeled the Vietcong terrorists (because they engaged in combat out of uniform and assassinated local officials), but opponents of the Saigon government did not. Nevertheless, a functional definition is more sensible than one conditioned on the identity of the perpetrators. For this article, terrorism refers to the illegitimate, deliberate killing of civilians for purposes of punishment or coercion. This holds in abeyance the questions of whether deliberate killing of civilians can ever be legitimate or killing soldiers can be terrorism.

In any case, for all but the rare nihilistic psychopath, terror is a means, not an end in itself. Terror tactics are usually meant to serve a strategy of coercion.[3] They are a use of force designed to further some substantive aim. This is not always evident in the heat of rage felt by the victims of terror. Normal people find it hard to see instrumental reasoning behind an atrocity, especially when recognizing the political motives behind terrorism might seem to make its illegitimacy less extreme. Stripped of rhetoric, however, a war against terrorism must mean a war against political groups who choose terror as a tactic.

American global primacy is one of the causes of this war. It animates both the terrorists' purposes and their choice of tactics. To groups like al Qaeda, the United States is the enemy because American military power dominates their world, supports corrupt governments in their countries,

---

[2]"The word has become a political label rather than an analytical concept." Martha Crenshaw, *Terrorism and International Cooperation* (New York: Institute for East-West Security Studies, 1989), 5.
[3]For a survey of types, see Christopher C. Harmon, "Five Strategies of Terrorism," *Small Wars and Insurgencies* 12 (Autumn 2001).

and backs Israelis against Muslims; American cultural power insults their religion and pollutes their societies; and American economic power makes all these intrusions and desecrations possible. Japan, in contrast, is not high on al Qaeda's list of targets, because Japan's economic power does not make it a political, military, and cultural behemoth that penetrates their societies.

Political and cultural power makes the United States a target for those who blame it for their problems. At the same time, American economic and military power prevents them from resisting or retaliating against the United States on its own terms. To smite the only superpower requires unconventional modes of force and tactics that make the combat cost exchange ratio favorable to the attacker. This offers hope to the weak that they can work their will despite their overall deficit in power.

PRIMACY ON THE CHEAP

The United States has enjoyed military and political primacy (or hegemony, unipolarity, or whatever term best connotes international dominance) for barely a dozen years. Those who focus on the economic dimension of international relations spoke of American hegemony much earlier, but observers of the strategic landscape never did. For those who focus on national security, the world before 1945 was multipolar, and the world of the cold war was bipolar. After 1945 the United States had exerted hegemony within the First World and for a while over the international economy. The strategic competition against the Second World, however, was seen as a titanic struggle between equal politico-military coalitions and a close-run thing until very near the end. Only the collapse of the Soviet pole, which coincided fortuitously with renewed relative strength of the American economy, marked the real arrival of U.S. global dominance.

The novelty of complete primacy may account for the thoughtless, indeed innocently arrogant way in which many Americans took its benefits for granted. Most who gave any thought to foreign policy came implicitly to regard the entire world after 1989 as they had regarded Western Europe and Japan during the past half-century: partners in principle but vassals in practice. The United States would lead the civilized community of nations in the expansion and consolidation of a liberal world order. Overwhelming military dominance was assumed to be secure and important across most of the domestic political spectrum.

Liberal multilateralists conflated U.S. primacy with political globalization, indeed, conflated ideological American nationalism with internationalist altruism.[4] They assumed that U.S. military power should be used to stabilize benighted countries and police international violence, albeit preferably camouflaged under the banner of institutions such as the United Nations, or at least NATO. They rejected the idea that illiberal impulses or movements represented more than a retreating challenge to the West's mission and its capacity to extend its values worldwide.

Conservative unilateralists assumed that unrivaled power relieved the United States of the need to cater to the demands of others. When America acted strategically abroad, others would have to join on its terms or be left out of the action. The United States should choose battles, avoid entanglements in incompetent polities, and let unfortunates stew in their own juice. For both multilateralists and nationalists, the issue was whether the United States would decide to make an effort for world welfare, not whether a strategic challenge could threaten its truly vital interests. (Colloquial depreciation of the adjective notwithstanding, literally vital U.S. interests are those necessary to life.)

For many, primacy was confused with invulnerability. American experts warned regularly of the danger of catastrophic terrorism—and Osama bin Laden explicitly declared war on the United States in his *fatwa* of February 1998. But the warnings did not register seriously in the consciousness of most people. Even some national security experts felt stunned when the attacks occurred on September 11. Before then, the American military wanted nothing to do with the mission of "homeland defense," cited the Posse Comitatus act to suggest that military operations within U.S. borders would be improper, and argued that homeland defense should be the responsibility of civilian agencies or the National Guard. The services preferred to define the active forces' mission as fighting and winning the nation's wars—as if wars were naturally something that happened abroad—and homeland defense involved no more than law enforcement, managing relief operations in natural disasters, or intercepting ballistic missiles outside U.S. airspace. Only in America could the nation's armed forces think of direct defense of national territory as a distraction.

---

[4]Rationalization of national power as altruism resembles the thinking about benign Pax Britannica in the Crowe Memorandum: "... the national policy of the insular and naval State is so directed as to harmonize with the general desires and ideals common to all mankind, and more particularly ... is closely identified with the primary and vital interests of a majority, or as many as possible, of the other nations.... England, more than any other non-insular Power, has a direct and positive interest in the maintenance of the independence of nations, and therefore must be the natural enemy of any country threatening the independence of others, and the natural protector of the weaker communities." Eyre Crowe, "Memorandum on the Present State of British Relations with France and Germany," 1 January 1907, in G. P. Gooch and Harold Temperley, eds., *British Documents on the Origins of the War, 1898–1914*, vol. 3: *The Testing of the Entente, 1904–6* (London: His Majesty's Stationery Office, 1928), 402–403.

Being Number One seemed cheap. The United States could cut the military burden on the economy by half after the cold war (from 6 percent to 3 percent of GNP) yet still spend almost five times more than the combined military budgets of all potential enemy states. And this did not count the contributions of rich U.S. allies.[5] Of course the margin in dollar terms does not translate into a comparable quantitative margin in manpower or equipment, but that does not mean that a purchasing power parity estimate would reduce the implied gap in combat capability. The overwhelming qualitative superiority of U.S. conventional forces cuts in the other direction. Washington was also able to plan, organize, and fight a major war in 1991 at negligible cost in blood or treasure. Financially, nearly 90 percent of the bills for the war against Iraq were paid by allies. With fewer than 200 American battle deaths, the cost in blood was far lower than almost anyone had imagined it could be. Less than a decade later, Washington waged another war, over Kosovo, that cost no U.S. combat casualties at all.

In the one case where costs in casualties exceeded the apparent interests at stake—Somalia in 1993—Washington quickly stood down from the fight. This became the reference point for vulnerability: the failure of an operation that was small, far from home, and elective. Where material interests required strategic engagement, as in the oil-rich Persian Gulf, U.S. strategy could avoid costs by exploiting its huge advantage in conventional capability. Where conventional dominance proved less exploitable, as in Somalia, material interests did not require strategic engagement. Where the United States could not operate militarily with impunity, it could choose not to operate.

Finally, power made it possible to let moral interests override material interests where some Americans felt an intense moral concern, even if in doing so they claimed, dubiously, that the moral and material stakes coincided. To some extent this happened in Kosovo, although the decision to launch that war apparently flowed from overoptimism about how quickly a little bombing would lead Belgrade to capitulate. Most notably, it happened in the Arab-Israeli conflict. For more than three decades after the 1967 Six Day War, the United States supported Israel diplomatically, economically, and militarily against the Arabs, despite the fact that doing so put it on the side of a tiny country of a few million people with no oil,

---

[5]At the end of the twentieth century, the combined military budgets of China, Russia, Iraq, Yugoslavia (Serbia), North Korea, Iran, Libya, Cuba, Afghanistan, and Sudan added up to no more than $60 billion. *The Military Balance, 1999-2000* (London: International Institute for Strategic Studies, 1999), 102, 112, 132, 133, 159, 186, 275.

against more than ten times as many Arabs who controlled over a third of the world's oil reserves.

This policy was not just an effect of primacy, since the U.S.–Israel alignment began in the cold war. The salience of the moral motive was indicated by the fact that U.S. policy proceeded despite the fact that it helped give Moscow a purchase in major Arab capitals such as Cairo, Damascus, and Baghdad. Luckily for the United States, however, the largest amounts of oil remained under the control of the conservative Arab states of the Gulf. In this sense the hegemony of the United States within the anticommunist world helped account for the policy. That margin of power also relieved Washington of the need to make hard choices about disciplining its client. For decades the United States opposed Israeli settlement of the West Bank, terming the settlements illegal; yet in all that time the United States never demanded that Israel refrain from colonizing the West Bank as a condition for receiving U.S. economic and military aid.[6] Washington continued to bankroll Israel at a higher per capita rate than any other country in the world, a level that has been indispensable to Israel, providing aid over the years that now totals well over $100 billion in today's dollars.[7] Although this policy enraged some Arabs and irritated the rest, U.S. power was great enough that such international political costs did not outweigh the domestic political costs of insisting on Israeli compliance with U.S. policy.

Of course, far more than subsidizing Israeli occupation of Palestinian land was involved in the enmity of Islamist terrorists toward the United States. Many of the other explanations, however, presuppose U.S. global primacy. When American power becomes the arbiter of conflicts around the world, it makes itself the target for groups who come out on the short end of those conflicts.

PRIMACY AND ASYMMETRIC WARFARE

The irrational evil of terrorism seems most obvious to the powerful. They are accustomed to getting their way with conventional applications of force and are not as accustomed as the powerless to thinking of terror as the only

---

[6] Washington certainly did exert pressure on Israel at some times. The administration of Bush the Elder, for example, threatened to withhold loans for housing construction, but this was a marginal portion of total U.S. aid. There was never a threat to cut off the basic annual maintenance payment of several billion dollars to which Israel became accustomed decades ago.

[7] The United States has also given aid to friendly Arab governments—huge amounts to Egypt and some to Jordan. This does not counterbalance the aid to Israel, however, in terms of effects on opinions of strongly anti-Israeli Arabs. Islamists see the regimes in Cairo and Amman as American toadies, complicit in betrayal of the Palestinians.

form of force that might make their enemies do their will. This is why terrorism is the premier form of "asymmetric warfare," the Pentagon buzzword for the type of threats likely to confront the United States in the post-cold war world.[8] Murderous tactics may become instrumentally appealing by default—when one party in a conflict lacks other military options.

Resort to terror is not necessarily limited to those facing far more powerful enemies. It can happen in a conventional war between great powers that becomes a total war, when the process of escalation pits whole societies against each other and shears away civilized restraints. That is something seldom seen, and last seen over a half-century ago. One does not need to accept the tendentious position that allied strategic bombing in World War II constituted terrorism to recognize that the British and Americans did systematically assault the urban population centers of Germany and Japan. They did so in large part because precision bombing of industrial facilities proved ineffective.[9] During the early phase of the cold war, in turn, U.S. nuclear strategy relied on plans to counter Soviet conventional attack on Western Europe with a comprehensive nuclear attack on communist countries that would have killed hundreds of millions. In the 1950s, Strategic Air Command targeteers even went out of their way to plan "bonus" damage by moving aim points for military targets so that blasts would destroy adjacent towns as well.[10] In both World War II and planning for World War III, the rationale was less to kill civilians per se than to wreck the enemy economies—although that was also one of Osama bin Laden's rationales for the attacks on the World

---

[8]Theoretically, this was anticipated by Samuel P. Huntington in his 1962 analysis of the differences between symmetrical intergovernmental war and asymmetrical antigovernmental war. "Patterns of Violence in World Politics" in Huntington, ed., *Changing Patterns of Military Politics* (New York: Free Press of Glencoe, 1962), 19–21. Some of Huntington's analysis of insurrectionary warfare within states applies as well to transnational terrorism.

[9]The Royal Air Force gave up on precision bombing early and focused deliberately on night bombing of German cities, while the Americans continued to try precision daylight bombing. Firestorms in Hamburg, Darmstadt, and Dresden, and less incendiary attacks on other cities, killed several hundred-thousand German civilians. Over Japan, the United States quickly gave up attempts at precision bombing when weather made it impractical and deliberately resorted to an incendiary campaign that burned most Japanese cities to the ground and killed at least 300,000 civilians (and perhaps more than half a million) well before the nuclear attacks on Hiroshima and Nagasaki, which killed another 200,000. Michael S. Sherry, *The Rise of American Air Power: The Creation of Armageddon* (New Haven: Yale University Press, 1987), 260, 413n43.

[10]The threat of deliberate nuclear escalation remained the bedrock of NATO doctrine throughout the cold war, but after the Kennedy administration, the flexible response doctrine made it conditional and included options for nuclear first-use that did not involve deliberate targeting of population centers. In the Eisenhower administration, however, all-out attack on the Soviet bloc's cities was integral to plans for defense of Western Europe against Soviet armored divisions.

Trade Center.[11] In short, the instrumental appeal of strategic attacks on noncombatants may be easier to understand when one considers that states with legitimate purposes have sometimes resorted to such a strategy. Such a double standard, relaxing prohibitions against targeting noncombatants for the side with legitimate purposes (one's own side), occurs most readily when the enemy is at least a peer competitor threatening vital interests. When one's own primacy is taken for granted, it is easier to revert to a single standard that puts all deliberate attacks against civilians beyond the pale.

In contrast to World War II, most wars are limited—or at least limited for the stronger side when power is grossly imbalanced. In such cases, using terror to coerce is likely to seem the only potentially effective use of force for the weaker side, which faces a choice between surrender or savagery. Radical Muslim zealots cannot expel American power with conventional military means, so they substitute clandestine means of delivery against military targets (such as the Khobar Towers barracks in Saudi Arabia) or high-profile political targets (embassies in Kenya and Tanzania). More than once the line has been attributed to terrorists, "If you will let us lease one of your B-52s, we will use that instead of a truck bomb." The hijacking and conversion of U.S. airliners into kamikazes was the most dramatic means of asymmetric attack.

Kamikaze hijacking also reflects an impressive capacity for strategic judo, the turning of the West's strength against itself.[12] The flip side of a primacy that diffuses its power throughout the world is that advanced elements of that power become more accessible to its enemies. Nineteen men from technologically backward societies did not have to rely on homegrown instruments to devastate the Pentagon and World Trade Center. They used computers and modern financial procedures with facility, and they forcibly appropriated the aviation technology of the West and used it as a weapon. They not only rebelled against the "soft power" of the United States, they trumped it by hijacking the country's

---

[11]In a videotape months after the attacks, bin Laden said, "These blessed strikes showed clearly that this arrogant power, America, rests on a powerful but precarious economy, which rapidly crumbled . . . the global economy based on usury, which America uses along with its military might to impose infidelity and humiliation on oppressed people, can easily crumble. . . . Hit the economy, which is the basis of military might. If their economy is finished, they will become too busy to enslave oppressed people. . . . America is in decline; the economic drain is continuing but more strikes are required and the youths must strike the key sectors of the American economy." Videotape excerpts quoted in "Bin Laden's Words: 'America Is in Decline,' the Leader of Al Qaeda Says," *New York Times*, 28 December 2001.

[12]This is similar to the concept of political judo discussed in Samuel L. Popkin, "Pacification: Politics and the Village," *Asian Survey* 10 (August 1970); and Popkin, "Internal Conflicts—South Vietnam" in Kenneth N. Waltz and Steven Spiegel, eds., *Conflict in World Politics* (Cambridge, MA: Winthrop, 1971).

hard power.[13] They also exploited the characteristics of U.S. society associated with soft power—the liberalism, openness, and respect for privacy that allowed them to go freely about the business of preparing the attacks without observation by the state security apparatus. When soft power met the clash of civilizations, it proved too soft.

Strategic judo is also apparent in the way in which U.S. retaliation may compromise its own purpose. The counteroffensive after September 11 was necessary, if only to demonstrate to marginally motivated terrorists that they could not hope to strike the United States for free. The war in Afghanistan, however, does contribute to polarization in the Muslim world and to mobilization of potential terrorist recruits. U.S. leaders can say that they are not waging a war against Islam until they are blue in the face, but this will not convince Muslims who already distrust the United States. Success in deposing the Taliban may help U.S. policy by encouraging a bandwagon effect that rallies governments and moderates among the Muslim populace, but there will probably be as many who see the U.S. retaliation as confirming al Qaeda's diagnosis of American evil. Victory in Afghanistan and follow-up operations to prevent al Qaeda from relocating bases of operation to other countries will hurt that organization's capacity to act. The number of young zealots willing to emulate the "martyrdom operation" of the nineteen on September 11, however, is not likely to decline.

ADVANTAGE OF ATTACK

The academic field of security studies has some reason to be embarrassed after September 11. Having focused primarily on great powers and interstate conflict, literature on terrorism was comparatively sparse; most of the good books were by policy analysts rather than theorists.[14] Indeed, science fiction has etched out the operational logic of terrorism as well as political science. Eric Frank Russell's 1957 novel, from which the epigraph to this article comes, vividly illustrates both the strategic aspirations of terrorists and the offense-dominant character of their tactics. It describes the

---

[13]Soft power is "indirect or cooptive" and "can rest on the attraction of one's ideas or on the ability to set the political agenda in a way that shapes the preferences that others express." It "tends to be associated with intangible power resources such as culture, ideology, and institutions." Joseph S. Nye, Jr., "The Changing Nature of World Power," *Political Science Quarterly* 105 (Summer 1990): 181. See also Nye, *Bound to Lead: The Changing Nature of American Power* (New York: Basic Books, 1990).

[14]For example, Bruce Hoffmann, *Inside Terrorism* (New York: Columbia University Press, 1998); Paul R. Pillar, *Terrorism and American Foreign Policy* (Washington, DC: Brookings Institution Press, 2001); Richard A. Falkenrath, Robert D. Newman, and Bradley S. Thayer, *America's Achilles' Heel: Nuclear, Biological, and Chemical Terrorism and Covert Attack* (Cambridge: MIT Press, 1998).

dispatch of a single agent to one of many planets in the Sirian enemy's empire to stir up fear, confusion, and panic through a series of small covert activities with tremendous ripple effects. Matched with deceptions to make the disruptions appear to be part of a campaign by a big phantom rebel organization, the agent's modest actions divert large numbers of enemy policy and military personnel, cause economic dislocations and social unrest, and soften the planet up for invasion. Wasp agents are infiltrated into numerous planets, multiplying the effects. As the agents' handlers tell him, "The pot is coming slowly but surely to the boil. Their fleets are being widely dispersed, there are vast troop movements from their overcrowded home-system to the outer planets of their empire. They're gradually being chivvied into a fix. They can't hold what they've got without spreading all over it. The wider they spread the thinner they get. The thinner they get, the easier it is to bite lumps out of them."[15]

Fortunately al Qaeda and its ilk are not as wildly effective as Russell's wasp. By degree, however, the phenomenon is quite similar. Comparatively limited initiatives prompt tremendous and costly defensive reactions. On September 11 a small number of men killed 3,000 people and destroyed a huge portion of prime commercial real estate, part of the military's national nerve center, and four expensive aircraft. The ripple effects, however, multiplied those costs. A major part of the U.S. economy—air travel—shut down completely for days after September 11. Increased security measures dramatically increased the overall costs of the air travel system thereafter. Normal law enforcement activities of the Federal Bureau of Investigation were radically curtailed as legions of agents were transferred to counterterror tasks. Anxiety about the vulnerability of nuclear power plants, major bridges and tunnels, embassies abroad, and other high-value targets prompted plans for big investments in fortification of a wide array of facilities. A retaliatory war in Afghanistan ran at a cost of a couple billion dollars a month beyond the regular defense budget for months. In one study, the attacks on the World Trade Center and the Pentagon were estimated to cost the U.S. economy 1.8 million jobs.[16]

---

[15] Russell, *Wasp*, 64. The ripple effects include aspects of strategic judo. Creating a phony rebel organization leads the enemy security apparatus to turn on its own people. "If some Sirians could be given the full-time job of hunting down and garroting other Sirians, and if other Sirians could be given the full-time job of dodging or shooting down the garroters, then a distant and different life form would be saved a few unpleasant chores. . . . Doubtless the military would provide a personal bodyguard for every big wheel on Jaimec; that alone would pin down a regiment." Ibid., 26, 103.

[16] Study by the Milken Institute discussed in "The Economics: Attacks May Cost 1.8 Million Jobs," *New York Times*, 13 January 2002.

Or consider the results of a handful of 34-cent letters containing anthrax, probably sent by a single person. Besides killing several people, they contaminated a large portion of the postal system, paralyzed some mail delivery for long periods, provoked plans for huge expenditures on prophylactic irradiation equipment, shut down much of Capitol Hill for weeks, put thousands of people on a sixty-day regimen of strong antibiotics (potentially eroding the medical effectiveness of such antibiotics in future emergencies), and overloaded police and public health inspectors with false alarms. The September 11 attacks and the October anthrax attacks together probably cost the perpetrators less than a million dollars. If the cost of rebuilding and of defensive investments in reaction came to no more than $100 billion, the cost exchange ratio would still be astronomically in favor of the attack over the defense.

Analysts in strategic studies did not fall down on the job completely before September 11. At least two old bodies of work help to illuminate the problem. One is the literature on guerrilla warfare and counterinsurgency, particularly prominent in the 1960s, and the other is the offense-defense theory that burgeoned in the 1980s. Both apply well to understanding patterns of engagement between terrorists and counterterrorists. Some of the axioms derived from the empirical cases in the counterinsurgency literature apply directly, and offense-defense theory applies indirectly.

Apart from the victims of guerrillas, few still identify irregular paramilitary warfare with terrorism (because the latter is illegitimate), but the two activities do overlap a great deal in their operational characteristics. Revolutionary or resistance movements in the preconventional phase of operations usually mix small-unit raids on isolated outposts of the government or occupying force with detonations and assassinations in urban areas to instill fear and discredit government power. The tactical logic of guerrilla operations resembles that in terrorist attacks: the weaker rebels use stealth and the cover of civilian society to concentrate their striking power against one among many of the stronger enemy's dispersed assets; they strike quickly and eliminate the target before the defender can move forces from other areas to respond; they melt back into civilian society to avoid detection and reconcentrate against another target. The government or occupier has far superior strength in terms of conventional military power, but cannot counterconcentrate in time because it has to defend all points, while the insurgent attacker can pick its targets at will.[17] The contest between insurgents and counterinsurgents is "tripartite," polarizing political alignments and gaining the support of *attentistes* or those in the middle. In today's principal counterterror campaign, one might say that the yet-unmobilized Muslim elites and masses of the Third World—those who were not already actively committed either to supporting Islamist radicalism or to combating it—are the target group in the middle. As Samuel Huntington noted, "a revolutionary war is a war of attrition."[18] As I believe Stanley Hoffman once said, in rebellions the insurgents win as long as they do not lose, and the government loses as long as it does not win. If al Qaeda-like groups can stay in the field indefinitely, they win.

Offense-defense theory applied nuclear deterrence concepts to assessing the stability of conventional military confrontations and focused on what conditions tended to give the attack or the defense the advantage in war.[19] There were many problems in the specification and application of the theory having to do with unsettled conceptualization of the offense-defense balance, problematic standards for measuring it, and inconsistent applications to different levels of warfare and

---

[17]Mao Tse-Tung's classic tracts are canonical background. For example, "Problems of Strategy in China's Revolutionary War" (especially chap. 5) in *Selected Works of Mao Tse-Tung* (Beijing: Foreign Languages Press, 1967), vol. i, and "Problems of Strategy in Guerrilla War Against Japan," in *Selected Works*, vol. ii (1967). Much of the Western analytical literature grew out of British experience in the Malayan Emergency and France's role in Indochina and Algeria. For example, Franklin Mark Osanka, ed., *Modern Guerrilla Warfare* (New York: Free Press, 1962); Gerard Chaliand, ed., *Guerrilla Strategies: An Historical Anthology from the Long March to Afghanistan* (Berkeley: University of California Press, 1982); Roger Triniquier, *Modern Warfare: A French View of Counterinsurgency*, Daniel Lee, trans. (New York: Praeger, 1964); David Galula, *Counterinsurgency Warfare: Theory and Practice* (New York: Praeger, 1964); Sir Robert Thompson, *Defeating Communist Insurgency* (New York: Praeger, 1966); Richard L. Clutterbuck, *The Long Long War: Counterinsurgency in Malaya and Vietnam* (New York: Praeger, 1966); George Armstrong Kelly, *Lost Soldiers: The French Army and Empire in Crisis, 1947–1962* (Cambridge: MIT Press, 1965), chaps. 5–7, 9–10; W. P. Davison, *Some Observations on Viet Cong Operations in the Villages* (Santa Monica, CA: RAND Corporation, 1968). See also Douglas S. Blaufarb, *The Counter-Insurgency Era: U.S. Doctrine and Performance, 1950 to the Present* (New York: Free Press, 1977); D. Michael Shafer, *Deadly Paradigms: The Failure of U.S. Counterinsurgency Policy* (Princeton: Princeton University Press, 1988); Timothy J. Lomperis, *From People's War to People's Rule: Insurgency, Intervention, and the Lessons of Vietnam* (Chapel Hill: University of North Carolina Press, 1996).
[18]Huntington, "Patterns of Violence in World Politics," 20–27.
[19]George Quester, *Offense and Defense in the International System*, 2nd ed. (New Brunswick, NJ: Transaction Books, 1988); Robert Jervis, "Cooperation Under the Security Dilemma," *World Politics* 30 (January 1978); Jack L. Snyder, *The Ideology of the Offensive: Military Decision Making and the Disasters of 1914* (Ithaca, NY: Cornell University Press, 1984); Stephen Van Evera, *Causes of War: Power and the Roots of Conflict* (Ithaca, NY: Cornell University Press, 1999), chaps. 6–8; Charles L. Glaser and Chaim Kaufmann, "What Is the Offense-Defense Balance and Can We Measure It?" *International Security* 22 (Spring 1998).

diplomacy.[20] Offense-defense theory, which flourished when driven by the urge to find ways to stabilize the NATO-Warsaw Pact balance in Europe, has had little to say directly about unconventional war or terrorism. It actually applies more clearly, however, to this lower level of strategic competition (as well as to the higher level of nuclear war) than to the middle level of conventional military power. This is because the exchange ratio between opposing conventional forces of roughly similar size is very difficult to estimate, given the complex composition of modern military forces and uncertainty about their qualitative comparisons; but the exchange ratio in both nuclear and guerrilla combat is quite lopsided in favor of the attacker. Counterinsurgency folklore held that the government defenders need something on the order of a ten-to-one advantage over the guerrillas if they were to drive them from the field.

There has been much confusion about exactly how to define the offense-defense balance, but the essential idea is that some combinations of military technology, organization, and doctrine are proportionally more advantageous to the attack or to the defense when the two clash. "Proportionally" means that available instruments and circumstances of engagement give either the attack or the defense more bang for the buck, more efficient power out of the same level of resources. The notion of an offense-defense balance as something conceptually distinct from the balance of power means, however, that it cannot be identified with which side wins a battle or a war. Indeed, the offense-defense balance can favor the defense, while the attacker still wins, because its overall margin of superiority in power was too great, despite the defense's more efficient use of power. (I am told that the Finns had a saying in the Winter War of 1939-40: "One Finn is worth ten Russians, but what happens when the eleventh Russian comes?") Thus, to say that the offense-defense balance favors the offensive terrorists today against the defensive counterterrorists does not mean that the terrorists will prevail. It does mean that terrorists can fight far above their weight, that in most instances each competent terrorist will have much greater individual impact than each good counterterrorist, that each dollar invested in a terrorist plot will have a bigger payoff than each dollar expended on counterterrorism, and that only small numbers of

---

[20]For critiques, see Jack S. Levy, "The Offensive/Defensive Balance of Military Technology," *International Studies Quarterly* 28 (June 1984); Scott D. Sagan, "1914 Revisited," *International Security* 11 (Fall 1986); Jonathan Shimshoni, "Technology, Military Advantage, and World War I: A Case for Military Entrepreneurship," *International Security* 15 (Winter 1990/91); Richard K. Betts, "Must War Find a Way?" *International Security* 24 (Fall 1999); Betts, "Conventional Deterrence: Predictive Uncertainty and Policy Confidence," *World Politics* 37 (January 1985).

competent terrorists need survive and operate to keep the threat to American society uncomfortably high.

In the competition between terrorists on the attack and Americans on the defense, the disadvantage of the defense is evident in the number of high-value potential targets that need protection. The United States has "almost 600,000 bridges, 170,000 water systems, more than 2,800 power plants (104 of them nuclear), 190,000 miles of interstate pipelines for natural gas, 463 skyscrapers . . . nearly 20,000 miles of border, airports, stadiums, train tracks.[21] All these usually represented American strength; after September 11 they also represent vulnerability:

> Suddenly guards were being posted at water reservoirs, outside power plants, and at bridges and tunnels. Maps of oil and gas lines were removed from the Internet. In Boston, a ship carrying liquefied natural gas, an important source of fuel for heating New England homes, was forbidden from entering the harbor because local fire officials feared that if it were targeted by a terrorist the resulting explosion could lay low much of the city's densely populated waterfront. An attack by a knife-wielding lunatic on the driver of a Florida-bound Greyhound bus led to the immediate cessation of that national bus service. . . . Agricultural crop-dusting planes were grounded out of a concern that they could be used to spread chemical or biological agents.[22]

Truly energetic defense measures do not only cost money in personnel and equipment for fortification, inspection, and enforcement; they may require repealing some of the very underpinnings of civilian economic efficiency associated with globalization. "The competitiveness of the U.S. economy and the quality of life of the American people rest on critical infrastructure that has become increasingly more concentrated, more interconnected, and more sophisticated. Almost entirely privately owned and operated, there is very little redundancy in this system."[23] This concentration increases the potential price of vulnerability to single attacks. Tighter inspection of cargoes coming across the Canadian border, for example, wrecks the "just-in-time" parts supply system of Michigan auto manufacturers. Companies that have invested in technology and infrastructure premised on unimpeded movement "may see their expected

---

[21]Jerry Schwartz, Associated Press dispatch, 6 October 2001, quoted in Brian Reich, "Strength in the Face of Terror: A Comparison of United States and International Efforts to Provide Homeland Security" (unpublished paper, Columbia University, December 2001), 5.
[22]Stephen E. Flynn, "The Unguarded Homeland" in James F. Hoge, Jr. and Gideon Rose, eds., *How Did This Happen? Terrorism and the New War* (New York: PublicAffairs, 2001), 185.
[23]Ibid., 185–186.

savings and efficiencies go up in smoke. Outsourcing contracts will have to be revisited and inventories will have to be rebuilt."[24] How many safety measures will suffice in improving airline security without making flying so inconvenient that the air travel industry never recovers as a profit-making enterprise? A few more shoe-bomb incidents, and Thomas Friedman's proposal to start an airline called "Naked Air—where the only thing you wear is a seat belt" becomes almost as plausible as it is ridiculous.[25]

The offense-dominant character of terrorism is implicit in mass detentions of Arab young men after September 11, and proposals for military tribunals that would compromise normal due process and weaken standard criminal justice presumptions in favor of the accused. The traditional liberal axiom that it is better to let a hundred guilty people go free than to convict one innocent reflects confidence in the strength of society's defenses—confidence that whatever additional crimes may be committed by the guilty who go free will not grossly outweigh the injustice done to innocents convicted, that one criminal who slips through the net will not go on to kill hundreds or thousands of innocents. Fear of terrorists plotting mass murder reversed that presumption and makes unjust incarceration of some innocents appear like unintended but expected collateral damage in wartime combat.

Offense-defense theory helps to visualize the problem. It does not help to provide attractive solutions, as its proponents believed it did during the cold war. Then offense-defense theory was popular because it seemed to offer a way to stabilize the East-West military confrontation. Mutual deterrence from the superpowers' confidence in their counteroffensive capability could substitute for defense at the nuclear level, and both sides' confidence in their conventional defenses could dampen either one's incentives to attack at that level. Little of this applies to counterterrorism. Both deterrence and defense are weaker strategies against terrorists than they were against communists.

Deterrence is still relevant for dealing with state terrorism; Saddam Hussein or Kim Jong-Il may hold back from striking the United States for fear of retaliation. Deterrence offers less confidence for preventing state sponsorship of terrorism; it did not stop the Taliban from hosting Osama bin Laden. It offers even less for holding at bay transnational groups like al Qaeda, which may lack a return address against which retaliation can be visited, or whose millenialist aims and religious convictions make them

---

[24] Ibid., 193–194.
[25] Thomas L. Friedman, "Naked Air," *New York Times*, 26 December 2001.

unafraid of retaliation. Defense, in turn, is better than a losing game only because the inadequacy of deterrence leaves no alternative.[26] Large investments in defense will produce appreciable reductions in vulnerability, but will not minimize vulnerability.

Deterrence and defense overlap in practice. The U.S. counteroffensive in Afghanistan constitutes retaliation, punishing the Taliban for shielding al Qaeda and sending a warning to other potential state sponsors. It is also active defense, whittling down the ranks of potential perpetrators by killing and capturing members of the Islamist international brigades committed to jihad against the United States. At this writing, the retaliatory function has been performed more effectively than the defensive, as the Taliban regime has been destroyed, but significant numbers of Arab Afghans and al Qaeda members appear to have escaped, perhaps to plot another day.

Given the limited efficacy of deterrence for modern counterterrorism, it remains an open question how much of a strategic success we should judge the impressive victory in Afghanistan to be. Major investments in passive defenses (airline security, border inspections, surveillance and searches for better intelligence, fortification of embassies, and so forth) are necessary, but will reduce vulnerability at a cost substantially greater than the costs that competent terrorist organizations will have to bear to probe and occasionally circumvent them. The cost-exchange ratio for direct defense is probably worse than the legendary 10:1 ratio for successful counterinsurgency, and certainly worse than the more than 3:1 ratio that Robert McNamara's analysts calculated for the advantage of offensive missile investments over antiballistic missile systems—an advantage that many then and since have thought warranted accepting a situation of mutual vulnerability to assured destruction.[27]

The less prepared we are to undertake appropriate programs and the more false starts and confusions that are likely, the worse the cost-exchange ratio will be in the short term. The public health system, law enforcement organizations, and state and local bureaucrats are still feeling their way on what, how, and in which sequence to boost efforts. The U.S. military will also have to overcome the natural and powerful effects of inertia and attachments to old self-conceptions and preferred

---

[26]See Steven Simon and Daniel Benjamin, "America and the New Terrorism," *Survival* 42 (Spring 2000): 59, 66–69, 74.

[27]Estimates in the 1960s indicated that even combining ABM systems with counterforce strikes and fallout shelters, the United States would have to counter each Soviet dollar spent on ICBMs with three U.S. dollars to protect 70 percent of the industry, assuming highly effective ABMs (.8 kill probability). To protect up to 80 percent of the population, far higher ratios would be necessary. Fred Kaplan, *The Wizards of Armageddon* (New York: Simon and Schuster, 1983), 321–324.

programs and modes of operation. Impulses to repackage old priorities in the rhetoric of new needs will further dilute effectiveness of countermeasures.

Nevertheless, given low confidence that deterrence can prevent terrorist attacks, major improvements in defenses make sense.[28] This is especially true because the resource base from which the United States can draw is vastly larger than that available to transnational terrorists. Al Qaeda may be rich, but it does not have the treasury of a great power. Primacy has a soft underbelly, but it is far better to have primacy than to face it. Even at an unfavorable cost exchange ratio, a number of defensive measures are a sensible investment, but only because our overwhelming advantage in resources means that we are not constrained to focus solely on the most efficient countermeasures.

At the same time, as long as terrorist groups remain potent and active, a serious war plan must exploit efficient strategies as well. Given the offense-dominant nature of terrorist operations, this means emphasis on counteroffensive operations. When terrorists or their support structures can be found and fixed, preemptive and preventive attacks will accomplish more against them, dollar for dollar, than the investment in passive defenses. Which is the more efficient use of resources: to kill or capture a cell of terrorists who might otherwise choose at any time to strike whichever set of targets on our side is unguarded, or to try to guard all potential targets? Here the dangers are that counteroffensive operations could prove counterproductive. This could easily happen if they degenerate into brutalities and breaches of laws of war that make counterterrorism begin to appear morally equivalent to its target, sapping political support and driving the uncommitted to the other side in the process of polarization that war makes inevitable. Whether counteroffensive operations gain more in eliminating perpetrators than they lose in alienating and mobilizing "swing voters" in the world of Muslim opinion depends on how successful the operations are in neutralizing significant numbers of the organizers of terrorist groups, as opposed to foot soldiers, and in doing so with minimal collateral damage.

PRIMACY AND POLICY

September 11 reminded those Americans with a rosy view that not all the world sees U.S. primacy as benign, that primacy does not guarantee

---

[28] For an appropriate list of recommendations see *Countering the Changing Threat of International Terrorism*, Report of the National Commission on Terrorism, Pursuant to Public Law 277, 105th Congress (Washington, DC, June 2000). This report holds up very well in light of September 11.

security, and that security may now entail some retreats from the economic globalization that some had identified with American leadership. Primacy has two edges—dominance and provocation. Americans can enjoy the dominance but must recognize the risks it evokes. For terrorists who want to bring the United States down, U.S. strategic primacy is a formidable challenge, but one that can be overcome. On balance, Americans have overestimated the benefits of primacy, and terrorists have underestimated them.

For those who see a connection between American interventionism, cultural expansiveness, and support of Israel on one hand, and the rage of groups that turn to terrorism on the other, primacy may seem more trouble than it's worth, and the need to revise policies may seem more pressing. But most Americans have so far preferred the complacent and gluttonous form of primacy to the ascetic, blithely accepting steadily growing dependence on Persian Gulf oil that could be limited by compromises in lifestyle and unconventional energy policies. There have been no groundswells to get rid of SUVs, support the Palestinians, or refrain from promoting Western standards of democracy and human rights in societies where some elements see them as aggression.

There is little evidence that any appreciable number of Americans, elite or mass, see our primacy as provoking terrorism. Rather, most see it as a condition we can choose at will to exploit or not. So U.S. foreign policy has exercised primacy in a muscular way in byways of the post-cold war world when intervention seemed cheap, but not when doing good deeds threatened to be costly. Power has allowed Washington to play simultaneously the roles of mediator and partisan supporter in the Arab-Israeli conflict. For a dozen years nothing, with the near exception of the Kosovo War, suggested that primacy could not get us out of whatever problems it generated.

How far the United States goes to adapt to the second edge of primacy probably depends on whether stunning damage is inflicted by terrorists again, or September 11 gradually fades into history. If al Qaeda and its ilk are crippled, and some years pass without more catastrophic attacks on U.S. home teritory, scar tissue will harden on the soft underbelly, and the positive view of primacy will be reinforced. If the war against terrorism falters, however, and the exercise of power fails to prevent more big incidents, the consensus will crack. Then more extreme policy options will get more attention. Retrenchment and retreat will look more appealing to some, who may believe the words of Sheik Salman al-Awdah, a dissident Saudi religious scholar, who said, "If America just let well enough alone, and got out of their obligations overseas . . . no one would bother them."[29]

More likely, however, would be a more violent reaction. There is no reason to assume that terrorist enemies would let America off the hook if it retreated and would not remain as implacable as ever. Facing inability to suppress the threat through normal combat, covert action, and diplomatic pressure, many Americans would consider escalation to more ferocious strategies. In recent decades, the march of liberal legalism has delegitimized tactics and brutalities that once were accepted, but this delegitimation has occurred only in the context of fundamental security and dominance of the Western powers, not in a situation where they felt under supreme threat. In a situation of that sort, it is foolhardy to assume that American strategy would never turn to tactics like those used against Japanese and German civilians, or by the civilized French in the *sale guerre* in Algeria, or by the Russians in Chechnya in hopes of effectively eradicating terrorists despite astronomical damage to the civilian societies within which they lurk.

This possibility would highlight how terrorists have underestimated American primacy. There is much evidence that even in the age of unipolarity, opponents have mistakenly seen the United States as a paper tiger. For some reason—perhaps wishfully selective perception—they tend to see retreats from Vietnam, Beirut, and Somalia as typical weakness of American will, instead of considering decisive exercises of power in Panama, Kuwait, Kosovo, and now, Afghanistan.[30] As Osama bin Laden said in 1997, the United States left Somalia "after claiming that they were the largest power on earth. They left after some resistance from powerless, poor, unarmed people whose only weapon is the belief in Allah. . . . The Americans ran away."[31]

This apparently common view among those with an interest in pinning America's ears back ignores the difference between elective uses of force and desperate ones. The United States retreated where it ran into trouble helping others, not where it was saving itself. Unlike interventions of the 1990s in Africa, the Balkans, or Haiti, counterterrorism is not charity. With vital material interests involved, primacy unleashed may prove fearsomely potent.

---

[29]Quoted in Douglas Jehl, "After Prison, a Saudi Sheik Tempers His Words," *New York Times*, 27 December 2001.
[30]See data in the study by Barry M. Blechman and Tamara Cofman Wittes, "Defining Moment: The Threat and Use of Force in American Foreign Policy," *Political Science Quarterly* 114 (Spring 1999).
[31]Quoted in Simon and Benjamin, "America and the New Terrorism," 69.

Most likely America will see neither absolute victory nor abject failure in the war against terror. Then how long will a campaign of attrition last and stay popular? If the United States wants a strategy to cut the roots of terrorism, rather than just the branches, will American power be used effectively against the roots? Perhaps, but probably not. This depends of course on which of many possible root causes are at issue. Ironically, one problem is that American primacy itself is one of those roots.

A common assertion is that Third World poverty generates terrorism. While this must certainly be a contributing cause in many cases, there is little evidence that it is either a necessary or sufficient condition. Fundamentalist madrassas might not be full to overflowing if young Muslims had ample opportunities to make money, but the fifteen Saudis who hijacked the flights on September 11 were from one of the most affluent of Muslim countries. No U.S. policy could ever hope to make most incubators of terrorism less poor than Saudi Arabia. Iran, the biggest state sponsor of anti-American terrorism, is also better off than most Muslim countries. Poverty is endemic in the Third World, but terrorism is not.

Even if endemic poverty were the cause, the solution would not be obvious. Globalization generates stratification, creating winners and losers, as efficient societies with capitalist cultures move ahead and others fall behind, or as elite enclaves in some societies prosper while the masses stagnate. Moreover, even vastly increased U.S. development assistance would be spread thin if all poor countries are assumed to be incubators of terrorism. And what are the odds that U.S. intervention with economic aid would significantly reduce poverty? Successes in prompting dramatic economic development by outside assistance in the Third World have occurred, but they are the exception more than the rule.

The most virulent anti-American terrorist threats, however, do not emerge randomly in poor societies. They grow out of a few regions and are concentrated overwhelmingly in a few religiously motivated groups. These reflect political causes—ideological, nationalist, or transnational cultural impulses to militant mobilization—more than economic causes. Economic development in an area where the political and religious impulses remain unresolved could serve to improve the resource base for terrorism rather than undercut it.

A strategy of terrorism is most likely to flow from the coincidence of two conditions: intense political grievance and gross imbalance of power. Either one without the other is likely to produce either peace or conventional war. Peace is probable if power is imbalanced but grievance is modest; the weaker party is likely to live with the grievance. In that situation, conventional use of force appears to offer no hope of victory, while the righteous indignation is not great enough to overcome normal inhibitions against murderous tactics. Conventional war is probable if grievance is intense but power is more evenly balanced, since successful use of respectable forms of force appears possible.[32] Under American primacy, candidates for terrorism suffer from grossly inferior power by definition. This should focus attention on the political causes of their grievance.

How are political root causes addressed? At other times in history we have succeeded in fostering congenial revolutions—especially in the end of the cold war, as the collapse of the Second World heralded an End of History of sorts.[33] The problem now, however, is the rebellion of anti-Western zealots against the secularist end of history. Remaking the world in the Western image is what Americans assume to be just, natural, and desirable, indeed only a matter of time. But that presumption is precisely what energizes many terrorists' hatred. Secular Western liberalism is not their salvation, but their scourge. Primacy could, paradoxically, remain both the solution and the problem for a long time.*

---

[32]On why power imbalance is conducive to peace and parity to war, see Geoffrey Blainey, *The Causes of War*, 3rd. ed. (New York: Free Press, 1988), chap. 8.

[33]Francis Fukuyama's thesis was widely misunderstood and caricatured. He noted that the Third World remained mired in history and that some developments could lead to restarting history. For the First World, the defeated Second World, and even some parts of the Third World, however, the triumph of Western liberalism could reasonably be seen by those who believe in its worth (as should Americans) as the final stage of evolution through fundamentally different forms of political and economic organization of societies. See Fukuyama, "The End of History?" *National Interest* no. 16 (Summer 1989); and Fukuyama, *The End of History and the Last Man* (New York: Free Press, 1992).

*The author thanks Robert Jervis for comments on the first draft. This article was originally published in *Political Science Quarterly* 117 (Spring 2002): 19–36.